# Understanding Management

**Jay W. Lorsch**
Harvard University

**James P. Baughman**
Harvard University

**James Reece**
University of Michigan

**Henry Mintzberg**
McGill University

**Harper & Row, Publishers**
New York, Hagerstown, San Francisco, London

Sponsoring Editor: John Greenman
Production Supervisor: Stefania J. Taflinska
Compositor: Maryland Linotype Composition Co., Inc.
Printer and Binder: The Maple Press Company
Art Studio: Vantage Art, Inc.

**Understanding Management**

Copyright © 1978 by Jay W. Lorsch, James P. Baughman, James Reece, and Henry Mintzberg

Library of Congress Cataloging in Publication Data
Main entry under title:

Understanding management.

    Includes index.
    1. Management. 2. Organization. I. Lorsch,
Jay William.
HD31.U514        658.4        78-674
ISBN 0-06-044042-2

# Contents

# Preface

This book is unique as an introductory text in management of the business enterprise. Each of the authors is an established specialist in his field: Baughman in business history and the relationship between business and its wider environment; Lorsch in the behavior of people in organizations and in the theory of organizations; Reece in control and accounting; Mintzberg in business policy and in the behavior of managers.

To use the terms employed in Section I, the book represents both a specialized and a coordinated effort by the authors. After several preliminary meetings, each specialist wrote his own section, communicating to the reader those ideas and knowledge he thought a beginning student would need. Then these sections were exchanged by all the authors to make sure that the approach was consistent and coordinated. Out of this process comes a book that we believe allowed each author to draw on his specialized knowledge and experience but still provides to the student a coherent view of the challenges and issues managers face in modern society, as well as providing an introduction to some of the tools managers use to deal with them.

Larry J. Bossman, Jr., of the University of Detroit has developed an instructor's manual to accompany this book that, besides providing summaries of chapter content and testing materials, includes an extensive annotated bibliography for each section. These bibliographies contain suggestions for collateral reading that extend and augment the basic concepts in each chapter and provide alternative points of view on the topics discussed.

In total, this book took almost five years to complete because of the competing time pressures on the several authors. We, therefore, especially appreciate the skill, dedication, and patience of Jack Greenman and his associates at Harper & Row. Without these qualities this book would never have become a reality.

Jay W. Lorsch

*Eastham, Massachusetts*

# 1

# Managers and the Habitat of Management

Why do we have managers? What are their functions? How can managers become more effective? Finally, what is management? How is it exercised? In what ways can it be made more efficient? This book attempts to deal with these questions. But first we must underscore some basic assumptions of this text. One is a simple but crucial truth: Managers are people—no more and no less. They share, with all of us, human strengths and weaknesses. They may look, but not see; hear, but fail to listen; speak, but not communicate; touch, but remain untouched themselves. They can lack belief or understanding or both. In reasoning, they may unwittingly obscure a problem rather than solve it, and lessons learned are sometimes easily forgotten. They can think without acting and, of course, act without thinking. Like other human beings, they too can create and destroy. Even when successful, they can sometimes fall short of their own expectations and aspirations or those others hold for them. They can fail, although often in failure they help prevent worse consequences for others or for themselves. They can be ridiculous or sublime. They can be heroes or fools. Because managers are human, they are fallible; thus there are good and bad managers and, as a result, efficient and inefficient management. But managerial ineffectiveness is never solely the result of fallibility. That management is a humanistic process, practitioners will do well never to forget.

A second basic assumption of this text is that managers are made, not born. Managers may start with certain innate characteristics, but there can and should be development through experience and education. Third, the art and science of management can be taught and, more importantly, learned. Fourth, management is not a spectator sport. Rather, managers are actively involved. Fifth, the main test for management is effectiveness, not elegance. Whether management techniques achieve results is what counts, not whether they follow textbook principles. Six, managers are accountable for their actions to others as well as to themselves. Seven, management is only a means to achieve the firm's goals, not an end in itself.

Consider the second and third assumptions. They assert, subject to the reader's own evaluation of the evidence and arguments to be presented throughout this book, that native ability or the desire to manage is not enough. To be sure, some individuals seem to have native intelligence, a sense of humanism, a certain amount of intuition, well-developed instincts, and positive traits. But to become a successful manager, even "the best and the brightest" individual has much to learn. "Child prodigies" are rarely found in management because there is a body of managerial knowledge and a set of managerial skills that can only be acquired through formal education and, further, that knowledge and those skills enhance natural talents only through practical and situational experiences. Ideally, the interaction among being, learning, and doing should continue throughout a manager's career: Little in management is learned "once and for all." Rather, management is a practical fusion of art and science that continually challenges one's creative resources with new puzzles to solve. Like diagnosis and prescription, it demands science. Like leadership, it demands art.

How, then, do managers solve problems? As most managers know, they definitely do not do it from the sidelines. They are players, not fans; actors, not the members of an audience; participants, not spectators. And chance—for good or bad—plays a role, too, and influences the outcome of problem-solving. But the process of managerial problem-solving, or decision-making, is much like working a crossword puzzle. One must bring intelligence, knowledge, commitment, and concentration to the task. And then one plunges in, beginning in any of a dozen places, and works on several elements simultaneously. At first, tackling a particular word may be an easier approach. Working "across" may be harder than working "down"—or vice versa. Gradually, however, success builds upon success until the puzzle is solved.

The process of solving crossword puzzles is, thus, like the managerial process in many ways. Both capitalize on native ability, formal education, and practical experience. In both, problems are interrelated and solutions are interdependent. Managers work simultaneously "across" with peers and "down" (or "up") with subordinates and superiors. Trial and error is an acceptable method of attack. Although each situation is different, one can transfer learning from one situation to the next. But there are important major differences. In the crossword puzzle, there is only "one best solution," and hence only perfection succeeds. In management, however, solutions are rarely perfect, because, unlike the crossword, the managerial puzzle is changing and not static. The "better way" is, therefore, infinitely possible; the "best way" rare. Further, people, of course, are not words: They react to the decisions of managers and can, as a result, inhibit as well as accelerate solutions to problems.

We should now consider, finally, basic assumptions six and seven mentioned previously, namely, that managers are accountable for their actions to others and themselves, and that management is only a means, not an end itself. Because its successful practice requires specialized training and demands moral and ethical behavior, management may properly be called a profession and its practitioners held to professional standards of excellence. Further, by definition, management is a service. If it serves only itself, it serves no one. In a sense managers are accountable to all whose lives they affect, shareholders, employers, suppliers, customers, etc. They make a contribution to all these interest groups.

Happily, opportunities for such contribution abound, and skillful, responsible managers are in demand. But what is a manager, anyway? How do we recognize one when we see one? Where do we look? Where do managers hang out? What are they likely to be doing? Who else is involved? Why? So what? Who cares? These are fair but difficult questions that should be easier to answer by the time we have come to the end of this book. But we can begin by exploring the natural habitat of management and reflecting upon who and what we find there.

## The Habitat of Management

*Habitat,* according to Webster, is the natural abode, the particular location where something grows or lives, that place where it is commonly found. Habitant is the thing living in that location. We can borrow these definitions and, like naturalists in the field, begin by noting the salient characteristics of the habitat in which managers flourish and by recording their obvious behavior. Much later, we can consolidate our conclusions about both habitat and habitant.

What, then, is the natural habitat of managers? We might think of it as those intersections of time and place where the production or distribution of goods or services commonly occurs. It may also be regarded as those organizations whose collective purpose springs from such production or distribution. The practitioners and tasks of management are inexorably entwined with the evolution of such intersections and with the external and internal relationships of such organizations.

Thus, while managers are indisputably prevalent, more often than not they are found at certain predictable locations. Also, they are more often found in groups than alone. The groups they frequent are purposeful, not casual, and appear to be self-perpetuating. They are not self-sufficient, however, for we can observe numerous competitive and cooperative transactions among them. Managers visibly participate in these external relationships as well as in the more inner-directed activities of their own group. But the intent and effects of their participation are less apparent than its nature and frequency. Managers appear almost continuously to be engaged in interpersonal transactions that somehow relate to group identity and effectiveness. Just how this is so and why will preoccupy us throughout this book.

To facilitate our inquiry, it will be helpful to focus our attention on particular groupings and situations within the habitat of management. For example, we might observe religious, military, or governmental organizations, for they and their activities have certainly contributed to the demand for management and the supply of managers. The church, the armed services, and the many branches of government produce and distribute services (and sometimes goods) on a massive scale. They generate many of the kinds of functions and relationships in which managers specialize. But within and around the private, profit-oriented firm, we find an even better site for observing managers engaged in the full range of functions and relationships that defines their speciality. Unquestionably, it is that activity called "business" that is most synonymous with the past, the present, and the future of management. Business is the most natural habitat of managers. Thus, to understand the practice of management and the profession of manager, one must first understand the functions and relationships of business and the vocational demands their performance and conduct generate. These functions and relationships are both external and internal to the firm. We shall begin with externalities, but will move to internalities in due course. Throughout, however, we should remember these elements of our basic vocabulary: Functions can create relationships and relationships can create functions; but, in either case, managers *perform* functions and *conduct* relationships.

## Buying and Selling: Functions and Relationships

The two fundamental external functions of business are buying and selling, and the most basic business relationship is that of buyer and seller. The performance of these functions and the conduct of this relationship generate, perhaps, the most basic demands for management. Further, an additional and a complex set of functions and relationships follows from *what* people buy or sell, from *why, where, when,* and *how* people buy or sell, and from *whose business* it is what, why, where, when, and how they do so. These additional functions and relationships must also be managed.

WHAT PEOPLE BUY OR SELL

We have already used the words "goods" and "services" as one means of describing what people may buy or sell. But what do these words actually mean?

*Goods.* We may think of goods as tangibles—objects that can be touched, such as goldfish, spacecraft, motorcycle helmets, and artichokes. Some are "durable goods," those that people expect to last, that may be worth maintaining and repairing rather than replacing, and that are bought only a few times in one's lifetime rather than often. Examples are homes, refrigerators, automobiles, and furniture. Other goods are "semidurable." We expect them to wear out, but not right away. We take care of them, but we buy them more frequently. Clothing, shoes, and toys are good examples. Then there are "nondurable goods," those bought for short-term consumption and, thus, more frequently. Food, gasoline, toothpaste, and laundry detergent are examples.

*Services.* Compared to goods, services are less tangible. We may think of them as helpful experiences—some last a lifetime, and others must be periodically renewed. Teachers, doctors, lawyers, and policemen provide educational, medical, legal, and security services to students, patients, clients, and citizens. Bankers, engineers, bus drivers, and social workers provide consumers with financial, technical, transportation, and welfare services. Communication, recreation, and entertainment are also services, as are tax collection, rubbish removal, and pollution control.

Do the distinctions between and within goods and services have any significance? Indeed they do. They are important because they give us our first evidence that the demands placed on managers can vary from situation to situation. Buying or selling goods can differ from buying or selling services. For example, goods usually can be inspected before they change hands; services, however, are more difficult to appraise until they have actually been performed. Goods differ among themselves. Buying or selling perishables is unlike buying or selling durables. Services differ, too. Personal-service transactions such as a haircut are managed differently from impersonal-service transactions such as broadcasting the weather report. Further, the various degrees of complexity alter the managerial task. Buying or selling simple goods like nails requires knowledge and skills different from those used in buying more complex products like microscopes. A simple service transaction such as making change demands talents different from those of a complex service such as insuring a supertanker.

Distinctions among what we buy or sell, thus, give rise to different management situations, each with its own particular kind of manager. Part of the managerial task is certainly to recognize such differences in kind or degree and deal with them accordingly. Paradoxically, however, another part of the task is to discover common characteristics among seemingly disparate goods or services that permit them to be similarly managed. The very fact that a category like durable goods or personal services can be identified suggests that a common approach may be possible within that category; what is learned in one transaction may prove to be useful in similar situations. Trash compactors and television sets are different products, but the act of buying or selling them is remarkably similar. And buying or selling tax advice turns out to be little different from buying or selling insurance, although the reasons for buying or selling these services are not the same.

WHY PEOPLE BUY OR SELL

Why *do* people buy or sell? An ancient conundrum asks: "Which came first, the chicken or the egg?" So one might ask of the history of business: "Who came first, the buyer or the seller?" Let us try to examine the puzzle a little more closely.

If Necessity's first child was Invention, her second must have been Trade. There have always been the "haves" and the "have-nots," and, thus, there has always been at least the possibility, if not the fact, of exchange between the two. In primitive or subsistence societies, barter fills the need with three possible exchanges: (1) goods for goods, (2) services for services, and (3) goods for services. Barter becomes business when profit and a medium of exchange enter the transaction and the three trade possibilities become: (1) money for goods, (2) money for services, and (3) money for money. And trade requires management to the extent that buyers and sellers specialize functionally and to the extent that the processes comprising the buyer-seller transaction are consciously anticipated by each side.

### HOW PEOPLE BUY OR SELL

What are the key processes of selling that must be managed? At a minimum, the seller must have or accumulate marketable quantities and qualities of goods or services; estimate their demand; care for them through consummation of the sale; publicize their availability for sale; estimate an offering price that the market will bear; set any terms of sale; conduct the sale itself; collect payment; and finally, deliver the goods (or services).

*The Seller.* Consider the seller's management problems as an interdependent sequence of decisions that must be made. Suppose you have a three-speed bicycle, in reasonably good shape, that you would like to sell. The money gained from the sale is to go toward the purchase of a new ten-speed model. Your first management problem is the estimation of demand in your "trading area," (i.e., where your likely customers are). Is it even realistic, you might ask yourself, to think of selling a three-speeder when there are so many ten-speeders around? Who would buy a used three-speed bike? Who needs it? Where is a buyer likely to be found? In management terms, you must "segment the market" into that place, time, and type of consumer that fit the quantity and quality of what you wish to sell.

Having completed your analysis of the market, you now begin to publicize the availability of your bike for sale. Perhaps you begin by using word of mouth among relatives and acquaintances. But after the bike remains unsold, you decide to put up a sign. But where should the sign be placed? Should you advertise more formally? Where? How long? At what cost? How do you word the advertisement to attract attention, inform, and persuade prospective buyers? What selling points do you emphasize? Appearance? Style? Reliability? Price?

What price are you asking? How much will you accept? Are you willing to bargain? Why or why not? Is cash only required, or will you give your customer credit? Where and when can the bike be inspected or tested by prospective buyers? How are you maintaining its condition and security pending sale? Will you make the deal by mail, over the telephone, or only face to face, or does how the sale is made make little difference to you? How will the deal finally be struck? When and where will you receive payment? When and where will you deliver the bike to its new owner? How much did you make, or what is your profit, on the sale?

*The Buyer.*   While the seller is occupied with such decisions, the buyer—in whose place you may now imagine yourself, having sold the used bike and about to buy a new ten-speeder—in turn, is managing a set of complementary processes. They include: the specification of need, the appraisal of the merits of goods and services available, the accumulation of the requisite cash or credit, the setting of purchase criteria, the conduct of the purchase itself, receipt of the goods or services, and payment.

As you get ready to buy the new bike, you are now a potential consumer. Consider the sequence of interdependent purchasing decisions you must manage. Why do you wish to purchase a new ten-speed bicycle anyway? Is it a necessity or a luxury? Are you sure? When do you want it? Can you afford to wait? How can you find out what models are available? Can you shop around? Will you? Is there any helpful information on buying bikes that you can read? Whom should you ask for advice? How do you make up your mind? In answering these questions, you as buyer are also segmenting the market into that place, time, and type of seller that fit the quantity and quality of what you wish to buy.

Still you must question further: How much money do you have? Is it enough? How might you make up the difference? Is credit appropriate? Is it available? What is the most you will spend? Can you bargain? For what? Lower price? Free delivery?

Service after the sale? A money-back guarantee? How will the deal finally be struck? When and where will you make payment? When and where will you take possession of the bike? Are you satisfied with the transaction?

### ISSUES IN BUYING AND SELLING

From these examples, it should be clear that, even in simple transactions between buyers and sellers, the need for management varies directly with the uncertainties involved. For example, management of selling is relatively easier if the goods or services involved "command a ready market," that is, if they can be sold whenever and wherever available, with little haggling over quantity, quality, price, or the terms of sale. Such "sellers' markets" may reflect spontaneous shortages (e.g., a sudden demand for umbrellas during an unseasonably rainy period); they may reflect a fad (e.g., a recording of the latest popular song can be difficult to find); they may reflect more chronic imbalances of demand over supply (e.g., fossil fuels); or they may reflect the pure luxury trade (e.g., "elegance is priceless"). In any of these cases, the management of selling is dominated by the seller's desire to enjoy what the market will bear and her need to keep up with a very "visible demand."

But consider how uncertainties can creep in to complicate the management of selling. Suppose consumer preferences are muted or obscure. Do *you* always know what you want when you go shopping? If you do not, how is someone else supposed to know? A shop proudly displays the finest in potential heirlooms, but you may come in looking for throwaways. Another may offer the best in contemporary pieces, but you may ask for something more old fashioned. You want something yellow; a store may have it only in blue. Or a boutique carries only small sizes; you may want something in a large size. Worse, regardless of what is being sold, shoppers may come and go, with no more result than, "Just looking, thank you."

Suppose instead that you are buying or selling nuclear reactors, commercial jet aircraft, a low-income housing project, investment advice, a research laboratory, crude oil, or high-fashion clothing. How do complexity and scale breed uncertainty in these cases? If you are the seller, you may not have enough of what customers want. They want a fleet, whereas you have only two vehicles. You may not have all of the options that a customer wants. He wants a complete package of goods and related services, but you sell only some of the goods and some of the services. Suppose a customer must buy now but can only pay later. How might time and money be managed? If you deliver now but receive payment later, what can you do? Repossess your goods? Suppose the customer has ruined them or consumed them. Suppose that services rather than goods are involved: Can you repossess services that have already been performed? Can you insure yourself against loss? Suppose one is selling in Latin America but delivering in Japan. How might distance and intervening national borders complicate matters? What trade regulations must be honored? How is transportation to be arranged? How are exchanges of currencies to be accomplished? Suppose the goods or services involved are perishable. How do buyers or sellers avoid getting stuck with rotten eggs or last year's calendar? Suppose you have more than one product. How do you sell several goods or services simultaneously?

Suppose potential customers are indifferent or skeptical. How do you attract their attention, inform them, and persuade them that your product or service is worthwhile? Do you depend on satisfied customers to tell others? Do you advertise? If so, where? On billboards? In newspapers? Magazines? On radio? Television? If sales have responded to advertising, how do you find the point where the number of sales dollars earned per advertising dollar spent is greatest? Suppose the more you charge for your goods or service, the less customers buy. Managers call these kinds of goods and services "price elastic." How do you determine the price that reverses the trend? How do sellers manage in "buyers markets," where similar goods or services are readily available, where the conditions of purchase dominate the terms of sale, and power over what the market will bear has subtly shifted to the consumer? Is it more difficult to sell or to buy a used car?

### WHERE PEOPLE BUY OR SELL

Why, what, and when people buy and sell, therefore, create abundant opportunities for managers and management. *Where* people buy and sell adds more. It is not easy to determine the best point of sale or the best purchase point for diverse goods and services. It takes skill, hard work, and some luck. Every locational decision is a compromise among the preferences of the seller, the preferences of the buyer, and the nature of the goods or services involved. If you grew strawberries, mined copper, manufactured sailboats, or taught skiing, where would you prefer to sell? If you wanted strawberries, copper, sailboats, or ski lessons, where would you prefer to buy? The eternal question faced and somehow resolved is: Is it easier to bring the goods or services to the people, or to bring the people to the goods and services?

The answer can be resolved in the market. If a market is a place where buyers and sellers get together to do business, consider how many different marketplaces one encounters in a year's time: stores and offices of infinite variety, factories, farms, service facilities, street vendors, door-to-door salespersons, mail-order catalogs, auctions—the list could go on and on. The length of the list is less important than the point its diversity underscores: The choice of a proper marketplace or, to use a more contemporary idiom, of an appropriate channel of distribution is a management problem of the first order.

Recent business history can provide us with an example of the choice of a proper marketplace. Swiss watchmakers in the 1950s and 1960s were committed to production of a handcrafted, high-priced product of heirloom quality. It seemed reasonable to them to restrict distribution of their watches to jewelry stores of impeccable standing. They did this for two reasons: (1) to maintain the quality image of their product and (2) to enlist the jeweler as their salesperson, someone who was both able and authoritative in explaining the true value of what was being sold. Jewelers were willing to cooperate because Swiss watches fit their self-image, were compatible with other goods and services they sold (such as rings or repairs), and because the high selling price gave them a handsome profit on each sale (the difference between the price the jeweler paid the watchmaker and the price the jeweler charged the customer is variously called "mark-up," "mark-on," or "margin." Swiss watches, in this sense, were "high-margin" items). Customers seeking excellence and elegance responded to this particular distributive system. In contrast, an upstart American watchmaker called Timex decided to mass-produce a low-priced, "throwaway" watch. To sell its product, Timex had to turn to supermarkets and drugstores. The reason was simple: jewelers would not handle the product. The Timex watch was well made, quite durable, but rather utilitarian in appearance. If and when it failed, buying a new one was cheaper than repairing a broken one. In fact, the low price encouraged the customer to buy several for different uses rather than one for posterity. The Timex did not fit the jewelers' self-image and was not compatible with their other goods and services. Most important, however, it was a low-margin item that did not turn much of a profit on its sale and offered no future flow of income from a lifetime of perpetual maintenance and repair. Thus Timex sold through mass distributors, instead. Both the Swiss and Timex had to find appropriate marketplaces that would accommodate the different nature of each product and be compatible with the preferences of the customers they sought to attract. In one sense, both successfully managed the locational portion of the selling process. That Timex's profits on a high volume of low-priced watches soon exceeded Swiss profits on a low volume of high-priced watches is another story—to be taken up again when we consider the management problems of *how*, not why, what, when, or where to buy or sell.

### HOW YOU PLAY THE GAME COUNTS

Buyers and sellers share at least one common purpose: to make a deal at the lowest cost to themselves. But they approach that purpose as adversaries—however amicable their trading behavior may be. It is true that no sale takes place until both the buyer and the seller are satisfied, but their intentions are opposed: The seller is present to maximize the price he receives, and the buyer is there to minimize the price she pays. But compromise is the essence of trade, and for that reason how much to give becomes a key management problem on both sides.

The problem is eased somewhat, however, when buyers and sellers agree upon units of quantity and quality and upon a medium of exchange. In barter transactions of goods for goods, services for services, or services for goods, consider the difficulties of "fair exchange." How many coconuts are worth how many pearls? How much rowing is worth how much carrying? How much digging is worth how many nails? How many fish are worth how much carpentry? These transactions are made easier in business societies by agreement upon standardized weights, measures, and grades for goods and services, and by the designation of one particular commodity as "money." This permits the translation of different quantity/quality mixtures of different goods and services proportionally into monetary values. But units of quality, quantity, and value merely allow the adversaries to keep score. They do not supplant the trading game itself.

Even if only two players are involved in this adversary situation, conduct of the buyer-seller relationship can be a sticky management problem from either side. The reason is simple. Although actions by either side influence the outcome, neither side can completely determine the outcome itself, except by withdrawing from the relationship altogether. Thus how you play the game very much determines whether you win or lose. The management problem becomes more ticklish when we realize that either the buyer or the seller can introduce new players into the game and still other new players can introduce themselves whether the buyer, the seller, or their associates like it or not.

## Middlemen: Functions and Relationships

Should anyone else be involved in the buyer-seller relationship? By asking a "should" question, we raise the possibility that either or both sides may find it advantageous to share their functions and their roles in the relationship with others. It we call these "others" "middlemen," let us examine some of the circumstances under which they might be asked to participate. We shall, in the process, also be examining two more external relationships of business: middleman-seller and middleman-buyer.

### THE ROLE OF MIDDLEMEN IN BUYING OR SELLING

Why, when, where, and how might a buyer or seller decide not to buy or sell for himself? When might a buyer use the services of someone else to help him buy something? Why might a seller choose to sell goods or services through someone other than himself?

Let us begin with some analogous examples closer to home. We might be able to grow our own food, design and build our own houses, make our own clothes, educate ourselves, care for our own health, and write our own wills. To be able, however, is not necessarily to be willing. Most of us find it more convenient to obtain these goods and services from specialists. This is also the case in trade. At almost every step, there are opportunities to forgo inside competence to benefit from outside expertise. Managers call these opportunities "make-or-buy" decisions. They challenge themselves, in a sense, to show cause why making goods or performing a service themselves is better than buying from another firm.

Why might it be better, for instance, to buy rather than to make? Sometimes it is because we are ignorant, inexperienced, or lack requisite skills—we simply cannot draw or do not know the law, for example. Other times, it is because we cannot find the time to upgrade our knowledge, skills, or experience, or we are just too busy to return to school. Or we might have the competence to do the job, but we prefer to use our time for other activities in which we feel more distinctly competent. We might be perfectly able to mow our own lawn, shovel our own snow, or rake our own leaves. But we may choose to hire these services because we can afford to pay for them from earnings made doing something else instead. We tend to buy when it is cheaper than doing it ourselves, and "cheaper" can usually be expressed as some combination of quality, quantity, time, convenience, and money.

Buyers and sellers also sometimes find it cheaper to share the functions and the conduct of their relationship with specialists. Managers tend to employ middlemen when the specialist knows something that the manager does not know or knows only superficially, or when the specialist can do something the manager cannot do, or perhaps cannot do as well, or simply does not wish to do. Consider some examples of activities relevant to buying and selling that might be hired rather than undertaken directly by the buyer or seller.

Both buyers and sellers require current information on quantities, qualities, prices, and preferences: the latter to forecast and segment demand; the former to forecast and segment supply. In this case, specialists in market research or product evaluation can help. For example, would you know how to suggest what colors or fabrics might dominate women's fashions next year? Sellers and buyers need to know the information this year so that they may anticipate both the demand and the supply. They typically seek outside advice. Would you know how to evaluate the merits and demerits of the light aircraft available in today's market? If not, the services of an engineering consultant or a test pilot might be well worth their cost. If you are selling cosmetics to students, a consumer panel of experts made up of teenagers and young adults might be helpful to you. When you are buying securities, an investment analyst might be of assistance. If you are considering alternative locations for a new store, you might consider commissioning special studies of population densities, age and income mixes, and commuting patterns. If you are buying fuel oil, careful forecasts of future availability and price, provided by experts, might improve purchasing decisions now.

Buyers and sellers also require communications: the seller to publicize availability; the buyer to publicize need. Advertising, promotion, and media specialists abound, as do the media themselves. Moreover, both buyers and sellers require transportation: the latter to the point of sale; the former to the delivery point. They can transport goods themselves, to be sure, but they also may seek out common carriers, who serve shippers at posted prices on regular schedules, or contract carriers, who will tailor transportation services to the needs of particular clients.

Both buyers and sellers require care of their goods: the latter, pending sale; the former, after purchase. It is quite typical for them to turn to middlemen for packaging, storage, maintenance, or security facilities superior to their own. Buyers need payment mechanisms; sellers need collection mechanisms; and either may require credit. Middlemen rise to meet these needs. Legal advice, like financial services, frequently comes from outside.

In the marketplace itself, sellers often find it advantageous to hire specialists to display their wares and to act as their agents in conducting the sale. Buyers also may find it useful to purchase through specialized individuals or organizations. Why else would stores, showrooms, salespersons, brokers, personal shoppers, merchants, agents, and a host of other marketplace middlemen appear?

### RELATIONSHIPS WITH MIDDLEMEN

How middlemen relate to buyers and sellers, and to buying and selling, must be managed as are the decision processes leading to their selection or rejection. In one sense, these are buyer-seller relationships, with the middleman as seller. But they are somewhat distinct from the classic buyer-seller relationship because they are not primarily adversary in nature. We might think of them more as skeptical. The buyer, in this case, tends to have somewhat of a "show-me" attitude and must be convinced that entering into a relationship with a middleman is, somehow, better than buying directly himself. Indeed, the appearance and the survival of any middleman depend upon her client's assessment of her indispensability. This produces, perhaps, the most extreme form of "buyer's market" and colors the resulting relationship accordingly. The relationship cannot be one of hostility, suspicion, or mistrust or it is doomed; but even the most capable middleman is still vulnerable to the manager's decision that, for whatever reason, he is expendable.

From this it follows that the degree to which buyers or sellers employ middlemen is a measure of the degree of functional specialization the buyer or seller chooses to adopt. Adam Smith, writing in the 1770s, observed that specialization is limited only by the size of the market. By this he meant that the more business transactions there are, the less likely will any one individual or organization try to do everything. Specialists in every function and every relationship will appear, as will specialists in every good and every service. What we might add to Smith's cogent observation, however, is that the process of specialization is not supernatural. It is the outcome of decisions made by human beings exercising managerial judgment as to whether or not they should involve others in their affairs. These decisions may be considerations of: Which middlemen, if any, are to be involved? How many? How often? For how long? How much authority and responsibility are to be shared? How should costs and benefits be shared with others?

To summarize briefly, the question whether anyone else should be voluntarily involved in the functions of buying and selling or in the buyer-seller relationship has led us to discover new opportunities for managers and management. The question whether anyone else *is* involved leads us to more.

Besides his counterpart and any middlemen who have been invited to participate, there are at least two other interested parties involved in the buyer-seller relationship whether buyers, sellers, or middlemen like it or not: competitors and regulators. And there are six others who may be involved: creditors, debtors, employees, peers, superiors, and owners. This means that there are more functions and relationships to be conducted, and more functions and relationships to be managed.

## Borrowing and Lending: Functions and Relationships

When borrowing and lending precede or accompany buying and selling, the managerial functions and relationships involved become more complex. As a purchaser of goods or services, consider some situations in which you might prefer to buy something now and to pay for it at a later date. We might distinguish among these situations by dividing them into two groups: those in which consumer credit is convenient and those in which it is imperative.

### BUY NOW, PAY LATER

Very few of us can pass up a "bargain" in quantity, quality, or price. And many times we will go temporarily into debt in order to seize an opportunity. We do not have enough cash at the moment, but we know there will be enough cash available from our future income to more than pay the price of something. Credit can be a real convenience to consumers, but when you use a credit card at a service station or a charge account at a department store you are creating a creditor-debtor relationship as well as a buyer-seller transaction. You are helping to create a new opportunity for management and managers as well.

Credit can also be imperative. Seasonal imperatives, for example, are quite common. Farmers must buy seed and fertilizer in the spring, but they may be unable to pay for them until their crops are harvested and sold in the fall; manufacturers of Christmas novelties must purchase supplies and finance most of their production costs well before they receive the sales income that will pay off their obligations; a college student may borrow school expenses in the fall, confident they can be repaid out of earnings from a job the following summer. Imperatives of obsolescence also occur. The old car simply does not run any more; the children's clothes no longer fit; the smoky chimney is no longer legal and must be replaced. Imperatives of scale, too, must be accommodated. The price of a home can more easily be afforded if spread over time; the price of a needed piece of equipment may exceed this year's earnings but can be paid for in installments out of future earnings (which might even be higher because of its purchase). And emergencies create additional imperatives. There might be an unexpected hospitalization, a destructive fire, a lost purse, political disruption, or spoilage of a critical stockpile.

For convenience or out of necessity, then, you may chose to buy now, pay later. A seller may provide this option free or for a fee, called "interest" or "carrying charges," and he thereby becomes your creditor as well as your supplier. The goods or services involved "secure" the loan in that they must be returned or will be terminated if the debt is not paid within the period stipulated by the lender.

Alternatively, a purchaser might go to a third party—a middleman—to borrow all or part of the price of the goods or services desired. For this assistance, the lender sets a price for the loan (interest), stipulates the repayment schedule, and usually requires the pledge of something of value to secure the loan until it is repaid. This something of value is typically the item purchased itself: an automobile, a house or other building, machinery, a boat, aircraft, or land. Additional or alternative security may be required in the form of some other asset owned by the borrower or pledged for the borrower by a "cosigner" of the loan. A cosigner is a person who assumes the obligation for the loan along with the borrower. The lender becomes the borrower's creditor in this process, and until the loan is repaid, the creditor has a continuing interest in the debtor's affairs and solvency.

SELL NOW, COLLECT LATER

Turning to the other side of the buyer-seller relationship, consider some circumstances under which someone might prefer to sell now, collect later. Again, one finds both reasons of convenience and necessity. There are sometimes tax advantages, for example, in deferring income from the present to the future. The availability of consumer credit may sometimes mean the difference between a sale and no sale at all. The income received from a successful credit transaction may be greater than that which would have been received for the same transaction in cash.

THE MANAGEMENT OF LENDING AND BORROWING

Having now identified lending and borrowing as frequent business functions that precede or accompany purchases and sales, and having recognized creditor-debtor relationships as frequent preconditions and/or byproducts of buyer-seller relationships, we may now suggest some of the vocational challenges presented by the management of lending and of credit and by the management of borrowing and of debt.

The management of lending requires the information and ability to evaluate the "creditworthiness" of prospective borrowers (how likely the borrower is to repay the debt); to assess the risks for the lender under different lending assumptions and against alternative uses of the lender's funds; to negotiate the loan on favorable terms; to establish procedures for data-gathering and data-processing, collection, cancellation, and (if necessary) foreclosure or repossession; and to provide contingency reserves for "bad debts." Has the borrower borrowed before? Has she met previous obligations? How much does she already owe? Is it a better risk to lend to this borrower or to that one? How much interest is legal? How much interest is appropriate? What security should be pledged? How can I keep track of the borrower during repayment? Can I insure against loss?

The management of borrowing requires the information and ability to assess the risks for the borrower under different borrowing assumptions and against nondebt alternative sources of funds; to negotiate the loan on favorable terms; to secure proper repayment of the loan through the dedication of specific assets and/or income to that purpose; to ensure that the "debt capacity" of the borrower is not exceeded. Debt capacity means the amount a person can borrow without risk of nonpayment of the debt and interest. Should I borrow or use savings? Can I afford the interest? Can I give adequate security? Am I sure I can repay? Am I too much in debt already? Can I insure against loss?

Although their functions are distinct and their interests opposing, lenders and borrowers confront many similar problems and call upon similar managerial skills to help solve them. This can also be said for buyers and sellers. All must gather and evaluate data relevant to their individual self-interest and apply the intelligence gained in collective relationships. All confront functional opposites and use bargaining and negotiating techniques to narrow differences. All can benefit from systematic analysis and orderly procedures. All must manage the problem of "liquidity," that is, the difficult economic task of having sufficient cash where and when one wants it. All must manage the problem of "profitability," of having income that will, hopefully, typically exceed expenses by an acceptable margin. All face the challenge and the threat of "innovation," of something being done better than the current "state of the art." And all face the difficulties of establishing and maintaining coherence in present actions and between the actions of today and those of tomorrow.

Because such opposing business functions and relationships still have so many problems in common, we might begin to ask ourselves for future reference in this book if there may not, indeed, be some core set of management skills that, once mastered, are portable from function to function and from relationship to relationship. Before we go too far, however, there are other functions and relationships that must be explored. Let us begin with the function of competition and its attendant competitive relationships and then move on to matters of regulation, employment, and ownership.

## Competition: Functions and Relationships

Business competition thrives on aggressive behavior and adversary relationships, but it is more like power politics than war to the death. There are winners and losers, to be sure, but rarely total victory or total defeat. There is frequently another chance, another time, or another place. For this reason, the conduct of competitive relationships demands astute managers and efficient management.

At one level, competition may appear to be a game. For example, we can recognize competing "teams" that exhibit distinctive offensive and defensive formations and some definite "plays" that vary the comparative quantity, quality, and price of available goods and services. Moreover, we can spot individual managers who, like chess masters or All-American halfbacks, have developed a personal repertoire of "moves." And we can also keep "score" in terms of sales volume, market share, and profitability.

There is more to competition than overt play, however. There is an accompanying, but more subtle, agenda of basically political choices: how to exploit strengths and buffer weaknesses; whether to observe or to act; when to speak and when to listen; whether to confront or to compromise; when to challenge and when to withdraw; whether to innovate or to imitate, that is, to lead or to follow; whether, in short, to ignore, anticipate, or react; and, if so, when, where, and how. Let us take two classic examples of how managers might think through some of the competitive elements.

Suppose a product that you offer requires the use of expensive raw materials. Although it is very costly to produce because of its scale and technological complexity, it is nonetheless clearly a necessity for a small but stable group of consumers. Examples of such a product might be a nuclear reactor, an electron microscope, or a supersonic jet plane.

Under these conditions, you assume that you will have few competitors because there are only a few customers and because entry into the market is difficult; that is, only a few people can make the same product. You assume also that you will have a large potential market share, but there will be few unit sales per competitor. You must charge high unit prices to cover high unit costs, but you know too that customers might pay an additional premium for extra quality and utility. You realize that competition in this particular market revolves much more around the quality and utility of competing products than their quantity or price. You probably will, therefore, tend to compete in areas such as design, installation, service, product modification after the sale, and replacement planning. Repeat business would be a long-term phenomenon, so that the profit per sale would have to be high enough for you to remain solvent in the interim between sales.

Suppose, on the other hand, a product that you offer uses cheap raw materials. It is very inexpensive to produce because of its uniformity and lack of technological complexity. But it is clearly a necessity for a large and stable group of consumers. Examples of such a product might be breakfast cereal, toothpaste, bleach, or laundry detergent.

Under these conditions, you assume that you will have many competitors because there are many customers and because entry into such a market is easy; that is, almost anyone can make the same product. Further, you assume that you will have a smaller potential market share than in the preceding example, but you now will have many more unit sales per competitor. You must charge low unit prices because unit costs are low and because the customer will not pay a premium for your product, since its quality and utility do not differ from those of your competitors. You would, therefore, assume that competition in this market would consist of, somehow, differentiating your product from others on dimensions other than price, quality, or utility. You might, for example, consider how competing toothpastes are differentiated: the use of brand names to create identity; the development of brand awareness through advertising; the use of flavorings; the convenience of a variety of sizes; distinctive packaging; and almost universal availability. Repeat business will be frequent, but the profit per sale will be low. But this means a high sales volume and a large market share will be imperatives for solvency.

In the first case, competition consists of selling a few high-priced items, to a few customers, infrequently, at a high profit per sale, and with much direct buyer-seller contact. In the second case, competition consists of selling many low-priced items, to many customers, as often as possible, with a low profit per sale, and with very little personal contact between buyers and sellers except through advertising and distributive middlemen. In current business terminology, managers would be well advised to use "personal selling" in the first instance, and a "mass-marketing" approach in the second.

These two examples do not cover all of the competitive situations managers may encounter. For example, most goods and services ultimately *do* compete on a price basis. Just because you decide to buy a luxury rather than economy car does not mean that you will not shop around for the best price. Even the finest of furs are more or less expensive. To cite another situation in which our two classic examples may disappear, consider the problems of competing during periods of rapid technological change. With the very nature of the product vulnerable to dramatic, almost daily change, traditional price-quality relationships become irrelevant. When transistors replaced vacuum tubes in utility, long-standing assumptions about the size, shape, quality, and price of radio and television receivers were replaced as well. The process accelerated further when solid-state circuitry replaced the wiring complexes of an earlier time. Inexpensive, hand-held, electronic computers were only a fantasy until they appeared to sweep bulkier, more expensive, slower, more simplistic products from the field.

The two classic examples presented previously do suggest, however, most of the typical competitive judgments managers must make: What consumer preferences, product characteristics, and technological imperatives constrain *all* competitors in my particular market? Which of these conditions of doing business might be responsive enough to innovation on my part to give me a competitive edge? Does it matter if someone else gets the innovation first? Is it necessarily unprofitable to be a follower? When should competition be a spectator sport? Have the rules of the game changed?

To highlight the complexity of the managerial task, let us look a little more deeply into the subtleties of competitive decision-making. We can begin by examining four simple, but typical, competitive plays: variance of price, variance of quality, new product development, and product diversification.

*Variance of Price.*   A manager must constantly ask herself: Can I lower (or raise) my price? How will buyers and competitors behave if I lower (or raise) my price? One way to lower my price might be to cut my margin. Can I afford to do so given my costs? If so, for how long before I lose money on each sale? Another way to lower my price is to cut costs themselves. Can I truly do so, or am I up against a technological or labor barrier? Even if I can cut costs and/or cut margin, will the number of sales I make increase if I lower my price? Will consumers really buy more if I charge less, or are they insensitive to price? What will my competitors do? Will they undercut my price, giving me the option of undercutting theirs once again? If I do trigger a price war, is my staying power greater than theirs? What if I raise my price? Will others follow, with little effect on the distribution of market share, or will they lag behind and gain sales at my expense? In short, the manager must constantly assess the risks of price leadership, whether up or down.

*Variance of Quality.*   A manager must also ask himself: What if I invest in a quality increase? Will consumers be able to perceive it? If they do not, can I increase their awareness? If they do, will they absorb some or all of my increased costs through a willingness to pay more for my better product? If consumers do not perceive an increase in quality, can I afford to continue selling at the old price but at the new costs? Assuming I can keep my old customers, even at a premium price, will my better product attract new customers who have never bought my product before and increase, thereby, my market share? What will my competitors do? Will they follow me up the quality scale? What will happen if they do? If they do not? On the other hand, what are the consequences if I reduce the quality of my product? How will my customers and competitors respond?

*New Product Development.*   Suppose now that I have developed an entirely new product. Nothing like it has ever been offered to the public before. When, where, and how do I introduce it for maximum market penetration and profit? Do I try a few test markets first? Have I estimated the price-quality mix that the market will bear? How vulnerable is my product to imitation?

Will my competitors be able to make it better or cheaper once they see it? Will I be able to recover my developmental investment as well as my production and marketing costs? What, in short, are the risks of product innovation?

*Product Diversification.* Finally, since each market for each product has such different profiles of consumer and competitive behavior, am I better off specializing or diversifying my product line? Should I concentrate my risk in a single product in a single market, or can I spread my risks over several products in several markets? Is it realistic to believe that the ups and downs of one market might be favorably offset by the ups and downs of another? Is it technically or legally possible to play one market against another, one competitive situation against another, or one portfolio of risk against another?

Competition and competitive relationships generate such questions. Managers resolve them just as they might resolve the questions generated by the functions of buying, selling, lending, borrowing, and intermediation and by their attendant relationships.

Consider a competitive experience from recent business history that combines almost all these problems and challenges. It is easy to recall the spartan, two-door, rear-engine sedan that the West German firm Volkswagen began to import into the American market after World War II. It sold for well under $2000, accommodated a family of three comfortably (plus one or two friends in a squeeze), came in assorted bold colors, got good gasoline mileage, and was easily driven and repaired. Its style changed little from year to year, and the idea was to drive the one you bought for a considerably longer period than was expected of postwar American cars. It had a noisy, homely appeal that was captured in various nicknames like the "Beatle" or the "Bug." It rapidly became the most popular imported car in the United States, and American sales soon accounted for over 50 percent of world Volkswagen sales. Buyers were happy and so was the seller. American competitors tried their best to dent this market, but they had little success.

At the height of its popularity, however, the Beatle's competitive world came unglued. First came a set of American automobile safety regulations that added weight (e.g., thicker steel in vulnerable spots like bumpers and fuel tanks), lowered performance, and raised costs. Next came a set of federal emission-and-noise-control regulations that bore heavily on the Volkswagen's notoriously "dirty" and noisy engine, and that could only be accommodated by reconfiguring the popular shape and further raising costs and reducing performance. Unit labor costs in Germany were rising, too. And during the early seventies appeared sportier, price-competitive Japanese vehicles, which began to gain an American market share. American manufacturers fought back, too, with more compact and economical cars.

Almost overnight (during 1970–1971), the manufacturers of Volkswagen automobiles saw their product's viability in its prime market seriously deteriorate. To survive meant the abandonment of traditional configuration, performance, and price. It also meant experimentation with new configurations, multiple models, and diverse performance and price alternatives characteristic of their product line since 1975. The result is yet uncertain, but without prompt and purposive management, Volkswagen might have been cut out of its most lucrative market.

## Deciding on Strategy

The Volkswagen example and our earlier discussion of choices of whether or not to buy, sell, use middlemen, lend, borrow, or compete suggest another underlying function performed by managers: self-determination. By this is meant the setting of limits on what activities they and those whom they choose to involve in relationships with them will perform. The philosopher or the poet might ask: Who am I? Who should I be? The more pragmatic manager, however, asks: What business am I in? What business should I be in? He also asks these questions in the future tense: What business shall I be in, and should I be in, tomorrow?

The definition of purpose and the limitation of intent, therefore, are difficult features of management because there are so many possibilities. For example, what to buy or sell, when to buy or sell, where to buy or sell, how to buy or sell, and whether to buy or sell at all can be answered in an almost infinite variety of ways. Self-determination—or "strategy formulation," as managers usually refer to the function—requires coherent decisions as to which set of answers one chooses to pursue, which to forgo or ignore, and which to avoid. Self-determination connotes a collective as well as an individual task. Not only is the manager responsible for his own individual identity (how he thinks about himself and his job), but he must also engage in the search for collective identity and purpose in the organization of which he is a part. How do members of his organization think about it and its purposes? (How a manager does this will be considered in detail in the Sections I and II of this book.)

This is not to cast the manager in some superhuman role, however, detached from day-to-day reality. Indeed, as we shall see in the other sections of this book, managers must spend a large portion of their time in solving daily problems, and they can search for an individual or a collective identity only as the pressures of the present permit. But they are not absolved of managerial responsibility, and even a catch-as-catch-can search is more beneficial to all concerned than no search at all.

Again, let us stress that this is not meant to depict the manager's role as one of complete isolation. Managers do not exist in a vacuum. The functions and relationships discussed so far do embody elements of choice and, thus, elements of voluntarism. But they also involve other people. Therefore, although every managerial decision calls for some degree of self-determination, that degree is influenced by the intentions and behavior of others—both inside and outside the manager's own organization. And just as the manager is accountable to himself, so, too, is he accountable to others. These additional ramifications of the manager's role may be appreciated more fully when we examine relationships generated by the functions of regulation, employment, and ownership.


## Regulation: Functions and Relationships

"None of your business" is probably one of the most common exclamations in the English language. If we speculate for a moment on why this is so, and on when it might be an accurate or inaccurate observation, we can begin to study the difficult subjects of regulation, employment, and ownership and their implications for managers and management.

### THE "PRIVACY" OF PRIVATE ENTERPRISE

The usual vehemence with which we are told "Mind your own business!" idiomatically signals a more pervasive ideological contention: that many of the functions and relationships of business are considered private by those who manage them. Is this contention legitimate? Why should such privacy be asserted?

The arguments for private enterprise rest on a variety of propositions, but three are central: To the extent that it is proprietary, voluntary, and competitive, business is asserted to be private. Let us examine each of these propositions in turn to develop the argument. Later we shall consider its legitimacy.

*Proprietary Argument.* The proprietary assertion rests on the sanctity bestowed upon personal property by Anglo-American philosophy and law: It is legitimate to strive to accumulate, conserve, employ, and transfer private property by legal means. The application of this theme to business should be understandable: To the extent that business represents the accumulation, conservation, employment, or exchange of property among its legitimate owners, it should be considered a private affair. Just as "a man's home is his castle," to utilize as he sees fit, so, too, one's business ought to be one's own, to manage as one pleases.

*Voluntarism.* The assertion of voluntarism springs from a particular interpretation of the nature of some of the very functions and relationships we have been discussing. It is argued that the relationships that accompany functions such as selling, buying, lending, borrowing, or intermediation are voluntary; either party can always withdraw. Sales and purchases are interdependent. We cannot have one without the other. They only occur because of mutual consent. No seller can force someone to buy; no buyer can force someone to sell; no lender can force anyone to borrow; no borrower can force anyone to lend; and middlemen are welcome by invitation only. The linkage with privacy should be obvious: Voluntary relationships should only be the concern of their participants.

*Competitiveness.* Sellers and lenders are the principal sources of the competitive assertion. The marketplace is open to all who choose to enter, they argue; Let each person do the best she can in the field, but preserve the game. Privacy is necessary here not because competitive relationships are voluntary, but precisely because they are not. In chess, the board, the pieces, and the positions are there for all to see. But it would ruin the game if each player divulged her current strategy prior to each tactical move. In cards, what would be the point of dealing and playing all hands face up? In business, the argument goes, the consumer benefits from competition. Hence why subvert the very purpose of the exercise?

### SELF-REGULATING BUYER-SELLER RELATIONSHIPS

The argument of privacy has one more stage that has significance for the performance of business functions and the conduct of business relationships. Not only should voluntary relationships among proprietors and involuntary relationships among competitors be private, but they should also, to many minds, be self-regulating. That is, the relationship should be governed by the parties involved, not by any external agency.

Are buyer-seller and lender-borrower relationships self-regulating? Are processes of intermediation by middlemen and processes of competition self-regulating? Were they ever? Can they be? Should they be? These are high-priority managerial and public policy questions to which we shall now turn.

The doctrine of self-regulation, while anchored in the doctrine of privacy, looks to the marketplace and the behavior of its participants as the mechanisms of control. Adam Smith called the market's tendency to regulate itself "the invisible hand." By this he meant that if prices rise too high or quality falls too low, consumers simply will not buy. Moreover, only those competitors able to tune their pricing and quality control to this "consumer sovereignty" will survive. Indeed, in the pure "free-enterprise" view, they are the only competitors worthy of survival.

Faith in the self-preservating instincts of consumers and competitors thus lies at the heart of the self-regulatory philosophy. Indeed, the old warning *caveat emptor* ("let the buyer beware") captures the spirit of this faith. Another characteristic of the self-regulatory philosophy is its disinterest in issues of equity. If a seller has sold something voluntarily and if a buyer has bought it voluntarily, then the terms of the transaction between them must have been agreeable to both. That is, the transaction is deemed a "fair" one. Similar logic is applied to lender-borrower transactions and intermediation relationships.

A final principle of self-regulation is that government has the right to tax property and business transactions to raise revenue, but that its power to tax for purposes of control is suspect if not illegitimate. The argument goes something like this: Let "free enterprise" be free of regulation, but tax the result —either in the form of transactions taxes (e.g., license fees, excise taxes, tariffs, sales taxes) or in the form of taxes on property, income, and/or profits.

We know that both the concept of business and the philosophical ideal of a self-regulating market are very old. But has such a market ever existed in reality? A thorough study of business history as far back as written records permit shows us that the answer is no.

### DRAWBACKS TO SELF-REGULATION

*Governmental Strictures.* In what ways has the ideal of the self-regulating market been eroded and why? Two ancient customs, vestiges of which survive today, probably began the process. The first was the prerogative of temporal rulers to reserve, within the boundaries of their domains, certain businesses as monopolies for themselves, their heirs, or their assignees. Because of its value as a preservative, for instance, commercialization of natural salt was often reserved by ancient rulers for their own benefit. To cite another example, newly discovered or conquered lands were typically reserved to the ruler until dispensed with or sold to favorites for commercial development. The Spanish, French, English, and Dutch colonies in North America began this way. Sometimes governments went further and actually subsidized developmental efforts for a share in the eventual gain. The practice of granting patents was and is another manifestation of this tradition. Patents grant an innovator a monopoly limited by time and place.

Regulation of entry to markets is very old in other forms,

too. Not only have governments typically controlled entry into certain reserved monopolies (or near-monopolies), they have always regulated the access foreign business people, goods, or services have to their national borders. Import licenses and controls and tariffs for revenue can be found throughout history. Tariffs for the "protection" of domestic business have been common over the past 400 years. Japan, even today, restricts most stringently the importation of foreign goods, services, and capital. Some governments have also favored "exit" restrictions, too, in the form of export licenses and controls on goods, services, and money.

Other regulations on entry into the marketplace can be found to date back as far as the laws enforced by the walled cities of antiquity. The conditions of entering the city to do business there were extensively prescribed according to hours of access, standard weights and measures, allocation of display space, sign control, display limitations, product quality standards, sanitation rules, rules of competitive behavior, and, sometimes, ceiling prices. Similar regulations are to be found in public marketplaces throughout subsequent world history, and virtually every modern consumer protection law has its ancient antecedents. Modern pure-food-and-drug laws are derived from ancient proscriptions against adulteration and contamination. Today's campaigns for "truth in advertising," "truth in lending," "truth in labeling," and "truth in packaging" all have historical precedents. Product liability and *caveat vendor* are newer regulatory themes, but not too new.

*Religious Customs.* A second ancient custom gave spiritual rulers the power of denying certain businesses to individuals of other religious persuasions. Jews were discriminated against in non-Jewish domains; Christians were restricted in non-Christian domains; Muslims were controlled in non-Muslim domains—the list is endless. And, of course, where church and state were one, the possibility of regulation doubled.

Where and when church and state have been one, the former has had other regulatory influences on business. Most religions address ethical and moral issues associated with buying, selling, lending, and borrowing, and religious philosophy has frequently been translated into political regulation. The exclusion of nonbelievers from some trades has already been mentioned and continues today—notably in the Middle East. Two other good examples that date from the Middle Ages are proscriptions against usury (i.e., excessive interest charged on loans) and doctrinal and economic debates over the "just price" and the "fair return." Almost every modern business executive in the Western world is somewhere subject to laws restricting excess interest or profits that are rooted in medieval Catholic dogma.

But regulation of business along class or religious lines eroded the self-regulating market ideal in two ways. First, it restricted free entry into the markets so reserved or monopolized. Second, it substituted "administered prices" for market prices to the extent that the prices charged by official monopolies were whatever the government decided they should be. Consumers still had the choice of buying or not buying, but they had no true alternatives. The granting of official monopolies or subsidies is, of course, still quite prevalent. But the reasons and their implications for management have changed. In earlier times, monopolies were created principally to increase public revenues and their managers behaved accordingly. A successful manager under these circumstances was one who could administer prices so as to maximize public profit. Today, public monopolies are created to minimize consumer costs for some vital community service (such as collecting and delivering the mail) or to undertake projects beyond the capacity of the private sector (such as exploring outer space). Prices are administered (hopefully) to maximize service. Semipublic monopolies (such as communications, transportation, lighting, and power companies) are also sanctioned to provide universal and uniform service at (again, hopefully) least cost to the public.

Evidence of direct price controls is also easy to find in Western economic and business history. Scarcity, for example, has always triggered regulation. Natural disasters like fire, flood, drought, or pestilence have almost always brought about the regulation of prices. Similarly, war has had the same result. The most persistent price controls, however, have been ceilings placed on interest rates. Until the twentieth century, such controls were extensions of ancient moral prohibitions against usury. In this century, this rationale has continued, but it has been joined by more economically based arguments respecting the relationship between interest rates and the propensity of individuals to save and invest rather than to spend. More typical earlier than today, however, were severe penalties (usually including imprisonment) against defaulting debtors.

We could go on and on and prove rather easily that the regulation of business is as old as business itself. There have been laws to protect consumers, borrowers, sellers, lenders, competitors, intermediaries, and even the environment. And not all have been thrust upon the concerned parties. Many of these laws have been embraced voluntarily by all parties for mutual benefit (the adoption of standard weights and measures is a good example). Also, not all of these laws have been thrust upon "business" by some nonbusiness interest. Indeed, even a casual examination reveals that many regulations are controls that one group of business people has been able to have imposed upon another group of business people (buyers upon sellers, or borrowers upon lenders, for example).

### THE CHALLENGE: UNDERSTANDING SELF-REGULATION

But this is not the challenge for managers and regulators. The greater challenges are to discover where, when, and how self-regulation works, and where, when, and how it does not; to recognize when regulatory precedent should control and when it should not; and continuously and constructively to adjust the elusive balance of private enterprise and public interest.

Regulatory relationships are, then, another vocational challenge for managers. But, they differ from those relationships we have discussed so far. First, they are not bilateral, but multilateral. Complex issues simultaneously involve multiple interest groups. Almost 2000 permits had to be secured and several years of hearings and litigation had to be weathered before construction could begin on the Alaska pipeline. Second, they are seldom "one on one." Dealing with consumers in general is quite different from dealing with a customer in particular. Third, regulatory relationships are not true adversary relationships. They might more accurately be thought of as "advocacy" relationships, in which today's adversaries may be tomorrow's allies, depending upon the issue of the day. American automobile manufacturers and the United Autoworkers of America can put aside their differences to lobby against the export of American jobs, or to support affirmative-action programs for hiring and training women, minority-group members, and the handicapped. Arch competitors may join together in proposing or opposing regulations they deem critical to their mutual survival. Otherwise highly competitive truckers band together to propose an expansion of the Citizens Band radio network, or to oppose the national 55-mile-per-hour speed limit.

CONSISTENCY OF REGULATION

Consistency in regulation is difficult at best. First, regulatory principles must be situationally interpreted. For example, the intent of the national Occupational Safety and Health Act passed in the early 1970s is exemplary, but the task of defining minimum standards of compliance, industry by industry, has been enormous and the process acrimonious. Does that law apply in this case? Will the decision be upheld? This situation has never come up before. Second, enforcement of regulation is selective. All situations cannot be monitored equally. All violations cannot be detected. All allegations cannot be investigated. Third, American law enforcement is, basically, reactive. A violation must occur before the remedy is applied, but the remedy is not always prompt or just. The burden or proof is on the aggrieved party or, in her absence, on the public, which is not always willing or able to persevere to a conclusion. Fourth, blame is sometimes difficult to apportion even though there might be a consensus that some violation has occurred. For example, a stream or a beach is obviously polluted in violation of the law, but it may be difficult to discover who is to blame. Fifth, in some special cases the potential to violate has been equated with a violation itself. For example, the Western Electric Company has been prohibited from selling components other than to its sister companies in American Telephone and Telegraph because their presence in this market would be disruptive to competition.

To understand better the complex web of regulatory functions and relationships performed and conducted by modern managers, we must now ask: Who regulates? Where, when, how, and why do they regulate? Some examples will also help to clarify, and permit us to highlight the major implications of the answers to these questions for managers.

Who regulates and where they do so can be answered in two ways. First, we can differentiate governmental from nongovernmental regulation and, then, we can distinguish among levels and jurisdictions of the former. Where regulation takes place—in either its public or private guise—is easily separable into local, state, national, and international examples.

A substantial proportion of the regulatory functions and relationships encountered by managers today are not public, but private, or nongovernmental. The major reason this is true is that most management transactions are conducted through actual or implied contracts with other private individuals or organizations. Contracts to buy, sell, lend, borrow, and employ are good examples. Although such contracts are and must be legal, they still represent the primary private means by which managerial organizations overtly regulate each other. The primary implicit form of self-regulation is of course, competition.

Besides contracts and competition, however there are other forms of private regulation, and, as management becomes more and more professional, this will continue to be true. For example, many managers must pass certification requirements set by industry-sponsored professional associations before they can rise too far in their specialty. Perhaps the most notable case in point is found in accounting, where strict standards must be met to qualify as whatever the local equivalent of the American "Certified Public Accountant" or the British "Chartered Accountant" may be. Analogs are to be found in other industries as well, such as among underwriters and actuaries in insurance. The setting of such vocational standards and their enforcement are forms of self-regulation by managers. Self-regulation takes other forms, too. For example, internal and external audits of financial performance typically impose industry standards of "best practice" besides complying with governmental rules and procedures. The same can be said for standards for worker and product safety developed by private, industry-sponsored underwriting organizations. Codes of conduct have also been voluntarily generated in many managerial groups—especially in the service industries.

There is no doubt, however, that the vast majority of regulatory transactions are between public agencies and private organizations rather than among private organizations themselves. Who the public regulators are—and how, when, what, and why they regulate—remains to be considered in greater detail.

Public regulators can be sorted by jurisdiction and by how and when they regulate. The public regulatory process separates into legislative, executive, administrative, judicial, and commercial modes, and transactions are usually taking place simultaneously in all five of these modes and at all four levels of government (local, state, national, and international). Public regulatory transactions can also be sorted into those that tend to be nonrecurrent (i.e., those that take place "once and for all"), and those that tend to be recurrent (i.e., those that occur with some degree of periodicity). For example, one managerial organization might be simultaneously testifying in favor of a new municipal zoning ordinance (local, legislative, and relatively nonrecurrent), engaged in rate hearings before a public-utility commission (local or state, administrative, and probably recurrent), selling goods to the public schools (local or state, commercial, and hopefully, recurrent), complying with a presidential wage-price freeze (national, executive, and, hopefully, nonrecurrent), appealing a lawsuit to the Supreme Court (national, judicial, and probably nonrecurrent), and negotiating an exclusive concession agreement to mine raw materials abroad (international, legislative, executive or administrative, and, hopefully, nonrecurrent). Another managerial organization might be appearing in tax court (local, state, national, or international; administrative or judicial; recurrent or nonrecurrent), buying surplus government property (local, state, or national; commercial; recurrent or nonrecurrent), seeking presidential intervention in a labor dispute (national, executive, and hopefully, nonrecurrent), and negotiating compensation for a recent expropriation of foreign assets (international, executive, and judicial, nonrecurrent).

Forty simple combinations of the five regulatory modes, the four regulatory levels, and the two regulatory frequencies are possible, and all might be going on at once. This complexity and simultaneity in public regulation begins to pose the managerial challenge. But we now must add some categories of what is publicly regulated and why.

### WHAT IS REGULATED?

What is being publically regulated can be summarized as structure, conduct, performance, or some combination thereof. Structural regulation concerns the organization of managerial units and the organization of the marketplaces in which they interact. Examples of structural regulations might be limitations on the size of firms or the number of firms in a given market. Examples of the regulation of conduct might be rules governing pricing, competitive behavior, or labor-management relations. Examples of performance regulation might be ceilings on profits (which are common in wartime) or environmental quality standards (which most likely are here to stay). Adding only these three gross categories of *what* is regulated, raises our number of simple regulatory combinations to 120, and we have not yet considered *why* public regulation takes place at all.

### WHY IS IT REGULATED?

There are at least six general reasons for public regulation of the private sector: (1) to grant private enterprise legitimacy; (2) to adjudicate private disputes; (3) to promote private enterprise; (4) to inhibit private enterprise; (5) to raise public funds from private enterprise; and (6) to do business with private enterprise. Let us look at some modern examples of each.

Governments legitimize private enterprise through incorporation, licensing, and concession procedures. These legitimations may range from the granting of a liquor or taxi license by a municipality, through the incorporation of a firm under state statutes, or the licensing of radio and television stations by the Federal Communications Commission, to concessions to business bestowed by national or international authorities. Governments typically must sanction the *public* issuance of equity (e.g., ownership shares) and debt (e.g., bonds) and oversee their exchange (trading) in public securities markets (private conveyances of property and private lending or borrowing need only be registered after consummation). And in each instance (subject, of course, to due process of law) what the government gives, in the forms of incorporation, license, or concession, the government can take away.

Public regulation also occurs to promote private enterprise, once legitimate. Examples would include patents to protect the profits of innovation, indirect investment and consumption incentives (usually in the form of tax cuts, rebates, or credits), subsidies for research and development (such as those associated with defense and space programs), subsidies for education and training, direct subsidies for investment and/or operation (as in the transportation and agricultural sectors). At the same time, a vast network of inhibitions is placed on aspects of the structure, conduct, and performance of private enterprises to tune them more to the public interest: for example, rules respecting fair employment practices, occupational health and safety, equal opportunity, environmental quality, fair competitive practices, public reporting, product liability, consumer rights, minimum wages, pure food and drugs, and the like. Further, public regulation is available to adjudicate private contractual disputes between buyers and sellers, lenders and borrowers, landlords and tenants, owners and operators, employers and employees.

The last two major rationales for public regulation of private enterprise are to do business and to raise revenue. Since the late 1930s, business transactions (buying and selling, lending and borrowing) between public and private organizations in the United States have increased about fivefold. This has meant increases in both government uses of funds for growth, welfare, and security and government sources of funds, and in both instances many more government-business relationships.

A FINAL ANALYSIS

In only this brief discussion we have still implied *at least* 720 possible simple public regulatory situations (5 modes × 4 levels × 2 frequencies × 3 objects × 6 reasons), and because we can sense many nuances in the examples given, we sense that the true number of combinations is definitely much higher. To round out the picture, consider that in each regulatory situation managers have the options of reacting or anticipating. For example, one might choose to wait and only react to a legislative, executive, administrative, judicial, or commercial situation, or one might seize the initiative and try to influence the outcome through all the legal, moral, and ethical means available. When we include these options, our *minimum* set of simultaneously possible public regulatory situations increases to 1440! No wonder the functions and relationships generated by government-business interactions play such a large role in modern management and in the lives of modern managers. They are complex, sometimes contradictory, and almost always ambiguous. Despite "free enterprise" and the ideal of self-regulation, these public-private interactions are necessary and increasing. They require perception, tact, judgment, and flexibility. The challenge is to deal with them realistically, rather than to long romantically for the simplicity of earlier days.

Two key sets of relationships remain to be introduced in this preview of management and managers: relationships that spring from employment and those that arise from ownership.


## Employment: Functions and Relationships

Employer-employee relationships must surely be as ancient as those of buyers and sellers. Working for others has been a fact of life for most of the human race. But what are some of the premises that the manager brings to this relationship? At the outset, we must remember that the employee's work is an output for the employee, but it is an input for the employer. In one sense, it is a means to an end for the manager and an end in itself for the worker. This basic difference in perspective is, of course, the basis for misunderstanding as well as for understanding.

The classic employer's point of view casts the employee as a subordinate and as a volunteer. Subordinates take orders, by definition, and volunteers can quit if they do not like the work or the boss. Also, "if they can be hired, they can be fired." These views follow from the basic premise, but, obviously, their truth cannot condone the propensity of some managers to treat their workers merely as costs to be minimized, as subordinates to be subordinated, as disposable raw materials, or as interchangeable parts.

Granting the best of intentions and good faith on both sides, there have always been large areas of contention between management and labor. Typically at issue are: pay and fringe benefits, hours of work, productivity, working conditions (e.g., health and safety on the job), grievance procedures, recognition of union representation, job security, training, promotion, and retirement. In the past, these differences were resolved (or not resolved) between owners (or their managerial designates) and each individual worker (usually on a "take-it-or-leave-it" basis). No third parties were involved except to break up strikes. Settlements with one worker did not set precedents for or constrain settlements with another. Equity across the work force was unknown. Management under these conditions was autocratic at worst, paternal at best.

However, the modern context for compromising these age-old issues is quite different. It revolves around the process of bargaining between designated managers and the duly elected representatives of their workers, and is periodically codified in a legal, multiyear contract that binds all individuals on both sides to the collective agreement. Hence what goes for one, goes for all. All managers are equally bound and all workers are equally bound to the provisions of the contract. The bargaining context, the contract provisions, and grievance procedures under the contract are all regulated by government agencies, as are most aspects of management-labor relationships. The potential for disruption and deadlock is always high, but the potential for cooperation and progress is always higher.

Although most managers do not participate in the negotiating of collective-bargaining agreements, all managers are involved in the implementation of the contract "on the job." Managers handle the day-to-day responsibilities of hiring, training, supervising, evaluating, compensating, and terminating workers. They are also responsible for worker health, safety, welfare, and morale. They are the interface between motivations and priorities of the workers and the objectives and priorities of the organization.

It should be remembered that the "bottom line" of the labor-management relationship must be productivity, that is, the output of goods and services per unit of labor-management input. Rising productivity is the only real source of steadily rising take-home pay and fringe benefits for employees and managers, and the only real source of steadily rising profits for the organization. In not-for-profit situations, rising productivity means better services to customers or clients at lesser cost. But productivity is difficult to raise, because it depends upon many subtle interactions among the quality of the workers involved, the quality of the tools available to them, and the quality of the management of these human and mechanical factors. The outcome depends in large part upon humane, enlightened, and innovative managers and upon intelligent, responsible, and effective workers. Without one, the other is doomed. The purpose here is not to glorify or chastise either management or labor. Rather, the intent is to suggest that the function of employment and relationships with employees are probably the most time-consuming yet challenging aspects of the modern manager's day-to-day life. Successful performance and conduct here are enormously worth the effort.

Consider some classic problems. One of the oldest management prerogatives was the power to hire and fire at will and without justification. Until the twentieth century, this power was virtually absolute. But modern managers have less autonomous authority. Governmental regulations proscribe discrimination in hiring practices and require that equal opportunity be afforded all qualified applicants. And these regulations are having an effect. Once an employee has been hired, both governmental regulations and labor-management contracts require equitable training opportunities, evaluation procedures, advancement processes, and termination criteria. The manager's actions and reactions are subject to contractual and judicial review as well as review by her superiors.

Similarly, another early management prerogative was the power to determine a "fair day's work and a fair day's pay." Work rules and work standards are now more often negotiated and regulated, especially in the Western world. Hours, productivity, and pay are constrained by laws respecting occupational safety and health and minimum wages and by contractual agreements regarding similar areas. Managerial discretion is still required, but its limits are more specifically set. Once again, the challenge

is to deal with reality rather than to retrogress. Workers' grievances always have some element of truth as do managerial
complaints. Finding and resolving the legitimate problems on
both sides is the essence of a productive employer-employee
relationship.

Consider also some of the human situations the manager
encounters and, hopefully, can improve. Here he finds, for
example, the "rookies": some eager, others reluctant; some
talented, others inept; some quick, others slow; some bright,
others dull; most feeling uncertain about the new work; all
on trial; all needing at least some training and encouragement;
and all looking for integration and evaluation. Over there, the
manager has the "veterans": some ambitious, others not; some
"superstars"; some "troublemakers"; most "solid citizens"; some
"has-been's"; some "never were's"; some "elder statesmen"; some
"goof-offs"; all with some combination of parents, children,
spouses, relatives, neighbors, creditors, friends, enemies, landlords, doctors, lawyers, preachers, teachers, cops, tax collectors;
complaints about the weather, aches, pains, and traffic; all of
which is competing against the manager for their attention and
commitment. How can he realize the best in them, for them, and
for the organization? And what of those with special needs:
women overwhelmed by men; men overwhelmed by women;
blacks overwhelmed by whites; whites overwhelmed by blacks;
the handicapped doing the best they can. How does one manage
all of these disparate elements and one's self at the same time?

## Manager-Manager Relationships

The relationship between employers and employees, while crucial
to the success of modern managers, should not obscure the importance of many similar relationships among managers themselves, especially those between superiors and subordinates, and
those among peers. If these are not effective, no organization that
depends upon them for purpose and direction will succeed.

Let us consider first superior-subordinate relationships. It
is too easy to dismiss them with platitudes such as: The function
of superiors is to lead; the function of subordinates is to follow.

There is some truth in these statements, but it is too simple. Of course, superiors must lead—by both inspiration and example. Of course, subordinates must follow—through both loyalty and respect. Leaders also have a legal sanction to lead and followers a legal obligation to follow. But all of these statements miss the true nature of this important manager-to-manager relationship.

Superiors and subordinates need each other and work through each other for mutual and organizational benefit. Superiors may have a better perspective and grasp of the whole, but subordinate managers usually are closer to the scene and typically possess intelligence data and technical expertise vital to the successful conduct of the enterprise. Managerial decision-making is most often a group activity involving all levels of management in constructive dissent. Each level is argued from its own particular vantage point, but most valuable of all are those rare individuals who can translate the language of headquarters into the language of the field or the language of the field into that understandable at headquarters.

Being a superior is both an art and a science. Section III of this book devotes considerable attention to ways of becoming "Number 1." For now, let us simply pose the issue of being a superior by recalling some games bosses play.

*Game 1: "True Grit."* Winters were colder, mountains were higher, burdens were heavier, and times were harder when the boss was young. The road to the top was especially perilous; it was rocky, twisting, and filled with tricksters and thieves. But "true grit" won out, and here is the boss to prove it, to extoll its virtues, and to doubt the worth of others not similarly tempered. But wiser still is the boss who recognizes when experience may be the worst rather than the best teacher.

*Game 2: "Follow the Leader."* This variation of Game 1 can turn superior-subordinate relationships into a spectator sport. Watch me, copy me, but never will I (or probably can I) teach you the tricks of my trade, the elements of my virtuosity, and the secrets of my success. Just do as I do, but do not ask questions. You will get the hang of it sooner or later. Or will you?

*Game 3: "Don't Do What I Do, Do What I Say."* The opposite of Game 2, this may prove to be equally fatal.

*Game 4: "Back to the Drawing Board."* This game can be made even more exciting if, each time it is the boss's turn, he says: "I don't know what I want, but I know this isn't it."

*Game 5: "I Want Solutions, Not Problems."* This amounts to a spectator sport for bosses and is usually played best on Monday mornings. It demands answers without permitting questions. It is charades without clues.

*Game 6: "Pulling Rank."* There are two versions of this game. One is called: "You do the work, and I'll take the credit." The other is called: "I'll do the work, and you take the blame."

*Game 7: "Do What You Think Best."* Depending upon the boss, this can be the kiss of life or the kiss of death.

These examples of poor top-management behavior mirror games subordinates play. Let us recall some that are popular among "Number 2 s":

*Game 8: "Me, Too."* Also known as "Weathervane" or "Whatever You Say, Boss," it is sometimes played with "Speak Only When Spoken to."

*Game 9: "Trusty Sidekick."* The most popular version of this game for subordinates is called: "The Boss Told Me to Wait Here." It is usually played out of doors, preferably in rain, sleet, snow, and dark of night. Another version is called "Sure, I'll Be Glad to Hold That Bag for You."

*Game 10: "It's Not My Responsibility."* This one is also known as "I Don't Want to Get Involved," "Passing the Buck," or "Who, Me?"

*Game 11: "Behind the Throne."* The key statements here are: "The real power around here is me, and don't you forget it." "I made the boss, and I can break the boss." "Bosses come and go, but I'll always be in charge."

*Game 12: "I Was Only Following Orders."* This is also known as, "The Devil Made Me Do It" or "Don't Blame Me."

Obviously, these games by superiors and subordinates are neither the rule nor the objective of management. They do, however, highlight some of the problems to be overcome in establishing more constructive and productive relationships based upon trust, mutual respect, and complementary expertise.

Managers also work continuously with peers whose knowledge and skills are complementary. In larger organizations this is a necessity, and it provides one of the main channels for the improvement of management practice and of individual and collective effectiveness. Line managers, for instance, consult staff managers for special advice. Production managers interact with marketing managers, so that what can be sold can be made and what can be made can be sold. Financial managers interact throughout the organization to match the sources and the use of funds and to control incoming and outgoing flows of cash, credit, debt, and equity. Personnel managers and "relations" managers (e.g., those who deal with public relations, employee relations, government relations, community relations, shareholder relations) provide mutual services and support. Managers of similar goods, services, or processes compare notes. Regional managers pool their experience. Domestic and overseas managers exchange insights.

Once again, the objective is constructive interaction for individual and collective growth and development. But once again, games are played:

*Game 13: "No Trespassing."* You do your job, and I'll do mine." "Stay out of my territory." "Stay out of my way." "That's none of your business." "Don't ask." "Don't interfere."

*Game 14: "The Grass Seems Greener on Your Side of the Fence."* "Gee, your job is so much more interesting than mine." "Hope you don't mind if I hang around so much." "I wish my boss understood me like yours understands you." "I never seem to do as well as you do in assignments."

*Game 15: "One-Up."* This is also known as "Can You Top This?" "Have you seen the new policies and procedures manual and what it does to your department? You haven't? Oh dear, I guess I let the cat out of the bag too soon." Another version is to preface all peer conversations with: "As I told the boss the other day. . . ." Better still is: "As the boss mentioned to me last evening. . . ."

*Game 16: "Gossip."* Anyone can play.

*Game 17: "Over My Dead Body."* "There is no way that you are going to get that promotion if I have anything to do with it."

"If he thinks he is going to get those supplies before I do,
he's sadly mistaken. I'm taking this all the way to the top."

*Game 18: "Non-person."* To win this game you must avoid all
sight, sound, presence, or thought of another manager
until he disappears.

*Game 19: "Stalemate."* "I'm not going to budge on this." "You're
the stubborn one." "I'm right—you're wrong."

*Game 20: "Don't Call Me, I'll Call You."* This is also known as
"I'll Get Back to You." It is often played in buyers' or lenders'
markets with sellers and borrowers. It is also commonly
played immediately after your promotion and incorporates
the games of "We'll Have to Have Lunch Sometime" and
"Be Sure and Come to See Me Upstairs."

## Education: Functions and Relationships

Employer-employee and manager-manager relationships underscore two additional functions of modern management—learning
and teaching—and an additional relationship—that of teacher-
student. Nothing characterizes management and managers more
than their almost continual involvement in education and training: employers training employees; "old hands" teaching new-
comers; specialists helping generalists, and vice versa; superiors
learning from subordinates, who in turn learn from superiors;
peers learning from peers; practitioners being taught by academics, and vice versa. How to teach and how to learn are part
of the requisite knowledge and skills of management today.

Consider some examples: A foreman teaches new workers
how to operate a machine efficiently and safely. A corporate
attorney explains tax or antitrust considerations to a board of
directors. A plant manager helps to improve interpersonal skills
in an encounter group. A financial executive brushes up on
quantitative analysis in night school. A company president trans-
lates social concerns into corporate priorities. A staff specialist
helps a sales manager to do research on consumer behavior. A
corporate economist and a marketing vice president compare
their alternative methods (and results) of forecasting demand.
To manage is to teach; to manage is to learn.

## Ownership: Functions and Relationships

There remains yet a final function and a final relationship of management. They are, paradoxically, perhaps the newest function and the newest relationship. Both are growing by leaps and bounds and pose interesting managerial challenges.

In ancient and even early modern times, the owner-manager relationship was virtually unknown. The reason is simple: There was virtually no separation between the two functions. Owners and managers were one and the same. If an owner wanted to delegate authority or responsibility over part of his property or affairs, a middleman was employed.

The middleman (typically a lawyer, a banker, a broker, or an agent) performed those functions or conducted those relationships that the owner wished to delegate. But there was no question that anyone but the owner had the last word. Middlemen identified options and executed orders, but it was owners who made the important decisions. Business archives are full of correspondence between middlemen and owners. Almost invariably, the middleman's closing sentence was some form of the phrase: "I await your instructions in the matter." If the owner wanted to buy, the middleman bought; if the instructions were to sell, the middleman sold; if the owner wished to borrow, the middleman borrowed; if the order was to lend, the middleman did so. Middlemen were compensated for their advice and services by some combination of annual retainer and cash commissions or fees on each transaction. The owner-middleman relationship can be likened to the client-lawyer relationship today. Either side could terminate, but authority to act lay only with the owner.

### THE GROWTH OF THE MODERN CORPORATION

With the rise of the modern corporation (which dates from the early seventeenth century), a significant separation of ownership and management began, as did a subtle redistribution of authority and responsibility. The corporation was created for economic purposes, but its rapid acceptance as the predominant form of business organization rests on three legal advantages it offers over alternative institutional forms.

First, the corporation permits the widespread sale of fractional ownership shares (in the form of "stock") and, thereby, increases the potential capital available to the enterprise. The private and public sale of stock made it possible to concentrate more capital than either the proprietorships or the voluntary partnerships that characterized premodern business.

Second, the corporate form limited the liability of each owner to only the amount of her "share" in the enterprise and provided a relatively easy means of liquidating that liability at almost any time through public sale in the stock market. Under most forms of partnerships, all partners were equally liable for the losses or debts of the enterprise and had no ready market for their liabilities except each other.

Third, the corporate form gave the enterprise more longevity and continuity. Partnerships have no life of their own. They must be dissolved and reconstituted each and every time a partner joins, withdraws, or dies. The corporation, on the other hand, is chartered for a long period of time—sometimes virtually in perpetuity. Owners may come or go through the purchase or sale of shares, but the identity or turnover of ownership has little impact on the day-to-day operations of the corporation. It has a life of its own for the duration of its charter: it can own property, buy, sell, lend, borrow, hire, fire, sue, and, in turn, be sued. The corporation is, in fact, an individual of superhuman age; and it is master of its own fate to the extent that the law and the market will allow.

The evolution of the corporate form gave both a push and a pull to the separation of ownership and management. To the extent that shareholders were unable or unwilling to involve themselves in the day-to-day affairs of the enterprise, they tended to push for the employment of a permanent, professional cadre of managers to whom they were willing to delegate authority as well as responsibility. And to the extent that the corporation was more tangible and perpetual than its numerous owners, there was a pull on these managers, once employed, to identify more with the institution itself and their role in its development than with the large, somewhat anonymous, relatively passive, and ever-changing population of shareholders.

So as the modern corporation grew, the management function and the owner-manager relationship changed. Management became less proprietary and more professional. Owners delegated more and more authority as well as the responsibilities that had always been there. Included were not only the responsibilities of buying, selling, lending, borrowing, or employing under orders, but also the authority to initiate purchases, sales, loans, and employment subject to ratification.

Modern, professional managers derive their authority, then, not from proprietary rights of their own, but from the consent of the actual ownership. They hold this authority "by proxy" and are subject to at least an annual vote of confidence from the shareholders. The reality, of course, is that only the top one or two managers are directly responsible to the shareholders and that turnover of top management as a result of shareholder dissatisfaction is rare. The shareholders of most corporations are content merely to ratify rather than direct the actions of their managers.

This suggests, therefore, the modern challenge for improvement in owner-manager relationships. Suppose you were a shareholder and, thereby, a part owner of General Motors. What rights and responsibilities do your shares convey? What voice would you expect to have in the management of "your" corporation? What influence do you have? What influence should you have? Suppose, on the other hand, you were a top manager of General Motors. What rights and responsibilities does your position convey? What voice would you expect to have in the management of "your" corporation? What influence do you have? What influence should you have? In both cases, should the owner-manager relationship be self-regulating? If not, how would you regulate it? Why? In whose best interest?

Consider the more distant but more typical relationship between shareholders and the lesser managers of a corporation. As a middle or junior manager, whom do you work for? Your boss? The corporation? The shareholders? Yourself? The public interest? From whence do you derive authority? To whom are you responsible?

## Social Accountability: Functions and Relationships

To a very large extent the success of modern managers in organizing and working through others depends upon their ability to manage themselves, their ability to project personal enthusiasms, personal aspirations and expectations, and personal values and standards. Personal example is one way to motivate others. Personal achievement is not necessarily incompatible with collective achievement. Individual talent and creativity have a multiplier effect. But managerial success also depends upon the ability to discipline personal enthusiasms, personal aspirations and expectations, and personal values and standards. Personal example can destroy others, too. Personal achievement can also be had at the expense of others. Individual talent and creativity can also have a divisive effect.

Thus although the ability to manage one's self is a crucial ingredient of successful management, self-satisfaction is not the objective or the standard of performance. Managers are also accountable to professional standards of excellence and to social standards of utility and responsibility. To be so accountable makes their accomplishments worthwhile.

Edgar H. Schein, in an article entitled "The Problem of Moral Education for the Business Manager,"* makes the brilliant point that the powers that accrue to any professional because of specialized knowledge and skills include the potential power to exploit his clients because of his superior expertise. It is this "vulnerability of the client" that generates the need for moral and ethical behavior by the professional in each professional transaction with clients. Schein goes on to identify the major clients of the professional manager: customers, stockholders, subordinates, peers, the enterprise itself, the management profession, and the community at large. The last, of course, includes all of the participants in the managerial process, innocent bystanders, and the physical environment itself. The challenge is, as always, "to do better."

Modern managers can, thus, be recognized by where they are most typically found—the business corporation—and by what they are doing—performing the classic business functions and conducting the classic business relationships with buyers, sellers, lenders, borrowers, intermediaries, competitors, regulators, employers, employees, superiors, peers, and owners. That

---

* Prepared for the 17th Conference on Science, Philosophy and Religion, August 1966.

many of the functions and relationships must be performed or conducted simultaneonsly only adds to the vocational complexity and excitement of their lives. How managers organize and carry out such functions and relationships is less easy to perceive than the need to do so. But there are methods of management, and it is to these that the remaining parts of this book are devoted.

# I

# ORGANIZATION: A BALANCING ACT

$O$UR discussion so far has focused primarily upon how business firms function in relation to: the consumers of products and services, the competitive firms, and the various governmental agencies that affect their existence. In essence we have described how business firms operate in the context of the economic, social, and political forces that make up any society. As important as this understanding is, it is only a first step to understanding what the profession of business administration entails. It is as if one were to try to understand the job of being a football coach with knowledge only of tactics and strategies within the rules by which football is played. Certainly understanding when to use the forward pass, when to run, or when to try a field goal are critical to developing an understanding of the role of the defensive and offensive teams, and of the various special teams. What must the players at various positions on these teams do? What kind of training do they require? Also one must understand how to develop a plan for the game and how to evaluate the performance of individuals and the various units that make up a football team.

In this and the next section of this book we want to take just such an internal look into business firms to explore how they are organized and managed so that the economic and social roles of business are performed. Our immediate concern in this section will be with the major issues facing organizations. In the next section we shall focus on how results, especially in financial terms, are measured, evaluated, and rewarded.

Upon looking inside any business firm, from the smallest corner pharmacy to the largest major multiproduct and multinational company, we find managers faced with three major issues. First they must provide incentives for employees to join the firm and make a contribution to its goals. Second, and not unrelated to the first issue, is the matter of dividing up the work of the organization, both among individuals and the organizational units to which they belong, while still providing for sufficient coordination so that the total effort fits together. Finally, managers must constantly deal with the issue of introducing changes in strategy, in procedures and techniques, and in personnel and organizational arrangements, without disruption of the firm's effectiveness.

As the title of this section suggests, dealing with these three

issues really requires managers to engage in a series of
balancing acts, not unlike a tightrope walker. A balance must
be achieved between meeting an employee's individual needs and
aspirations and achieving the goals of the firm. Similarly, a
balance must be attained between the way work is divided and
the need for coordination of all the parts of the firm. Finally,
the need to keep up with the times and introduce change must be
constantly balanced against the firm's traditional ways of
operating, which often have contributed to its past success and
also have probably been effective in meeting many employee
needs.

Our purpose in the pages ahead is to describe how managers
try to accomplish these balancing acts. We should emphasize
again that unlike many other management texts, we are not
arguing for how this should be done. Rather, our purpose is to
expose the reader to current management practices so that
she will understand how managers have sought to achieve such
balances and what implications this has for the challenges and
frustrations of a managerial career. In fact, we should
emphasize at this early point the authors' belief that the constant
struggle for balance in these issues is an essential component
of any manager's job, and one that can provide a great deal
of challenge as well as many headaches.

Of course, there is no question that managers become more
involved in decisions about these organizational issues as they
progress in their careers. Nevertheless, we feel they need central
attention in an introductory management course for several
reasons. First, we share the hope with many of our readers, that
they will be, in the not-too-distant future, at a high enough level
in business firms to be concerned with such issues. But long
before reaching this stage of one's career, understanding these
issues can be important. First, the way these issues are dealt
with by the managers for whom they work will have a major
impact on the challenge and satisfaction students will find
in careers in business. Understanding how managers deal with
these issues can provide an important perspective on whether the
reader is apt to find a career in business rewarding. Similarly,
this understanding can help one more intelligently assess
whether a particular firm's practices in this area are likely to
make it a satisfying and challenging place in which to work.

# Individual Goals and Organizational Purposes

In Chapter 1, major attention has been devoted to the issues of organizational purposes. It is not our intention here to recover this ground. Rather, we shall assume that the reader already has an understanding of the organization's purpose, and shall devote our attention to the goals of individual employees and how managers try to harness their goals toward the purposes of the firm. In essence we want to answer this question: Why do people join business firms and work in them?

## Reasons for Working

Why do we work? There are two vantage points from which one can answer this question—from a societal perspective and from the perspective of the individual employee. As industrial societies have developed, the most widely held assumption about why people worked, both among managers and writers on management, has been to earn a living; that is, people work for money. Since shortly before World War II, and especially afterward, there has been a growing realization among many researchers and educators in the field of business administration and among some managers that this assumption was not entirely valid. Man and woman do not work for bread alone.

Rather, according to this more recent view, people work for a complex set of reasons, the exact nature of which may vary from one individual to another. For one thing, people work because they enjoy social contact with others. Most of us have some deeper psychological desire for affiliation with our fellows, and the work organization is one place in which social interaction can be found. A second psychological need that explains why people work is their enjoyment of having power over others or being in relationships to persons who have power over them. In the early years of our life these power games are played out in relationships to fathers and mothers, brothers and sisters, and eventually friends—particularly in school. But after one leaves school, an important place to develop relations of controlling others and being controlled by them is in work organizations.

A third reason that has been identified as important in leading persons to join organizations and work effectively in them is the intrinsic satisfaction that comes from the work itself. The very act of performing a job can make a person feel good. Such satisfaction does not only come to the research scientist or engineer who solves a complicated technical problem, or to the executive who finds it rewarding to see a program on which he has worked lead to economic gain for his firm. Such intrinsic reward can also come to hourly workers or clerical workers who enjoy working with the rhythm of more repetitive jobs in a production plant or office. More recently the argument has been made that these so-called blue- and white-collar workers will gain more satisfaction from work if they are given more complex jobs over which they have more control. We shall say more about this shortly.

At this juncture, however, we should emphasize that the suggested explanations for why persons join organizations and work effectively in them are not necessarily complete, nor would all authorities use the labels we have selected. Our purpose here has been only to expose you briefly to a few of the multiple factors that researchers have reported as sources of satisfaction for people at work. One way to summarize much of this work is to say that people appear to work and to work effectively when their jobs provide a confirmation of the person's self-worth and self-esteem. Thus persons work effectively when they gain feelings of competence from their work; they work effectively when they feel their effort is enabling them to belong to a compatible group of peers; they work effectively when they believe that their efforts are enhancing their status in relation to others; and they work effectively when they believe that the products or services they are producing are valued by others. In all of these ways, work contributes to the important psychological goal that most people have of feeling worthwhile.

While this view of why people join organizations and what motivates them to work has been developing in the groves of academia, the practicing manager has not abandoned his long-standing belief that money is an important, if not the most important, source of reward for employees. "Man may not work for bread alone, but it isn't unimportant in the total scheme of things," still seems to be the prevailing attitude among managers. We can see this if we turn to look at where business firms tend to put the emphasis as they design the set of rewards they use to attract and motivate employees.

## Intentional Steps in Linking Employees to the Organization

### COMPENSATION

At the top of any list—whether it is a small struggling lunch counter trying to hire a dishwasher or a large commercial bank trying to recruit junior loan officers—is the question of financial compensation. In either case, the manager involved in the hiring process will consider existing wage rates for alternative positions in their locale and within their firm, the abundance or scarcity of candidates for the job, and the economics of the job for the company. Out of this consideration will come a decision about how much the prospective employee should be offered.

Does this emphasis on financial remuneration mean that the academics who argue against economic motivation are wrong? Not necessarily, and for two reasons. First, money is not only important because of what it buys but also because it provides feedback to the individual about his self-worth and status in relation to others. Second, as important as money is in the practice of trying to motivate employees, it is not the only tool used. We shall turn to some of the other tools in current use shortly, but first we want to deal more fully with the concept of money as a source of feedback to the individual about her work. Managers recognize this when they design the specifics of compensation schemes.

The exact form that compensation can take varies depending upon the organizational level of the employee, the nature of the job, and whether the employee is a member of a union. In spite of the variety of possible payment plans, it is helpful to categorize them into two basic types. One is payment for time at work. Whether the employee is a machine operator paid on an hourly basis or an executive paid on annual salary, the basic understanding is that the employee will be paid for the time he puts in, and there is no direct connection between the results achieved and the pay received. In contrast, the other basic type of compensation scheme makes a very explicit effort to tie payment directly to results accomplished. There is a wide variety of these plans: The payment may be a percentage of sales volume commission to salespersons; a piece-rate incentive to machinists; a group-incentive plan for clerical employees; a profit-sharing plan for all employees; or a stock option program for top managers. In all cases, however, the underlying assumption is that there should be a direct connection between the results to which the employee contributes and her pay.

Although these two pure categories can be found in practice in many companies, it is perhaps just as common to find that financial compensation takes the form of a combination of the two types. For example, steelworkers in a rolling mill may be paid a basic hourly wage, plus a group bonus for the tonnage of steel produced in the mill on their shift. Similarly, salespersons are often paid a basic annual salary plus a commission on sales volume, whereas executives frequently are compensated with an annual salary, plus a bonus based on the profitability of their unit or of the total firm. Mentioning these two basic forms of compensation, however, re-emphasizes the fact mentioned that money is an important reward, not only for what it can buy, but also for its psychological meaning. For example, when income is tied directly to performance, it provides the individual with concrete feedback about how well he is performing his job. In this the bonus or commission statement might be likened to a score card in a golf match. If on the other hand, an individual is paid only for her time, money can still be an important measure of her status vis-à-vis others.

FRINGE BENEFITS

In addition to financial payments of the kind just described, almost all companies in the United States provide a set of benefits such as pension plans, medical insurance, and life insurance. These so-called fringe benefits are also seen by many managers as a tool for tying the employee to the firm and encouraging his contribution to organizational goals. However, even more so than in the case of current compensation, there is a question as to how much these benefits interact with the employees' perception of their personal goals. In the first place, the similarity of these benefit programs from one company to another means that they do not provide a comparative advantage for any one employer. Second, particularly for the younger and middle-aged employee, the issue of current compensation is of much greater importance, both as a source of feedback about performance and as a means of meeting their material needs. However, they can be important in motivating older employees to stay with a company, since the benefits often cannot be transferred. But whether they also encourage such employees to make an extraordinary contribution to the firm is an open question. In fact, there is much anecdotal evidence that suggests that such fringe benefits may make older employees, who might like to make a change in employers, unwilling to do so, because they would lose valued fringe benefits. Such employees may then stay on, but with a reduced interest in their work. This suggests that at least in some cases these benefits work to neither the advantage of the company nor that of the employee. However, irrespective of whether these benefits are really effective tools for linking employees to organizational goals, they have become such an expected feature of employment that companies have no choice but to continue and even improve them.

### PROMOTIONAL OPPORTUNITIES

Although one may question the utility of fringe benefits as a motivational tool, there are two other tools that managers do use to motivate employees and that, at least for many employees, seem to have more impact. These are opportunities for promotion and performance evaluation schemes. Both of these tools provide employees with data about higher management's evaluation of their current performance and their future performance. We shall first discuss the issue of promotion and then turn to the question of performance appraisal practices. However, the reader should bear in mind that there is a close relationship between the two, since performance appraisal schemes are often the mechanisms that are intended to provide employees as well as upper management with data about how immediate superiors see employees' future potential.

In describing the importance of promotional opportunities as a motivational tool, it is useful to emphasize that every person is motivated to work by various combinations of internal and external forces. We make this point here because many of our readers are apt to assume too quickly that there is universal and equal interest in advancement by everyone who joins business firms. However, to an important extent the desire for advancement is based upon goals set as a result of early childhood experience in the family. In this regard one's relationship with parents and other adult figures can have an important impact on how far one expects to advance in one's career. Of course, such expectations are tempered by the experience a person has at school and on the job. For example, a factory worker may enter a company aspiring to advance to foreman or beyond, because adult influences have emphasized the value of such advancement.

However, contact with other workers, union leaders, and the fact that few promotional opportunities may exist could cast doubt on these aspirations. If so, the employee really has two choices—to look elsewhere for advancement or to give up this aspiration. Similarly, college graduates entering a business firm may hope to rise to the vice-presidential level of management but gradually may scale down their expectations as they see the number and quality of competitors for these positions.

All of this is intended to put the role of promotional opportunities into proper perspective. However, it is in no way intended to minimize their importance, because for many employees, particularly those in supervisory and managerial positions, advancement is an important, if not the most important, goal. Such advancement allows them to live up to their idealized view of themselves and to gain the self-esteem they seek, as well as to achieve increased monetary rewards.

To provide advancement opportunities for employees is a goal managers often strive for in planning organization structure, and achieving this end is often not too difficult for a firm when its operations are expanding. In fact, the excitement and enthusiasm apparent in a growing firm are often shared by employees at many levels because of the increased opportunities provided for them as a result of expansion. However, when a company is faced with the prospects of a more stable level of operations—either because of its own particular situation or because of general economic conditions—opportunities for advancement can dry up and even disappear. (Such conditions affected a number of firms in the economic downturn of 1970–1971.) Lower- and middle-level managers in such firms find it difficult to accept with equanimity the notion that the firm faces a period of slowed or even zero growth. Their frustration and displeasure expressed to higher management, may be one factor that creates continual pressure within many firms for constant striving for growth.

PERFORMANCE APPRAISAL

As we suggested previously, the medium that is supposed to be used to communicate to employees how well they are doing, and what their prospects for advancement are, is a performance appraisal system. We may regard such schemes as analogous to receiving report cards or grades in a school or university. The feedback tells the students (employees) how well they are doing from the teacher's (boss's) perspective. The process of gathering the data for this feedback enables the teacher (boss) to determine who is ready for advancement.

But even this simple analogy between grading in schools and performance approval schemes in business firms can quickly be carried too far. For one thing, in most firms there is an attempt to provide verbal feedback to the employee, rather than having it only in writing. For another, there is usually a much clearer set of standards about what constitutes effective performance in a school setting than in a business setting. If the student completes certain papers, takes certain quizzes and exams, and demonstrates certain knowledge in a process, she has met the requirements of the course. However, for many jobs in business firms it is very difficult to determine appropriate standards of performance. These two aspects of performance appraisal schemes—face-to-face feedback and the difficulty of determining performance criteria—have made this area a highly problematic one in most businesses. Evidence of this concern can be seen by perusing tables of contents of business journals such as the *Harvard Business Review*. Hardly an issue of this journal has gone by in the past 15 years without some article on this topic. Similarly, groups of executives in any management development program are quick to admit that this is a most troublesome area for them personally and for their companies.

The reason that face-to-face interaction makes the process of evaluation so difficult can be easily understood. The basic premise is that personal contact between a superior and a subordinate will give both parties the greatest possible understanding of the situation. This contact is also supposed to provide the superior with an opportunity to counsel the subordinate on steps he should take to improve performance. This makes good sense and seems highly desirable. But what is overlooked are the psychological forces that surround these encounters. The superior is asked to tell subordinates how she judges them, and this creates a position that is possibly uncomfortable and that may even make her feel guilty. The subordinate, for his part, is asked to hear what an important and powerful figure things of him. Since most people like to maintain a positive image of themselves, the subordinate's tendency, when he hears negative data about himself, is to become defensive. Either he "turns off" and does not really hear what he is being told, or he becomes argumentative and refutes it. Even when the data are positive, the subordinate tends to be so concerned about possible negative appraisals that he may not accurately hear the feedback he is receiving.

*Poor Application of the Performance Appraisal Scheme.* This set of phenomena has led to two typical patterns of behavior in many firms. One pattern is that superiors tend to give positive feedback to all their subordinates while avoiding the painful process of giving negative data. Instead a superior tells all subordinates that they are doing a "fine" job or an "adequate" one. An example of this problem can be found in the U.S. Army, where the efficiency report (performance appraisal scheme) for officers has been revised frequently, because of a tendency for superior officers always to rate their subordinate officers at the top of various scales. This meant that it was difficult for top-level personnel officers to use this form for meaningful promotion decisions.

Neglect of the performance appraisal procedures (which are usually drawn up at some expense and effort by a personnel group) is the second common behavior pattern that firms engage in. Supervisors find that using these schemes is so painful, that they "forget" when the process is supposed to be done and they find "more important" activities that delay evaluations. No matter which of these patterns develops, the result is the same: performance appraisal is not provided in an effective manner, and the chance to motivate employees by letting them know how well they are doing their current jobs and what their chances for promotion are, are lost.

The problem is further complicated by the difficulty of measuring performance in a variety of jobs and for many different employees simultaneously. Because of the diversity of jobs and people, it is difficult, if not impossible, to arrive at a uniform set of evaluative standards for employees in any one company. It is obvious, for instance, that the standards used to evaluate first-line production supervisors must be different from those used to evaluate sales representatives. What is not so obvious is that persons such as sales representatives, who at first glance seem to be performing the same task, also may be facing quite different conditions. For example, in one territory sales representative A may face fierce competition, whereas representative B, who is across the state line, faces less competitive pressure. On the basis of results, B may look far superior to A; yet a closer examination of the two situations would reveal that A has worked more diligently and effectively even though the results achieved were not as visible as B's.

*Approaches to Performance Appraisal.* Another related issue is the problem of using the evaluation of a person at a lower organizational level as the basis for describing whether that individual has the ability to perform a higher-level job effectively. To continue with the example of the sales representative, one of the most persistent problems in managing sales forces is the question of which sales representative would make a good sales manager. Top managers with experience in their area have come to recognize that the star sales representative who is highly successful at obtaining orders is not necessarily going to be the most effective leader of other sales personnel. The job of selling is sufficiently different from that of leading salespersons to require individuals with somewhat different skills, interests, and abilities. For example, the job of sales representative may require someone who likes working alone and persuading customers about the merits of the company's products. Such a person may also thrive on the direct concrete evidence of results obtained when sales orders are received. The sales management job, in contrast, may require an individual who is content with less frequent feedback, who gains a sense of satisfaction from watching others grow in their abilities, and who is good at developing and motivating others to achieve results.

These kinds of variability among different jobs, therefore, have created certain difficulties in developing effective performance appraisal schemes. Schemes based only on absolute results achieved do not enable comparisons across levels or functions. Thus, many firms have tried approaches that emphasize evaluating "personality traits." Was the employee honest? Did he follow instructions? Did he provide leadership for others? And so on. The problem with this approach, however, has been that the managers who have been the "raters" have found it difficult to see a clear connection between any of these traits and the performance of individuals in their present job and particularly the next job.

*Management by Objectives.* Out of these types of issues a new approach to performance appraisal has emerged, one that is currently in vogue in many companies. *Management by objectives*, as it is generally labeled, places emphasis on the employee and her supervisor, jointly establishing certain performance goals for the subordinate. The employee's performance is then measured in terms of how well he achieves these objectives. Such goals can be stated not only in terms of results achieved for the company (sales increases, cost reductions, quality improvements) but also in terms of personal development goals for the individual (e.g., improved ability to work with persons in other departments; improved skills in statistical analysis, etc.). The underlying advantage of a management-by-objectives approach, according to its proponents, is that it involves the individual in setting his own goals. This builds into each employee a psychological commitment to strive for these goals. Achieving the goals is satisfying to the individual's need to feel competent and worthwhile. Since the goals are also worked out in the context of the firm's objectives, ideally the approach should also lead to the employee contributing more of his efforts to the firm's ends.

As sound as the concepts underlying management by objectives seem to be, it would be incorrect to portray this approach as a panacea. Like any new management tool, it creates a new set of challenges. For example, one difficulty with many attempts of *management by objectives* has been to get supervisors genuinely to permit subordinates to participate in the goal-setting process. Because of their own need to maintain control, and because they frequently feel they have superior knowledge about what goals should be, the supervisor often tends too heavily to stamp his imprint on the goals of his subordinates. Another general problem is that there is often so much emphasis on goals that can be quantified and easily measured, that the qualitative goals around developing the individual are often given limited, if any, attention.

A final issue worthy of mention is the question of whether financial rewards should be tied to the performance appraisal process. Should the employee's salary increases and/or incentive compensation be tied to the evaluation of his performance under the management-by-objectives scheme or any other performance appraisal scheme? The argument against tying compensation and evaluation together is based on the premise that this so increases the employee's psychological concern that he is even less likely to hear the feedback his boss is trying to give him. The argument for maintaining such a connection seems to rest on the fact that, as we pointed out previously, money is an important piece of feedback to the individual about how he is doing and it cannot be realistically separated from the performance appraisal process.

In spite of these problems and unresolved questions, there seems to be an increasing trend toward using performance appraisal schemes that are based on the management-by-objectives approach. Although it is not our intent in this book to suggest solutions to such problems, the interest in the issue seems so strong that it may be useful at least to mention briefly two factors that we feel are crucial in determining whether this approach will ultimately be successfully applied. First is the skill and dedication managers have in making it work. If they make it a part of their day-to-day management activities and find it a useful tool to guide not only their subordinates' work but also their own, it may be a very effective tool. Second, if the performance appraisal scheme is carefully and intentionally related to the company's other measurement and planning schemes and its connection or lack thereof to compensation is spelled out, it is most likely to become an enduring and a useful management technique.

## Unintentional Steps in Linking Employees to the Organization

So far our focus has been upon those explicit steps managers take in trying to achieve a balance between meeting employee needs and achieving the goals of the organization. Managers intentionally develop compensation schemes, benefit packages, promotion policies, and performance appraisal schemes with an eye toward encouraging employees to contribute to the ends of the enterprise. But as we have suggested earlier, there are complex factors that underlie employee motivation to work, and some of these factors are not tapped by the tools most companies intentionally use to try to motivate their employees. For example, as we pointed out previously, many employees are motivated to work because of the intrinsic satisfaction they derive from the work itself or because of the pleasure they derive from the friendships they establish at work.

Until very recently, managers have not attempted to consider explicitly how they might meet such needs. Yet it would be misleading to suggest that employees have not been achieving such satisfactions from their work. In fact, often without management intending it, such satisfactions have been available to many employees. Workers in factory settings, for instance, frequently report that an important source of satisfaction at work is membership in an "informal" group working in proximity to them. It has been found that such groups develop a rich set of rules and procedures around which they enforce member behavior. These so-called norms of acceptable behavior and group performance can either be supportive of the company's goals or opposed to it. Although such groups have been most deeply studied in factory settings, even a casual observer will become aware that similar groups are present in the research laboratory, the accounting office, and the executive suite.

Similarly, it is also obvious that many employees have achieved a keen sense of personal satisfaction from the intrinsic work they are doing. The most dramatic examples may be seen among research scientists absorbed in problem-solving, or highly skilled craftworkers turning out a high-priced sports car. Yet such satisfactions are also important for many other employees, whether they be men and women working on electronic circuitry or operating a steel-rolling mill.

Evidence of the importance of these sources of motivation has been building in research studies and in the management literature for almost 50 years, ever since the pioneering studies done at the Western Electric Company. More recently, because of increased concern about worker motivation and the so-called blue-collar "blues" and white-collar "woes," some firms have devoted more effort to designing intentionally organizations that facilitate a broader range of satisfactions for employees, and in the process increase their propensity to work toward organizational goals.

## Innovative Work Organizations

These innovations in work organizations most frequently focus on designing jobs, procedures, measurement, and compensation arrangements to create more opportunities for employees to gain satisfaction from the intrinsic nature of their work and/or from belonging to a viable work group. Although most of these innovations have taken place in factory settings, there have also been some attempts in settings involving clerical and office employees.

A typical example of such innovation is a new pet food manufacturing plant built in 1971 by a major U.S. food-processing company. In this plant, explicit attention was devoted to creating an organization in which factors such as the intrinsic nature of the job and the nature of work groups were emphasized (Walton). For example, they created work teams whose membership consisted of workers on a particular piece of the process. Members of these teams were expected to derive satisfaction from belonging to them. These teams were given considerable autonomy to decide how they could carry out the work. Team workers were expected to rotate among a wide range of jobs from maintenance, cleanup, and shipping to those dealing with actually operating the equipment. From this it was hoped that they would be able to overcome the boredom of the less complicated jobs and also would be able to gain a sense of identification with the whole task of operating a major step in the process. To reinforce this notion, pay increases in the plant were related to the workers' ability to master a progressively wider range of jobs. Other unique features of the design of this work organization are attempts to reduce status differences between workers and supervisors by eliminating special parking places and entrances for management, and by equipping office areas, workers' locker rooms, and recreation spaces with identical furniture and carpeting. Preliminary results in this small plant (70 employees) are encouraging; productivity is higher than comparable plants, and employee turnover is lower.

This is only one example of several similar experiments in the United States, Western Europe, and Japan. Another is the work restructuring in many factories of the Volvo company in Sweden. One of the most interesting facets of these changes is that management has virtually eliminated the traditional assembly line. All seem to have the shared goals of intentionally tapping into the motives to work connected to the job itself and group membership, which have been largely ignored by more traditional management approaches to linking employees to their work.

These experiments have sprung from an increased concern in many quarters (management, government, academic, and labor) over what appears to be a decline in productivity and an increasing alienation of workers from their work and the companies that employ them. This trend has been particularly visible in the United States and in certain Western European countries (especially Sweden), but the concern with the issue has been contagious and now encompasses most non-Communist industrial nations as well as some Communist ones.

In spite of the lively interest in this topic, it is difficult to predict now the significance of these innovations in work organization. One school of thought argues that these really are the forerunners of an important trend. Like Frederick Taylor's ideas about work simplification and industrial engineering in the early part of the twentieth century, these innovations from the behavioral sciences may gradually become the basis for management practices throughout the industrialized world.*

The counterargument, however, is that these ideas have only been applied in very specialized atmospheres. Frequently, these applications have been in smaller, newer plants having carefully selected managers and workers who are comfortable with greater autonomy and more participation in decision-making. These newer plants also do not have the history of animosity in labor-management relations that often characterizes larger plants. When attempts are made to apply these ideas in larger plants that have managers and supervisors who want to retain their traditional control over operations, where there is considerable mistrust between manager and workers, and where many workers themselves may not want more involvement in the work, the experimenters may find that their ideas are not borne out in these situations.

It is not our intention here to try to resolve the problem of

* Frederick W. Taylor, *The Principles of Scientific Management* (New York: Harper & Brothers, 1911).

worker alienation. Rather, we have wished to show what appears to be one of the major challenges that will face managers in the next few decades. Clearly, there is a problem in terms of employee attitudes and productivity, and it is not confined to factory workers. Each manager who is involved in supervising others will have to determine his own answer for these issues.

In essence the question boils down to whether more of what has worked in the past is the answer. Can employees continue to be motivated by explicit attention to financial compensation, fringe benefits and promotional opportunities? Or must more explicit attention be given to factors such as the intrinsic nature of the job itself and to the opportunity to work in compatible work groups? To do this must new approaches be found that take account of the dissenting position on these organizational innovations, as was outlined previously? Can they be applied in larger factories in which there are unions and a history of labor-management mistrust?

In answering such questions, managers of the future will find one of the most interesting challenges of their careers. The answers can obviously have an important impact on the economic progress of the United States and on the quality of life in this society. But it is worth also emphasizing that solutions to these questions will have an obvious impact on which individual firms grow and thrive and which stagnate and shrivel. Somehow the managers of firms that wish to be in the former category must find a way to balance the goals of the firm against the needs and expectations of their employees so that there is a mutually satisfactory equilibrium.

# Structure: The Organizational Skeleton

We now turn to the second major issue that managers must face in trying to achieve a balance in their organizations. This is the problem of obtaining both an efficient division of work and the necessary coordination of effort to assure that the various parts of the enterprise are moving in the same direction.

## The Division and Coordination of Work

The nature of this issue can be observed in any organization. Take, for example, the problem of conducting a large multisection course in a university. The professor in charge must first decide and get agreement from the section assistants as to what she will try to accomplish in the large lecture sessions and what they in turn will try to accomplish in the section meetings. This division of work will probably be planned in such a way that, ideally, the professor and the section assistants, by carrying out their individual activities, should together meet the teaching goals of the course. In essence, an attempt will be made to plan the division of the work so that it will lead to a coordinated effort if everyone does his assigned part.

Although such an attempt is admirable in theory, however, it does not usually work out in practice. For example, one section assistant finds his students are having more difficulty with a topic than was anticipated. Or the professor finds that a particular topic elicits more questions in the lecture session than she had anticipated. All of this is likely to cause the professor and her assistants to digress from their agreed-upon plan for dividing the work. They now find that the plan they have devised for dividing the work does not automatically take into consideration problems of coordination. Therefore, they must utilize some further mechanism for coordinating their efforts. This may take the form of meetings to resolve the issues or the exchange of written memos outlining necessary adjustments in each person's activities, and so on.

### THE ISSUE IN BUSINESS

The same set of issues is present in any business firm once it has more than one employee. For example, the proprietor of a lunch counter must decide how to organize the work of preparing the food and serving customers. Several alternatives are present: The same employees can wait on a few customers and prepare their food, or one set of employees can wait on customers and another set can prepare the food. Or some combination of these alternatives can be used. Implicitly or explicitly the owner of such a shop will be considering what is the most efficient (least costly) way to get the work done and what arrangement will be most apt to lead to smoothly coordinated service to the customers. If the owner is at all enlightened, he may also wonder which arrangement is apt to give his employees an interesting job—one that will be satisfying to them so that costly employee turnover is reduced.

This example, like the one of the university course, shows that the issues of the division of work and its coordination are clearly intertwined. Managers begin by trying to design the work so that the partial efforts of individual employees will add up to the total coordinated effort necessary for a successful operation. But so many unexpected events occur that there must be ways of adjusting activities and work loads in an even fashion. One way this is typically handled in small organizations is for the manager, through her own direct contacts with her employees, to give them instructions that keep their activities coordinated. This is what we might expect to see in the lunch counter example. The proprietor would ask individual employees to alter their activities to handle variations in work load, customer flows, and so on.

In larger business firms the basic issues of division of work and work coordination are not much different from those in the two examples given previously. What is different, though, is the complexity of the issues. One source of the added complexity is the fact that more than one individual is usually performing the same task. This makes it necessary to divide work among groups of employees doing quite different things. In both cases the requirement for coordination must also be taken into account.

DIVISION OF WORK

A helpful way to understand how managers engage in dealing with these issues is to review briefly some of the early management literature on these topics. The authors of what has come to be called classical organizational theory were themselves either practicing executives or close observers of actual management practices. These early authors tried to lay down principles of organization that they believed would lead to the greatest degree of efficiency. It was their view that organizations should be structured to maximize specialized effort. This meant that each employee would have a limited set of activities that his intelligence and skill would enable him to master. Having mastered this activity, he would be able to perform it in a repetitive and an efficient manner. Such specialization also meant that groups of employees doing similar work would be utilizing similar equipment, and this would also result in the most efficient use of machinery. It is important to note that this view does not take account of the motivational issue discussed in Chapter 2.

*Work Division by Function.* This emphasis on narrow definitions of work and efficient utilization of equipment led to an organizational principle that generally stated that work should be divided by *function*. Each organizational unit should have a specialized set of activities to accomplish. Theoretically, these functions were assigned so that if the employees in each unit did their assigned work, the total effort would lead to the coordinated results that met the firm's strategic goals. According to these early authors, any misunderstanding about who was to do what, or about needed shifts in assignment among units or within a unit would be handled by the common boss. The classical writers who laid down principles such as these have been criticized from many quarters. Their ideas have been seen as not taking sufficient account of the complexity and variability of human motivation to work. Similarly, these principles have been criticized as not recognizing variations in work requirements that make it necessary for firms operating in different businesses to consider organizational arrangements that are at variance with them.

Although there is validity to much of this criticism, there also is no question that as a statement of how business firms are organized, the emphasis on organizing by functions was accurate at the time these authors were writing and is still quite valid today. The foundation of the organizational structure of most business firms is a functional division of work. For example, in a typical company with a relatively narrow line of products, the work of the organization is divided into selling, manufacturing, design (research and engineering), finance, and personnel.

The explanations offered for this reliance on functional division of work in modern companies include several. The "classical" writers, as mentioned previously, have offered the explanation that this is the most efficient form of organization. Since, in their view, business people are essentially rational decision-makers, they develop the structure that is most efficient.

As another explanation, historians have noted that the earliest major business enterprises were often railroads, which lent themselves quite well to a functional organization. More recently, the explanation has been offered by sociologists that the functional basis of organizations actually has its roots in preindustrial economic organizations in which the production, distribution, and planning/administration functions were separated. Finally, psychologists could argue that in modern organizations one reason for a functional organization is that it builds established career identities that are now institutionalized not only in companies but also in business or other professional schools.

It is not our purpose here to unravel or explore these explanations in depth. It is quite likely that all of these facts play a role in influencing the predominance of a functional division of work. While there is a heavy reliance on the functional basis of organizations, it is not the only basis used. Gulick, one of the early writers, noted this himself. He pointed to the possibility of also organizing by product, territory, or time. And in fact any examination of organizational structure in business firms will quickly reveal that all of these dimensions are used—often simultaneously in the same company.

MULTIPLE ORGANIZATIONAL DIMENSIONS

If we take as an example a medium-sized firm manufacturing wearing apparel, we can illustrate this (Figure 3.1). Referring to the top management of the firm, we see a combination of a functional and product organization. The various activities reporting to the administrative vice president are broken down by function. However, each of the three vice presidents and general managers reporting to the president is responsible for a product division. That is, their organizational units each focus on the designing, manufacturing, and selling of particular sets of products (women's wear, men's wear, and children's wear). Within each of these product divisions, the primary division of work is on a functional basis. This is illustrated by the more detailed breakdown of activities within the women's wear division.

In this division there are three manufacturing functions: (1) merchandising (including planning and designing the prod-

**Figure 3.1 Organizational Structure of a Medium-Sized Company**

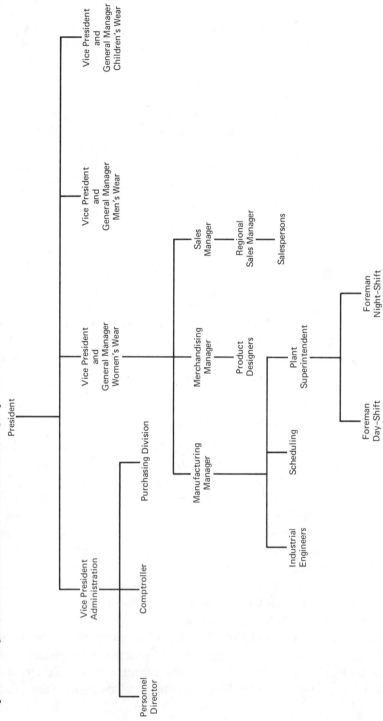

uct line), (2) manufacturing, and (3) selling. Within the manufacturing activity we find a breakdown not only by function (including engineering scheduling and plant), but within the plant we find a division of work based on time (shifts). Within the sales department the work is subdivided according to the part of the country in which the salespersons operate (regions).

*Product Division.* This highly simplified example is intended to be illustrative only of the way managers combine the use of these various bases for dividing work in developing organizational structure. Apparently, there are several reasons why they use each of these bases of dividing work. As we pointed out earlier, the functional division is usually the first to appear as a firm grows. However, if the firm expands its product line, the pressure for a product division of work emerges. This is so for at least two reasons.

First, the various functional managers (such as the manufacturing manager or sales manager) and the people working for them find it too difficult to deal with several products simultaneously. Perhaps the new product is not gaining the attention it needs because managers are overly concerned with the established product. Or possibly they become so excited and involved with the new product that they neglect the older product line. In either case the underlying problem is that the employee, whether he is a top functional manager, a salesman, or a foreman, finds that the scope of the work involved in dealing with a broadened line of products is too difficult. The obvious way to deal with this is to create separate product divisions, and this is the pattern observed in such situations. The endeavor to make such a product breakdown is intensified when the new product is substantially different from existing products. When the new product is sold to a different set of customers or when it requires new manufacturing processes, such situations provide an added incentive to create a new organizational entity to handle them.

The second reason for the emergence of product division is that the new product line also creates more problems for the chief executive of such a growing firm. Formally, he has probably been working directly with his key functional managers to coordinate their activities. With the advent of a new set of products and more decisions, he may see the need for help in this activity. Creating product divisions can give him two sub-ordinate divisional managers to aid in this coordinating work.

*Work Divisions by Time or Territory.*  The reasons for di-viding work by time or territory are not so complex as dividing work by products. Dividing work by time is usually the result of a desire to utilize costly equipment and provide necessary service for a longer-than-normal work day. Thus we generally see multiple shift operations in manufacturing and service facilities in which maximum utilization of equipment is desired. The territorial division of activity stems from the basic problem of providing service or customer contact in a defined area. The least costly way to handle this type of work usually is to have one person deal with a given area, thus minimizing his travel time and expense. Supervision is then provided over several contigu-ous areas, again limiting the travel time and cost for the supervisor. As suggested in the case of the apparel firm, the most typical example of this division is found in selling organizations.

While the use of territorial organization for sales forces has a long history, the question of geography as a basis for organiza-tion has become increasingly important in recent years with the tendency for more firms to operate on an international basis. As many large and even medium-sized U.S., European, and Japanese firms spread their activities around the world, they have had to consider how to manage these operations in widely separated parts of the world. One method that has been tried is to divide the world into areas (for example, the United States, Europe, South America, etc.), with managers responsible for operations in their location.

*Line and Staff Roles.*  There is one other aspect of the division of work that should be mentioned. This is the distinction that is usually made between line and staff activities in the class-ical literature. Line managers, according to the classical theorists, are persons involved in the chain of command who receive delegated authority and responsibility from above and in turn pass it on to subordinates. Although the classical theorists were less clear on what they meant by staff roles, the generally ac-cepted definition was persons in an advisory or service function to the line. Examples of such functions might be a personnel department or a legal department. The distinction made in the management literature has been widely accepted by managers, and they frequently describe the distinction between line and staff work.

However, close observation of how organizations actually function somewhat blurs this distinction. The staff actually develops an important influence over decisions because of its technical expertise. Take, for example, the decisions about hiring a new salesperson. According to the generally accepted distinction between line and staff, the decision should rest with the line manager, and the personnel department (the staff) should only find the candidates, gather data about them, and perhaps screen them in a preliminary way. In the process, the staff personnel executive, theoretically, can also offer advice to the line manager. In practice, however, since the personnel executive may have more experience with selection and is more knowledgeable about those candidates who are more likely to be successful, his "advice" begins to have a considerable influence on the final decision of the candidate to be selected. Stated another way, the staff personnel executive's expertise gives him considerably more influence on decisions than the traditional view of the staff role would suggest. In fact, in the areas where their expertise is relevant, such staff—whether they are personnel or financial experts or whatever—may carry as much authority as line managers. Therefore, while the division of work along this dimension may be a useful way of thinking about who is supposed to have *primary* responsibility for directing operations, it is misleading to give too much credence to the idea that staff units are not in a position to exercise considerable influence over areas where they have relevant expertise. It is important to recognize however, that the extent to which they influence affairs will depend upon the extent to which they have developed expertise that is both helpful and useful.

*Conclusions.* At this point we wish to summarize our discussion of the varied bases for dividing up work. The major point we have made is that historically, and even presently, the functional basis of dividing work has been predominant. But, increasingly, it is supplemented and complicated by the division of work according to product, time, and territory. Further, the division of work between line and staff is much more blurred in practice than much of the classical literature would suggest.

For the student considering a managerial career, there are at least two implications to be drawn from this discussion. First is the fact that all of these ways of dividing work can make life in such organizations both complicated and challenging. It is complicated in the sense that reaching decisions often requires that multiple persons be consulted. This requires a great deal of time, patience, and an enjoyment of the process of give and take. The challenge comes from negotiating this complexity and reaching decisions that make sense to the firm as a whole and have the support of those who must implement them. The second implication of this discussion is the fact that as managers move ahead in their careers, they will be faced with the necessity of making choices among these bases for dividing work in building and managing the organizations for which they have responsibility. This requires not only an understanding of the available options, but also of their strengths and limits. In the preceding discussion, we have emphasized some of the reasons for the ways of dividing work in various combinations. The basic problem resulting from any division of work, as we stated at the outset, is that it creates certain problems of coordination. It is to this relationship between the division of work and coordination that we now turn.

### THE PROBLEM OF COORDINATION

The reason that dividing work into parts leads to problems of achieving coordination is not difficult to understand. In a very small enterprise, for example, a so-called mom-and-pop grocery store, the proprietor can keep the various facets of the operation in her head and make necessary adjustments to keep things moving smoothly on her own. However, once a firm becomes larger and has a functional breakdown of work, the manager of each function and his subordinates begin to develop a more specialized point of view about how things should be done.

This is so, first of all, because implicitly or explicitly, in dividing up the work, each unit is given a set of goals that the top manager expects its members to achieve: "The sales force is to achieve a sales volume of $1.2 million." "The plant manager and his subordinates are to reduce costs 10 percent below last year." "Engineering is to develop a product design that will be better than competitive products in performance and appearance." Thus the efforts of employees in each unit become focused on their particular set of goals. If each unit meets its goals, the result should be the profitable operations desired by top managers and the owners. However, as we saw in the simple example of the multisection university course, unexpected events can occur that make it difficult for one or another unit to achieve its goals.

Further, it frequently happens that what is necessary for one unit to achieve its objective impedes another from reaching its goals. For example, for the sales manager to achieve his department's goals of higher sales volume, he may request that special manufacturing attention be given to the order of a large customer. That is, he may ask the plant manager to interrupt his production schedule and place the new order ahead of some other orders. The plant manager, whose primary concern is keeping manufacturing costs down, may object to this proposal because interrupting his production schedule will introduce inefficiency into the plant operations, which raises costs. This is only one of many such examples of conflicting goals that can develop between managers responsible for different functions, products, or territories. For the firm to achieve its total results, these conflicts must be resolved. In a nutshell, this is what the issue of achieving coordination is all about.

It is worth emphasizing that although the types of conflicts just mentioned emerge around the differing goals of various organizational units, they are apt to be exacerbated by other differences in the points of view of managers in various units. For one thing managers in different units may have different time horizons in mind as they think about decisions. For example, the design engineer has long-range plans and may be thinking several years into the future, while the sales manager is primarily worrying about current problems. When persons with these different time perspectives must work together, such differences can be a source of conflict. Similarly, managers in different units may be working under different managerial styles and with different measurement and work procedures. This too can create misunderstandings. For instance, the research manager may be accustomed to situations in which he and his subordinates have considerable freedom to do what they want, when they want to. In contrast, the plant manager may be used to running a more rigid organization in which things are done according to a fixed set of practices. When these two individuals come together in the work situation, these differences can be an added source of misunderstanding and conflict.


### ACHIEVING COORDINATION

Given the tendency for organizations to be full of conflict as a result of the division of work, the next question is how managers resolve conflicts to achieve coordination. As was suggested earlier, the ordinary approach in smaller organizations is for the common boss to sit down individually or jointly with the persons who are in disagreement and have them discuss, and thereby solve, their difficulties.

In fact, the common boss, as an arbiter of cross-functional conflicts, was the prescription that classical management writers used to handle the problems of coordination in an organization of any size. Their basic aim was that the work of the organization should be divided so that the goals of the parts added up to the goals of the whole. When any discrepancies, which they predicted would be infrequent, did occur, these conflicts were to be resolved by the common boss of the units in disagreement. Thus, according to this view, if a sales manager and a production manager were in disagreement over production schedules, their boss, the president of the firm, should resolve this issue.

Even though this view of the frequency of interdepartmental conflict and how it should be resolved through the hierarchy is overly simplistic, there is no question that it is not too far off base as a description of how many firms have tried to achieve coordination among their parts. In smaller firms with single-product lines, it can work well; and also in larger firms the hierarchy is an important mechanism for achieving coordination. However, in recent years, particularly as firms have been faced with more rapid change in markets and technologies, and have expanded their product lines and the parts of the world in which they operate, it has been found that the hierarchy alone cannot carry out the burden of achieving coordination. As a result of more changes in many firms' environments and their expansion in size, managers in the hierarchy who are responsible for coordination of activities among several functional or product units have found that they can no longer handle the amount of information and decision-making required of them. Decisions are delayed, or, even worse, none are made at all. This is a result of a sharp increase not only in the number of decisions but also in the number of players. More and more people must be involved in decisions as more products and geographic areas are involved.

As we saw in discussing the division-of-labor issue, one way to handle this coordination problem is to develop a new division of work by product. In essence, the company establishes a new kind of manager in the hierarchy who is responsible for coordinating activity around a set of products. This approach still retains the principle of coordination through the hierarchy. However, even after this step is taken, today's manager finds that the problems of coordination often still cannot be handled exclusively through the management hierarchy. The span of products in one division and the number of functions involved in a product division may be too complicated for one product divisional general manager to handle. Further, in many companies, several products are sold through one sales force and manufactured in one production plant; therefore, creating another new product division is not economically sound.

### COORDINATING POSITIONS

Faced with this situation, one solution that many companies have used is to develop special coordination positions outside the management hierarchy. The persons in these positions do not have direct positional authority for the various functions whose activities they are supposed to coordinate. That is, they are not the official bosses of individuals in the various functions who contribute efforts to the success of their products. As a way of achieving coordination and resolving conflict, persons in these coordinating roles must rely on their personal skills to resolve differences of opinion and must achieve influence over other functions through their expertise and ability.

The two most prominent examples of such positions are product managers in consumer products companies and program managers in the aerospace industry.

*Product Managers.* The product manager is not only responsible for planning the marketing strategy for her products, she is also expected to coordinate the efforts of other functions to the accomplishment of her plan. This coordination can involve not only the sales force but also the manufacturing plants that must deliver the products in the correct packages and in the correct quantities, on time, the research department that may be developing modifications in the product's characteristics or even new products, as well as so-called staff functions (legal, market research, finance), all of which provide expert opinion and information.

*Program Managers.* In the aerospace industry, program managers typically consolidate the efforts of many engineering and scientific functions involved in the designing of the product, and also the activities of the manufacturing functions. They may also have responsibilities for contact with the contractor and numerous subcontractors. In even a relatively small program this can involve them in contacts with perhaps a dozen functions.

Trying to understand all of the ramifications of this way of achieving coordination is beyond the scope of this book. In fact, it might require a book of its own. Rather our purpose here is only to use the roles of product and program management to illustrate one means business firms have developed to achieve coordination when the management hierarchy becomes overburdened.

### A MATRIX STRUCTURE FOR DIVIDING AND COORDINATING WORK

The use of these special coordinating roles, whatever label they are given, really has created a new organizational form, which is a fusion of the product and functional basis of dividing work. This is called a matrix or grid structure (Figure 3.2). The so-called program manager has the responsibility for coordinating the efforts of the various functional resources working on their product or program. On the vertical axis, therefore, the work is divided by product or program, while the coordination is achieved *across* functions. The functional managers along the horizontal axis are responsible for the efficient operations of their functions.

Figure 3.2 Matrix Structure Functional Resources

Functional Resources

| Programs | | Manufacturing | Sales | Research | Development | Purchasing | Control |
|---|---|---|---|---|---|---|---|
| | Program 1 | x | x | x | x | x | x |
| | Program 2 | x | x | x | x | x | x |
| | Program 3 | x | x | x | x | x | x |
| | Program 4 | x | x | x | x | x | x |

Along this axis the work is divided by function, and the coordination is *within* the function to assure that effective resources are available for all products. The persons in the middle of the grid (represented by *x*'s) have responsibility both to their functional boss and to their program managers. Thus one disadvantage of this organization is that a person must learn to work with at least two superiors. In practice, however, this does not seem to be an impossible problem, particularly if the two bosses cooperate enough and avoid putting the subordinate in unnecessary conflict. In fact, the analogy of the nuclear family is relevant here. The subordinate in a matrix structure is like the child in the family with a mother and father both giving directions. The child can prosper and grow as long as mom and dad work to give relatively consistent signals about what they expect. The same is true for the subordinate living in a grid structure. Life may not be easy or simple in such a structure, but the growth and complex product lines and technologies of modern firms have made such structures a necessity.

COORDINATING TEAMS

Coordinating positions are only one mechanism that has been developed to supplement the basic hierarchy in achieving coordination. Another widely used device is the formation of a team of managers representing various functions and working on a common product. Such teams can take a variety of forms depending upon the underlying structure of the organization and the nature of its business. A common example of such a team is the executive committee of a company, which includes the chief executive of the company and her major subordinates. The function of such committees is to provide overall coordination of the company at the highest level. Obviously, the exact composition of the committee and the topics dealt with will vary depending on the size of the company and its product line. For example, in a large multi-product firm, the membership might include the chief executive officer, the product divisional manager, and corporate staff officers. The topics at issue would be overall corporate strategy and the allocation of resources across product divisions. In a smaller, single-product company the membership might include the chief executive and the leader of the several functions. Because they are close to day-to-day operations, the members of such a group might deal with coordinating issues more related to operations.

These two examples are drawn from structures of either a product type or a functional type. However, coordinating teams can also be, and often are, an important part of a matrix structure. In such cases the program manager is the chairperson, and the membership includes the key functional personnel on the horizontal axis working on the product or program in question.

How these coordinating teams are actually used in practice can also vary depending on the nature of the problems they face and the predilections of their leaders and members. For example, some managers prefer to work with the whole group together, believing that this facilitates a free flow of information and assures that all the relevant parties have a say in decisions and feel committed to them. In contrast, other senior managers feel more comfortable usually dealing with the members of such teams on an individual basis. Their argument for this approach is that it saves time, because all members do not need to be involved in every issue.

So far we have discussed these teams or committees as if they were formally designated bodies. Although this is often the case, such teams can and frequently do emerge based on the members' need to get together without formal sanction from top management. For example, in a major chemical company people in research, development, sales, and manufacturing at the middle level of the organization working on a new product began to meet together to coordinate their efforts. Their meetings began informally because the individuals involved felt that this was a more efficient way to reach decisions and spread the word, rather than making frequent telephone calls and calling individual sessions. Gradually, as the members of the group worked together, top management became aware of its existence and its effectiveness in solving problems. When the new product was placed on the market commercially, higher management formally legitimized the group by designating one member as its chairperson and by giving it profit responsibility for the new product.

Whether such a group is formally recognized or not, and whether its meetings are between two individuals, or among all the members, or some combination of different meetings, the major point is that such groups have the important function of providing a medium for enhancing the coordination of the work effort where the hierarchy alone cannot do the job. As we have suggested earlier, the question of whether management by committee is good or bad is a moot one. Rather, the issue today is whether the coordinating issues in the organization are sufficiently complex to require this mechanism for coordinating the work of the various parts of the firm.

### PLANS AS COORDINATING MECHANISMS

So far we have discussed two coordinating devices—coordinating positions and teams—both of which involve face-to-face interaction among key managers to achieve coordination. Another coordinating device that is frequently utilized to support the hierarchy in achieving coordination is the development of plans and schedules. In those areas it is possible to forecast the future accurately, laying a careful plan or schedule of activity can enable each function to carry out its work load so that the total effort is well coordinated. The area in which plans are probably most frequently utilized is between manufacturing and sales departments. Here sales departments make estimates of the amount of products they will require, and manufacturing departments then determine whether and how they can turn out this volume of output. Once the plan is agreed upon, it provides a framework for these two functions to handle their individual efforts in a coordinated manner. The results of a period's activities are measured against the plan, and forecasts for future activities can then be updated.

The comparison of plans or schedules against actual results also implies the measurement of actual results and a process of management control. These are topics that will be examined in the next section of this book, but the important point at this juncture is to recognize that plans and schedules are also an important method for achieving coordination in an organization. In this sense they can play an important supplementary role to the management hierarchy. The use of plans as coordination devices does not eliminate the requirement for personal contact among representatives of the various units affected by the plan. They must work together to share the plan in the first place and then to make adjustments in the plan as they become necessary.

## Organizational Structure: A Multilevel Balance

We now have some understanding of the ways in which work is divided in business firms and of some of the means that managers have found useful in coordinating the activities of the various parts of the firm. It is important here to emphasize two connected points that have been left largely implicit in the discussion to this point.

The first is that we have been primarily describing how the work gets divided among the major units of the firm. As we have already implied, a firm of almost any size may use several bases of division of work simultaneously. Similarly, to achieve the necessary coordination, firms use various combinations of the coordinating mechanisms we have just described.

In essence then, in seeking a balance between the division of work and the coordination of work, managers have found it necessary to use combinations of the whole range of ideas for designing organizations that we have discussed.

The second closely related point is that, at a given level of the organization, the horizontal division of work is among product divisions or functions or territories (Figure 3.3), and so on. Reporting to the Chief Executive are product divisions, which in turn are divided by function, within various functions work is

Figure 3.3  A Typical Multilevel Organizational Structure

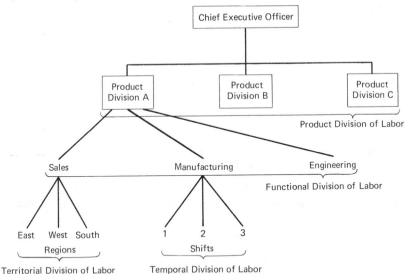

further divided by time or territory. In one sense then the management hierarchy, as we have suggested, is a coordinating mechanism to facilitate the coordination of effort among the organization's parts. But in another sense the management hierarchy also represents a division of activities among managers at various levels. The classical scholars of organization were very clear on this point. In their view, the hierarchy represented a division and delegation of authority and responsibility from the top of the organization to subordinate management levels and finally to the workers on the firing line. How much authority and responsibility were delegated to these subordinate levels is usually referred to as the degree of decentralization in the particular organization.

## Centralization Versus Decentralization

The question of how much centralization or decentralization represents a sound organizational approach has been a much argued point in management literature. In fact there seems to be something like a pendulum effect in these discussions. In some companies, there is a trend toward decentralization for a period and then the pendulum swings back to an emphasis on more centralization. There seem to be several reasons for this oscillation. Some concern the economic conditions the firm is facing. When the firm is facing a favorable economic climate, top managers seem to have more confidence in subordinates and are often more inclined to delegate authority and responsibility to them. When business conditions become more rugged, there is a greater tendency for top management to want to retain control, because the trust in subordinates has a tendency to evaporate.

Another reason for this indecision concerns an oversimplistic view of what decentralization and centralization mean and involve. The classical writers created an impression that top managers could delegate as much or as little authority to subordinates as they chose as long as authority was equal to responsibility. This notion of having complete control over how much authority and responsibility they retained or delegated was very comforting to many managers, and they have acted as though it were true. More recent descriptions of how organizations function, however, has suggested that this set of assumptions is fallacious.

As we have already indicated in describing the situation of product and program managers, there are several bases of authority in an organization. One is certainly the legitimate positional authority defined by upper management in the organization charts, procedural manuals, and so on. But equally important sources of authority, as we have shown in discussing staff functions, are the personal ability of various managers and how much information various individuals have. Persons with more information about the situation and who are perceived as being competent tend to have more influence over decisions. What this suggests, then, is that top managers cannot decide solely on their own where authority should reside in an organization and expect automatic compliance.

Another shortcoming in the traditional management views about centralization and decentralization is a failure to recognize that the issue is really one of a vertical division of labor and coordination. Therefore, it is not just a question of dividing authority and responsibility up and down the hierarchy, but it is also a question of organizing the flow of information and coordinating devices such as plans and reports, meetings, and so forth, to keep the divided work of managing the firm tied together.

In sum, it is important to recognize that, when we discuss centralization versus decentralization, we are dealing with issues of dividing up and tying together the coordinating processes that take place through the hierarchy. This requires a recognition of not only the complex issues of how power and authority are achieved in a firm but also attention to the central theme of this chapter: that management must constantly strive for a balance between dividing work in an efficient fashion and coordinating effort so as to keep all of the parts welded together.

## The Pattern of Structure and Strategy

Our discussion in this chapter has focused on the options available to managers as they plan the organizational structure of their firms. It has also provided an outline of the reasons why managers may select one or the other pattern of dividing the work and coordinating it. At the most general level it has been suggested that the particular pattern of structure that is appropriate for a firm depends upon the nature of the work that top management intends to accomplish. What are the cost constraints that must be considered in dividing up the work? How much coordination is required? At what levels of the organization and among which units is coordination needed?

In essence, to return to the terminology of Chapter 1, we have been arguing that the particular structural pattern that a firm develops must be consistent with the strategy the firm is pursuing. As we have seen, whether a firm pursues a strategy of producing and marketing a single product or has a diverse product line can affect not only the basis of dividing up the work but also the coordinating issues that must be managed. Similarly, whether a firm develops a strategy of worldwide operations or one of operating in a more limited geographical area also has an impact on the balance of the division of labor and coordination that must be achieved.

But beyond these more obvious implications of strategy on structure, there are more subtle ways in which the firm's structure must be related to its strategy. The strategy a firm undertakes defines the information environment with which managers must deal to reach decisions. The nature of this information, how predictable it is, how rapidly it changes, what functional specialists are required to handle it, and how frequently they must work together—all have an impact on the structural pattern that the firm needs to develop.

It would be misleading however to leave the impression that the structure of a firm follows from its strategy without an effect in the opposite direction. Clearly, the structure of the firm is an important constraint upon the strategic options that managers can consider. For one thing, the structure of the firm channels the information that reaches managers who are considering strategic issues. Thus they may find that the future options that they perceive are significantly shaped not only by the structure of the firm's current organization but also by the measurement and reward practices that accompany the structure. A second way structure influences strategic choice is because the capability of a firm to develop, produce, and market certain products and services is heavily constrained by the capabilities of its current organization. In this sense the organizational pattern the firm has evolved represents as real a resource to be utilized as the pool of talents of organization members, the technology the firm owns, and its financial assets.

In emphasizing this relationship between strategy and structure, we should not lose sight of the fact that effective structure must also be compatible with the needs of the human resources inside the firm. As we pointed out in the preceding chapter, the way individual jobs are designed can have an important impact on the motivation of employees to work toward the goals of the firm. The structural choices that are made must thus achieve a balance between the division of work and the coordination of work efforts to meet the firm's strategic requirements; but they must also meet the needs of its members.

## Implications for the Reader

This description of how organizations are structured may seem on the surface to have more relevance for persons well along in their managerial careers than it does for the beginning student. Yet, as we have already suggested, we believe that there are important reasons for beginning students to become acquainted with these issues.

First, and perhaps most obvious, many of the readers of books such as this will eventually be in positions where issues of planning organizational structures will be of concern to them. Even in firms of relatively small size, the primary way managers assure that the work of employees is in the direction of the company's goals is by designing not only organizational structure but also reward practices and measurement schemes that encourage such behavior. This is the dominant theme that connects this position of the book with Chapter 1 and the sections that follow it, because it means that one of the central tasks of any manager is to manage a system of organizational, measurement and reward practices.

Equally important, it is hoped that this discussion gives the reader a framework that will be helpful in understanding better the day-to-day activities of managers at all levels of an organization. As we have seen, the complexity of most modern organizational structures involves managers in an intricate web of interpersonal relations that he must manage. He must be prepared to resolve conflicts with peers, subordinates, and superiors. This involves not so much a capacity for compromise as it does a willingness to face up to tough differences of opinion and to work at resolving them in the best interests of the firm's objectives. Although this work is time consuming and often frustrating, it can also be challenging. As we shall point out in more depth in the final section of the book, it is a major element in showing what managerial work is all about.

# II

# MANAGEMENT CONTROL: MAKING THINGS HAPPEN

# Introduction to Management Control 4

In Chapter 1 of this book, we have discussed the "conditions of doing business," that is, the reasons why there are businesses in our society and other societies, and the roles of customers, competitors, third-party agencies, and society as a whole in shaping the conditions under which a business firm operates. In Section I we have looked at the issues surrounding three organizational "balances": that between the individual employee's needs and organizational requirements; that between the division of work and the coordination of effort; and that between tradition and innovation in performing organizational tasks. Thus at this point we have a notion of the complexity of the social, economic, and political environment in which a firm operates and of the way a firm organizes the skills and talents of individuals so as to be able to accomplish its objectives.

## Planning and Control

In this section of the book, we shall examine the process that involves:

1. How a firm decides what activities it is going to undertake;
2. How the firm establishes in specific terms what those activities are expected to accomplish during a given time period and how it allocates the resources that are necessary to make possible these accomplishments;
3. How, during the given period in which the firm operates, it measures how it is actually performing ("results");
4. How it evaluates these results, rewards desirable performance, and tries to correct undesirable performance.

Taken as a whole, these four activities comprise a process commonly referred to as *planning and control*.

As the reader can quickly see from the preceding description, planning and control is a massive and complex process that ultimately involves managers at every level of the organization. The following examples illustrate the range of decisions and analyses within each of the four activities that comprise this process. (Firm names in the following list are fictitious.)

1. Deciding on activities to be undertaken.

   **Based on the recommendations of top management, Alpha Corporation's board of directors decides that Alpha should enter the computer industry, and prepare itself to manufacture large, multipurpose computers.**

   **The president of Beta Corporation decides that Beta should begin a program to attract more minority-group students into the field of engineering.**

   **The vice president of marketing of Gamma Industries decides that the company should add metal tennis racquets to its sporting-goods line.**

The factory manager of Delta, Incorporated, decides to undertake a program to reduce factory administrative expenses.

The superintendent of the assembly department at Epsilon Electronics decides to reorganize the department so that workers can work in teams to assemble a complete item, rather than having each person perform only one small task on the item. The foreman of work station 22 at Zeta Manufacturing decides to begin efforts to improve the morale and esprit de corps of the unionized work group that the foreman manages.

2. Establishing specific target accomplishments and allocating required resources.

The board of directors of Alpha Corporation endorses a proposal for undertaking 13 different computer research and design projects. They approve a budget of $25 million to fund these projects over the next 12 months.

Beta's president approves a plan calling for the expenditure of $0.5 million this year to be used for magazine advertisements and preparation of a 30-minute movie dealing with minorities' career opportunities in engineering. The plan also calls for Beta personnel to contact in person the guidance counselors in at least 1000 high schools with significant enrollments of minority students.

The vice president of marketing of Gamma Industries submits a sales budget indicating that this department will be striving to sell 29,000 metal racquets over the next 12 months. The vice president requests $125,000 to fund this marketing program for the new racquets and, after discussions with the budget committee, agrees to attempt this proposed program with a reduced budget of $116,000.

The Delta factory manager sets a goal of a 5 percent reduction in factory administrative expenses. Of the total projected savings, $5500 will result from approving a request from the accounting supervisor to spend $2000 for electronic calculators for use by several clerks; the increased clerical efficiency will preclude the necessity of hiring a new clerk at $7500.

The assembly department superintendent at Epsilon Electronics submits a departmental budget request that includes $1500 for the purchase of new work tables and the dismantling of a conveyor belt system. The factory manager approves the request, based on statements that the department rearrangement will increase output this year by 12 percent without hiring more employees.

The foreman of work station 22 at Zeta Manufacturing submits a plan to the general foreman with a target of a 50 percent decrease in grievances filed by the foreman's employees over the next six months. The foreman asks for $50 to use for the purchase of tickets to a hockey game for the work crew. The request is approved.

3. Measurement of results.

Alpha's board of directors receives a report from the head of the new computer division, highlighting progress on the 13 computer research and design projects currently under way, and indicating that expenditures are as predicted.

Beta's president receives word that the new film on engineering careers has been produced, that an advertising program will be run in Ebony, and that 200 high school visits have been made during the first two months of this engineering career program.

The marketing vice president at Gamma receives a monthly sales report indicating that metal racquet sales are running 18 percent above the budgeted sales level.

Delta's factory manager learns that factory administrative expenses for the first three months are running 7 percent below the previous year's level.

The assembly department superintendent at Epsilon Electronics learns from last week's output report that production that week was 25 percent over plan, utilizing the budgeted number of employees.

From a notebook kept by Zeta's work station 22 foreman, the foreman knows that in the months January through March there have been only half as many grievances filed by the station's unionized workers as were filed during the same three months the previous year.

4. Evaluation, rewards, and corrective action.

A member of Alpha's board of directors remarks to Alpha's president that it is difficult to evaluate progress on the company's new computer projects because no one had ever stated how far along each project was to have been by this time.

The president of Beta, after receiving numerous letters from high school principals praising the firm's efforts to interest minority students in engineering careers, commends the Beta employee in charge of the program and adds $50,000 to the program's budget to extend the program to college freshmen.

After some investigation and analysis, Gamma's vice president of marketing concludes that the over-budget metal racquets sales results are not a reflection of too pessimistic a budget, but rather of the creativity of the racquet product manager. The vice president awards the product manager a salary increase, and the product manager also receives a personal letter of commendation from Gamma's president.

Delta's factory manager discovers that the reason factory administrative costs are 7 percent below budget rather than the planned 5 percent is that some order-processing clerks who left were not replaced. Unfortunately, order processing is falling behind as a result. The factory manager instructs the order-processing supervisor to fill the vacancies immediately, and chastises the supervisor for risking the company's customer goodwill by "trying to look good on the budget report."

Epsilon's assembly department superintendent calls the department's workers together, and praises their previous week's performance. The superintendent urges them to "keep up the good work" and assures them their increased output has not gone unnoticed by the production manager.

The general foreman shows the foreman in Zeta's work station 22 a copy of a letter the general foreman has sent to the director of industrial relations, praising the foreman's efforts in reducing labor grievances among station 22's workers.

The foregoing examples reflect not only the range of managerial levels and organizational units involved in the planning and control process but also the wide diversity of kinds of decisions and types of information flow that comprise this process. Later in this chapter we shall subdivide the planning and control process into three subprocesses and thereafter focus on only one of the three. Before further delineation of this process, however, let us try to gain a clearer understanding of the importance of planning and control in any organization or organizational unit.

## Example: An Airline Flight

Because the planning and control process is complex, any example that briefly tries to illustrate the full process will necessarily be oversimplified. With that forewarning, let us take as an example of a business "enterprise" a specific airline flight, Flight 126 from Boston to Los Angeles, and look for the manifestations of planning and control. This enterprise is relatively easy to understand, because it has a finite (and short!) life.

Our example is also easy to understand in terms of activities to be undertaken, largely because Flight 126 itself *is* the activity. The decision to have a Boston–Los Angeles flight—that is, the decision to undertake this activity—presumably was made by airline management based on analyses of the movement of people between the two cities, competitive flights, and the availability of aircraft for this flight.

Next, what are the desired accomplishments for the flight? The airline's printed schedule tells some of these: The flight is to leave Boston at 5:30 P.M., EST, and to arrive in Los Angeles at 8:15 P.M., PST (i.e., flight time is 5 hours and 45 minutes). Other important but not explicitly stated objectives for this flight are to: provide a smooth flight, serve appetizing food, and in general to create and/or maintain customer goodwill. Also, there presumably is the desire on the part of the airline's management to operate the flight at a profit. Finally, at a more detailed level, based on forecasts of the environmental conditions, the cockpit crew has developed a very specific route or flight plan that it expects to accomplish.

To achieve these results, airline resources must be committed to the flight. The airline has devoted a DC-10 "plant" to the flight and has assigned a "work force" in the persons of the flight crew. Other resources allocated to our "business" include meals, beverages, magazines for the passengers, and fuel for the aircraft. The allocation of the plane, crew, and fuel was made after analysis showed that our enterprise (i.e., a nonstop flight from Boston to Los Angeles leaving at 5:30 P.M.) was expected to be profitable. (A full plane would have 44 first-class passengers paying $209 each and 196 coach passengers paying $161 each, for a total revenue of $40,752; the business can break even at about 50 percent of capacity, or 120 passengers. Expected volume is 180 passengers.) The allocation of meals was based on an estimate of the number of passengers ("sales forecast") made a few hours before flight time.

At 5:30 P.M. the actual results of our enterprise can begin to be measured. A count of the passengers in each section of the plane is made, which is equivalent to measuring the flight's revenues. The actual take-off time is noted. As the flight progresses, various instruments in the cockpit measure direction, air speed, fuel consumption, altitude, and so on. The flight attendants are also measuring results with respect to customer satisfaction, though less explicitly and less formally: Passengers comment to them on the food, the smoothness of the flight, the cabin temperature, and so forth. These same customer satisfaction results are also measured more formally, by providing each passenger with a brief post card questionnaire that can be completed optionally and mailed to the airline's home office.

Clearly, these various measurements are of limited use without some benchmarks against which to compare them. Specific performance standards were set in the second stage of the planning-and-control process, as were resource consumption standards. Combined with the measurements of the third stage, we are prepared to carry out the last step in the planning-and-control process: the evaluation of results. Table 4.1 is a partial listing of some of the aspects of our flight that we can try to evaluate.

In using Table 4.1 to arrive at an evaluation of our enterprise, Flight 126, we soon discover that this critical fourth step in the planning-and-control process is not so easy or automatic as we might have hoped it would be. For example, the unfavorable revenue "variance" of $1,477 ($30,564–$29,087) was essentially out of our flight crew's control; hence we must be careful not to chastise, say, the pilot because the flight attracted fewer passengers than anticipated. The revenue item also demonstrates the complexity behind analyzing a variance: The $1,477 is actually the net result of an unfavorable first-class revenue variance of $2,926 ($6,897–$3,971) and a favorable coach variance of $1,449 ($25,116–$23,667). If this pattern were to continue flight after flight, we might conclude that first class's superior seating, legroom, meals, and free drinks and movies must be promoted more heavily.

## Table 4.1  Flight 126 Results

| Item | Plan | | Actual | |
|---|---|---|---|---|
| Revenue | 33 first class | $ 6,897 | 19 first class | $ 3,971 |
| | 147 coach | 23,667 | 156 coach | 25,116 |
| | Total revenue | $30,564 | Total revenue | $29,087 |
| | (75% of capacity revenues) | | (71.4% of capacity revenues) | |
| Take-off time | 5:30 P.M., EST | | 6:05 P.M., EST | |
| Arrival time | 8:15 P.M., PST | | 8:26 P.M., PST | |
| Flight plan (major cities flown over) | New York City, Pittsburgh, Louisville, Tulsa, Amarillo, Phoenix | | New York City, Pittsburgh, Indianapolis, Omaha, Denver, Las Vegas | |
| Fuel consumption | 17,910 gals | | 19,880 gals | |
| Complimentary alcoholic drinks served | 38 drinks (2 per actual first-class passenger; coach passengers to pay $1.50 per drink) | | 257 drinks provided without charge | |
| Questionnaire returns | Favorable: 12% (i.e., 12 per 100 passengers) Unfavorable: 5% | | Favorable: 27% Unfavorable: 2% | |

Next, consider the fact that the plane was 35 minutes late in leaving. The report tells us that this happened, but not *why* it happened. Perhaps it was the crew's fault: For example, the pilot's car ran out of gas on the way to the airport, and the pilot's late arrival delayed the take-off. Or perhaps it was no one's fault: Logan Airport in Boston had been closed part of the afternoon because of fog, and there was a long line of planes at 5:30 P.M. waiting to take off. Only some verbal information in conjunction with the numbers (i.e., 5:30 P.M. vs. 6:05 P.M.) will clarify this.

Now let us look at the remaining items in Table 4.1. Can you see a pattern that leads us to an educated guess as to what happened after take-off? Try to make such a guess before reading any further.

Here is what really happened. Because of the late take-off, which was due to bad weather, the pilot made two decisions concerning the flight. First, the pilot decided to try to make up the lost time so as to arrive in Los Angeles on time. Second, to "cheer up" the passengers, who had had to sit on the plane 40 or more minutes prior to actual take-off, the co-pilot announced that "drinks are on the house." Then en route the plane's radar indicated severe thunderstorms along the planned flight path; the crew revised the plan, resulting in a more northerly route that would help the plane avoid the storms and hence save the passengers a bumpy ride.

Because of the first two decisions, the flight "gave away" $328.50 in drink revenues ([257 − 38] × $1.50) and consumed 1970 extra gallons of fuel, worth $551.60. (Note that the sum of these amounts, $880, is equivalent to about 5½ coach tickets for the flight.) Because of the longer route taken to avoid the storms, not all of the time from the late take-off was made up. However, the passengers seemed to appreciate the gesture of free drinks and the pilot's making up all but 11 minutes of the late take-off: The number of passengers taking the time to complete the post cards and making favorable comments was more than twice that normally expected, and the number of unhappy passengers apparently was less than half that on a usual flight. The flight attendants also commented to the cockpit crew that the passengers were "an unusually happy group."

## Complexity of Planning and Control

With the data in Table 4.1 now supplemented with the results of further analysis and investigation, we may be willing to conclude that all things considered, our enterprise, Flight 126, was successful. Let us highlight a few important things about the process of arriving at this conclusion:

1. To know how well we did, we had to know how well we were supposed to do; that is, we needed to know our planned accomplishments and planned resource consumption.
2. The process involved several dimensions, not all measured in monetary terms; for example, we measured revenue dollars, gallons, and times.
3. The process involved both formal and informal measurement; for instance, we used measurements given by cockpit instruments, and flight attendants' personal observations.
4. We were willing to deviate from plans when conditions were different from those anticipated; the late take-off and

thunderstorms along the normal flight path are examples of such conditions.

5. There were different time horizons involved; we were willing to sacrifice profit on this flight (extra resources consumed) to keep customers happy so that they would ride our flights (rather than those of competitors) in the future.

6. We could not make a final evaluation without "looking behind the numbers;" that is, some of the factors relevant to our evaluation, such as the bad weather in Boston, were not reflected in Table 4.1.

All of these six observations hold true in the planning and control of almost any enterprise or of many activities within that enterprise.

Hopefully, we now have some notion of the complexity of the planning-and-control process. It was not a simple process even in our oversimplified enterprise. Moreover, there were other factors that made our flight easier to evaluate: All of the resources we had counted on were available at the times and places when needed; the crew was a stable, well-defined organization, in which each person knew his responsibilities and was properly trained to carry them out; the objectives of the airline apparently were clear to the crew—otherwise, how would the crew members have known whether or not to consume $880 worth of extra resources in order to maintain customer satisfaction? Let us imagine, then, the complexity of the planning-and-control process for the airline's top management, which *does* have to worry about, among other things, obtaining and allocating resources, hiring and structuring properly trained people into organizational units, and setting and communicating organizational objectives.

## Activities

Thus far, in trying to understand planning and control we have dealt with very concrete examples. To facilitate a deeper understanding, however, let us now approach this process somewhat more abstractly. These abstractions, or "models," should enable us more readily to understand planning and control in a wide variety of organizational settings.

The focus of our abstraction will be an *activity,* which we shall define as an entity that performs work, that has an intended objective or *output,* and that requires certain resources, or *inputs.* Diagrammatically, we can illustrate an activity thus:

We shall treat the internal structure of the activity as a given (perhaps one that is not well understood) and focus on the activity's inputs and outputs.

A simple (nonorganizational) example of an activity is an automobile engine. It has an intended objective or output called "power," which is harnessed to propel the vehicle in which the engine is placed. The engine has, of course, other outputs, including heat and carbon monoxide, sulfur dioxide, and the other ingredients that make up its exhaust. There are also several inputs. One of them, gasoline, is consumed rapidly as the engine operates. Other inputs, which are consumed in a somewhat different sense, include spark plugs, oil, water, and antifreeze. Before we leave this example, however, we should consider the many meaningful statements that can be made about an engine based on its inputs and/or outputs without any reference to (or knowledge of) the engine's internal structure and workings.

Let us turn now to an example of an organizational activity, the gift-wrapping service desk of a large downtown department store. In addition to the people doing the wrapping, this activity's inputs include boxes, wrapping papers, ribbons, bows, brown paper, twine, and mailing labels. A typical wrapping job consumes some of each of these inputs, including consuming some of the gift wrapper's time. Other resources that are required for a wrapping job but that are not perceptibly "consumed" by the job include: the floor space the service requires; the necessary counter space and storage shelves; paper, tape, and ribbon dispensers; and so forth. The gift-wrapping service desk's output is, in a narrow sense, nicely wrapped packages, and, in a broader sense, satisfied customers who will shop in the store partly because of this convenient service.

Before utilizing our concept of an activity, one further aspect should be noted: What we label as an activity is arbitrary; as long as we can define an entity that has input(s) and output(s), we may call it an activity. Furthermore, if one thinks about it, it becomes apparent that an activity can be a collection of other activities, or "subactivities." For instance, in the department store example, we could define any of the following as activities:

- The task of wrapping a single package;
- The gift-wrapping service desk;
- The customer service department, which includes gift-wrapping, check-cashing, and gift-counseling services, as well as providing information and making adjustments;
- The particular downtown department store in question as a whole;
- That store plus all of its suburban branches;
- The nationwide chain of stores of which that store and its branches are a part; or
- The retailing industry in the United States as a whole.

Thus activities are hierarchical, as we have already noted in a previous section of this book in discussing organizational structures.

## Activities and Planning and Control

We can now formalize in more detail our previous discussion of the planning-and-control process, giving names to each of the four steps in the process we have identified.

1. *Deciding on activities to be undertaken.* This step can now be seen as one of *planning* an activity's *outputs.* Of course, this also requires *establishing* (or continuing) the appropriate *activities* to produce these outputs. We shall call this step "programming."
2. *Establishing specific desired activity accomplishments and allocating the necessary resources.* This step is one of *setting output standards* for an activity, as well as providing inputs into the activity. Since there is usually a clear target level for the amount of these inputs, this step is also one of *setting input standards.* Also, in many instances we are

interested in setting a target for the relationship between inputs and outputs. This step of standard setting we shall call "budgeting."

3. *Operating and measuring results.* Operating means simply an activity's *performing* its *planned tasks.* To be able to evaluate this performance, we must *measure* the activity's inputs and/or outputs. We shall refer to this measurement step as "accounting." (Because we are accounting for an activity while it is "doing something," we shall occasionally emphasize this fact by calling this third step "operating/accounting.")

4. *Evaluating results, rewarding good performance, and correcting undesirable performance.* This fourth step, which culminates the planning-and-control cycle for an activity, is simply one of *comparing measured results* (actual inputs and/or outputs) from the accounting step *with planned standards* set during the budgeting step. This comparison may—but does not necessarily—result in the aforementioned rewards or corrections. We shall call this final step in the planning-and-control process "evaluation."

## Feedback

Figure 4.1 illustrates our four-step process, which is often referred to as the "control cycle." The figure emphasizes the sequential nature of the four steps of the control sysle. It also illustrates that as a result of the fourth step, evaluation, three different things can happen. Let us consider these in order of lengthening time horizon.

First is the dashed arrow labeled "corrective action," leading back to the operating/accounting step. This suggests a short-term, relatively minor change in the operations of an activity, where the evaluation step has indicated the need for such a change. This is most simply illustrated by a mechanical device like a home furnace thermostat. By setting the thermostat, one has "budgeted" a desired result—room temperature. A mechanism in the thermostat then measures (or "accounts for") the actual temperature. If the thermostat's comparison of the budgeted and actual temperatures indicates a significant discrepancy, a signal

Figure 4.1   The Control Cycle

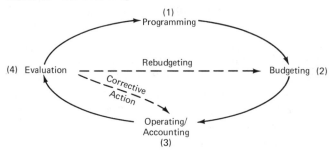

is sent to "operations" (the furnace) to take corrective action, that is, to shut off if the temperature exceeds the budgeted temperature, or to turn on if the reverse is true. The principle is that the evaluation leads to changed operations if budgeted and actual levels differ significantly. Though the corrective process in businesses is not usually so automatic as in the example of the thermostat, the same principle applies.

The thermostat example can also illustrate the nature of the dashed arrow in Figure 4.1 labeled "rebudgeting," leading from evaluation back to budgeting. In this instance, it is the person in the room, not the thermostat, who is making the evaluation. That person may decide that the room is generally too warm; hence by moving the thermostat lever or dial, he "rebudgets" to a lower level of temperature. The thermostat and furnace then continue to perform their functions with respect to the new budget he has set. (Note that rebudgeting occurs much less frequently than does corrective action.) In the same way, businesses on occasion alter budgeted input and/or output levels and then control to the new budget levels.

The "corrective action" and "rebudgeting" arrows in Figure 4.1 respectively suggest changes in our operations and performance standards, *prior to* the intervention of another programming step. This relooping through part, but not all, of the control cycle is often called a "feedback" process, and this cycle within a cycle is called a "feedback loop." The furnace, the thermostat, and the wiring connecting them constitute such a loop. A person, his hands, and the hot and cold water taps in his shower are another example.

The final Figure 4.1 arrow emanating from evaluation leads back to programming, representing the beginning of a new control cycle. To continue our simple home-heating analogy, suppose that no matter how many times the furnace is cycled on and off, or how many times one resets the thermostat, one cannot make the room comfortably warm without overheating the rest of the house. One now faces a new programming decision, with two obvious alternatives: (1) to stop trying to heat the room (e.g., shut off the radiator or close the hot-air vent) and (2) to find a new means of heating the room (e.g., by buying a plug-in space heater). In either instance, an activity is eliminated: heating the room using the existing central furnace. Or we might say that one is considering two alternatives: either not replacing the former activity (i.e., not heating the room) or beginning a new activity (i.e., heating the room with a different heat source).

It is more likely, of course, that a person *can* comfortably heat his room using the existing central furnace. In this case the "new" programming decision is to continue the present activity unchanged. For businesses, too, most activities in a given year are satisfactory performers, and thus are continued into the next year. Hence program changes are the exception rather than the rule.

Therefore, just as "exceptional" ("out-of-bounds" or "off-standard") performance for an activity resulted in changed operations or rebudgeting in the shorter run, so too in the longer run does performance *either* above *or* below the expectations for an activity lead to the exceptional decision in the programming step of whether to alter or eliminate that activity. In either instance, managers are recognizing that they would be "overloaded" if they continually examined every activity in detail; thus they must focus their attention where it appears to be needed most. This mode of focusing attention on activities that seem to be out of bounds is called *management by exception*.

## When Is an Organization "Out of Control"?

To emphasize the importance of the planning-and-control process, let us consider what can happen to organizations that fail to pay sufficient explicit attention to the control cycle. Here are some examples that provide at least circumstantial evidence of such failures. For each example, try to determine whether the failure is one of programming, budgeting, accounting, or evaluation, or some combination of these.

- In a period of two years, Super Enterprises, Incorporated, rapidly acquired the following: a small chain of tourist-oriented gift shops; a health and beauty aids products distributor; a chain of small 24-hour grocery stores; and a small chain of so-called catalog showrooms. In addition, Super opened on its own additional catalog showrooms and several medium-sized discount department stores, and started another company to import inexpensive goods from all over the world to be sold to its own stores, as well as to certain competitors. Super filed for bankruptcy when disastrous financial results clearly indicated that it had neither the financial nor management resources to support all of these activities.

- Calizona University's Graduate School of Business began establishing a doctoral program in 1973, even though published data indicated that the increasing supply of doctoral graduates in business would overtake the leveling demand for these graduates within two or three years.

- Giant Gyroscope Company decided to introduce a new children's "toy" gyroscope in time for the upcoming Christmas buying season. The price was set at $3.95. The item was a huge success, but unfortunately Giant learned the following February that it had cost $4.17 to make each gyroscope.

- New Massavania University, a private educational institution, kept its 1977–1978 tuition charge at the same level as in 1976–1977. Unfortunately, the university administration overlooked a cost-of-living increase clause in all faculty and unionized employee contracts. In March 1978 an emergency appeal was made to all alumni to raise money to cover the projected deficit between receipts and expenditures.

- Atelier Designers is a 70-person architectural firm that specializes in university and medical facilities. It has never bothered to collect customer satisfaction data from its clients, assuming that if the architect who designed the building was pleased with the result, so would be the client.

In early 1978 new school and hospital jobs virtually ceased for Atelier. Some investigation revealed that at almost every national convention of either university facilities planners or hospital administrators, people seeking an architect were told by their colleagues to "avoid Atelier—they're a bunch of prima donnas who design 'monuments' instead of functional buildings."

- Bernard Riesman was president of the Dress-Rite Company, a small manufacturer of womens' high-fashion belts. His firm was truly a "one-man show," with Riesman personally directing almost every aspect of the business. He prided himself on being able to "keep my hand on the pulse of this business," and he disdained what he called the "red tape" of detailed accounting records. When his outside accountant submitted the 1977 financial statements in late March 1978, Riesman was shocked to learn that the firm had made practically no profit for the year. This left inadequate funds to pay off a bank loan due April 15. The bank would not extend the loan and forced Dress-Rite into bankruptcy and liquidation.

- A project manager at Astro Aerospace never bothered reading the accounting reports indicating costs expended to date on the project, saying that the records were "too complicated." At completion, the actual project costs exceeded the customer's price by 25 percent, and Astro sustained a loss of $2 million on the project.

- The production manager at Harwood Manufacturing boasted of having the ability to manage operations through personal observation. This manager never took Harwood's budgetary control system seriously, claiming that "I know everything that goes on at least three weeks before it shows up in some report." The production manager was fired after an outside consultant's report indicated that Harwood's factory labor efficiency was by far the lowest in Harwood's industry. The firm's per-unit production costs were reduced by 20 percent within a year under the direction of the new production manager.

In all of these instances, the organization neglected to consider, or considered carelessly, some aspect of the planning-and-control process. In every case, the result was serious, if not disastrous. In most such instances in organizations, the disruptive impacts are felt by many people, from the highest to the lowest levels. It is to avoid such potentially fatal disruptions that many—though by no means all—organizations take the planning-and-control process seriously.

## Three Levels of Planning and Control

A quick review of the planning-and-control examples in the first segment of this chapter, and of the hierarchy of activities suggested in the department store gift-wrapping example, serves to remind us that Figure 4.1 is applicable to all kinds of activities, ranging from performing a single simple task to running an entire company. In every instance, the basic control concepts are the same: Decide what to do; set standards; measure; and then evaluate. However, in this introductory book we cannot deal with this full range of organizational activities, and we need to "carve out" a subset for more detailed study.

In his classical study of planning and control,[1] Robert N. Anthony suggested one way of categorizing the totality of planning and control. He defined these three processes as follows:

> *Strategic planning* is the process of deciding on objectives of the organization, on changes in these objectives, on the resources used to attain these objectives, and on the policies that are to govern the acquisition, use, and disposition of these resources.

> *Management control* is the process by which managers assure that resources are obtained and used effectively and efficiently in the accomplishment of the organization's objectives.

> *Operational control* is the process of assuring that specific tasks are carried out effectively and efficiently.

These definitions are not easy for someone without extensive business experience to understand. Table 4.2 gives some illustrations of the kinds of business activities that fall under each

---

[1] Robert N. Anthony, *Planning and Control Systems: A Framework for Analysis* (Boston: Division of Research, Harvard Business School, 1965).

**Table 4.2  Examples of Business Activities Included under Planning and Control Processes**[a]

| Strategic Planning | Management Control | Operational Control |
|---|---|---|
| Choosing company objectives | Formulating budgets | Controlling materials usage |
| Designing the organizational structure | Planning staff levels | Controlling hiring of workers |
| Setting financial policies | Planning cash flows | Controlling extension of credit |
| Setting marketing policies | Formulating advertising programs | Controlling advertisement placement |
| Setting production policies | Deciding on plant arrangement | Scheduling production |
| Choosing new product lines | Choosing product improvements | Purchasing product components |
| Acquiring a new division | Acquiring a new machine | Acquiring a new desk chair |
| Measuring, appraising, and improving overall company performance | Measuring, appraising, and improving management performance | Measuring, appraising, and improving workers' efficiency |

[a] Based on Anthony, op. cit., p. 19.

category. As these definitions and illustrations suggest, strategic planning is an activity carried on by a very small number of people at the highest levels of the organization. This is not to say that the process is unimportant to other people in the firm— indeed, the decisions made as part of the strategic planning process have an impact on literally everyone in the organization. However, with the exception of those who become involved in family-owned or other small businesses, it is not likely that most readers will actually become participants in the strategic-planning process of any firm for many years to come. Thus we shall not explore further the nature of that process, except to the extent that it impinges directly on management control.

On the other hand, operational control focuses on specific tasks, any one of which tends to be limited in scope. Control of these tasks obviously is crucial to the firm's success. That is why specific techniques such as PERT charts, economic order quantity

(EOQ) formulas, time-and-motion studies, credit-rating scoring systems, quality-control tests, and so on, have been developed as aids in operational control for certain tasks. Often these operational control efforts are so well developed that the firm has manuals on standard operating procedures that describe in detail how certain operations or tasks are to be performed and controlled. Although it is important for a manager to be familiar with the variety of techniques available for use in operational control, it is beyond the scope of this introductory text to discuss them further.

What we shall deal with here is the subject of management control, the middle level of the three planning-and-control processes that we have identified. Management control is a process in which—as the name implies—virtually all of a firm's managers are involved. You, the reader, probably aspire to hold a managerial position within a reasonable time after graduation. And the process of management control must be of interest to you. But whether or not you ever become a manager, as an employee at any level in any organization you will feel the impacts of that organization's management control system virtually every day of your working life. A knowledge of management control will prepare you to understand these impacts on you and on your co-workers.

## Management Control and Financial Accounting

One reason an organization's management control system has these pervasive impacts on employees is because the management control process encompasses the entirety of the organization's operations. In the process of programming, budgeting, measuring, and evaluating the organization's activities, various summaries and comparisons of these activities' inputs and outputs must be made. But how does one combine, say, labor hours and tons of raw materials so that they can be compared with salespersons' commissions? Some common denominator must be used—and the only feasible common denominator available is money. Thus management control systems tend to be based on monetary measurements of inputs and outputs. This is not to say that nonmonetary measurements such as the number of customer complaints, the number of new accounts opened, the number of employees added, and so forth, are not also important in management control. But, again, because management control is so all encompassing in an organization, and because the various separate organizational parts must be combined and compared in controlling the organization as a whole, the great bulk of information reported to managers in the organization is in the form of financial accounting reports. Thus, before we can extend our understanding of management control, we must first gain some knowledge of the discipline known as accounting.

# Accounting: The Language of Management Control

*Asking "What would happen if every vestige of accounting were wiped out?" is almost like asking "What would happen if there were no food or water or government?" As a matter of fact, if by some magic every accounting document and record were made to vanish, the chaos and confusion resulting would mean that there would be little food or water for most people. A society organized by individual initiative operating in free markets (a rough description of our own economy) is so dependent upon its accounting machinery that paralysis of the accounting machinery would have about the same catastrophic consequences as a 100 per cent effective general strike. It would virtually eliminate specialization of labor and exchange of products. We would be reduced to a small population living in a primitive culture of small, self-subsistent groups. Recovery would depend upon reestablishment of an effective accounting machinery.[1]*

[1] Billy E. Goetz and Frederick R. Klein, *Accounting in Action* (Boston: Houghton Mifflin, 1960), pp. 663–664.

## Accounting's Historical Antecedents

The history of accounting would seem to bear out the rather dramatic assertions of the preceding paragraph. We cannot know, of course, when man began keeping accounting records in his head, but symbols recording transactions between tribes have been found to date back to 5000 B.C. The Sumerian civilization in Mesopotamia kept such records on clay tablets beginning about 3200 B.C., and more than 3000 years ago scribes in Babylonia and Egypt actually received what in effect was formal accounting training in schools. Persia under Darius (521–486 B.C.) had government scribes who performed "surprise audits" of the accounts of the provinces, and similar audits were made in the Hebrew civilization, in which the chief scribe was the second highest position in government. However, in ancient Greece (c. 1400 B.C.) it became customary to use slaves as scribes and auditors; it was assumed that statements from slaves, who could be tortured, would be more reliable than those from freemen, whom the law protected from such drastic auditing techniques.

Accounting later became more prestigious in Greece, however, and records of the construction costs of government buildings were carved on the structures. One such tablet indicates that the Parthenon cost 469 talents of silver, or about $1 million at today's prices. (By way of comparison, the Pyramid of Cheops, in Egypt, cost 1500 talents of silver, according to accounting records inscribed on the pyramid and reported by Herodotus.) In the Roman Empire in about 200 B.C. quaestors in the territories were responsible for supervising the local government accountants. The quaestors' reports to Rome were given in person and heard by an examiner, a practice that gives us our modern-day term of "auditor" (from Latin *audīre*, to hear). In the Byzantine Empire, Constantine (early fourth century A.D.) founded a public administration school in which accounting was taught. The Holy Roman Empire under Charlemagne (A.D. 742–814) continued the Roman and Persian examples of government accountants and auditors; after his death this group was disbanded, and the disintegration of the empire soon followed.

Accounting declined in the Middle Ages but was revived in Italy during the Crusades. Full-blown double-entry bookkeeping appears in Genoese records of 1340, and the Office of Exchequer (from an Old French word meaning a counting table covered with a checkered cloth) developed in England. In the fifteenth century branches of the Medici Bank were required to submit annual balance sheets to the main office in Florence. In 1631 an accountant was sent from Holland by the financial backers of the settlement at Plymouth (Massachusetts) to investigate the colony's increasing debt, and the new Americans experienced their first audit.[2]

## Accounting for Managers

For centuries accounting on any large scale was primarily associated with governmental activities (particularly tax collection). The Industrial Revolution, however, brought additional accounting needs. Large-scale enterprises required vast amounts of money to finance them, and increasing numbers of people to direct their operations. Thus the owner-manager combination, which in small businesses was (and often still is) personified in one individual, gave way to two distinct groups: investors and managers. The former group put demands on the latter to know how the firm was protecting and utilizing the resources entrusted to it—that is, the investors wanted "an accounting" from the managers. In the United States today the primary manifestation of this "stewardship" accounting is the corporate annual report, which contains summary-level financial statements and is sent to the shareholders of the firm and to others who request it. Financial statements of corporations are also used by lenders (e.g., banks and insurance companies), relevant regulatory agencies (e.g., the Securities and Exchange Commission and public utilities commissions), and, of course, the Internal Revenue Service (IRS). (In the case of regulatory agencies and the IRS, financial statements usually differ from those presented to the public, in part because of special reporting requirements levied by these agencies.)

Until now our description of corporate reporting has focused on the informational needs of parties other than the firm's man-

[2] Information in these three paragraphs was drawn from Willard E. Stone's "Antecedents of the Accounting Profession," *Accounting Review*, April 1969, pp. 284–91.

agers. But, as we shall see, the information reported to these "outsiders" is also of great use to management. With relatively few exceptions, the principles underlying the manner in which financial data are gathered and reported to shareholders also provide the most useful framework for gathering financial information and reporting it to managers. Indeed, for the vast majority of American companies, the "corporate financial reporting system" is essentially identical to the "management financial reporting system," the only significant difference being in the level of detail and the frequency of reports. For this reason, what we are about to learn concerning financial statements can help us either as interested observers of a corporation or as members of that firm.

## Resource Flows

Financial accounting[3] is a process of measurement, and the outputs of that process are the financial statements that we wish to be able to understand. These statements are based on a set of ground rules common to all business accounting, much as all oral or written statements in English are based on a set of rules or grammar; indeed, accounting is often called "the language of business." But just as a study of the English language would be rather meaningless if we had no notion of the surroundings and activities that we use language to describe, so too is an understanding of accounting statements predicated on some knowledge of just what it is accounting measures.

Basically, accounting measures resources and their flows through an organization. We shall utilize the diagram in Figure 5.1 to try to gain a better understanding of the nature of these resources and how they flow.

---

[3] For simplicity, we shall usually call "financial accounting"—that is, accounting for things in monetary terms—simply "accounting," as is done in common usage. However, the reader should remember that the accounting process at times deals with nonmonetary factors, too—for example, the number of units produced, the number of cases in stock, the number of hours worked, and so on. Because these nonmonetary measurements are usually converted to a monetary common denominator very quickly in the accounting process, in fact most accounting information is financial in nature.

**Figure 5.1 Resource Flows in a Manufacturing Firm**

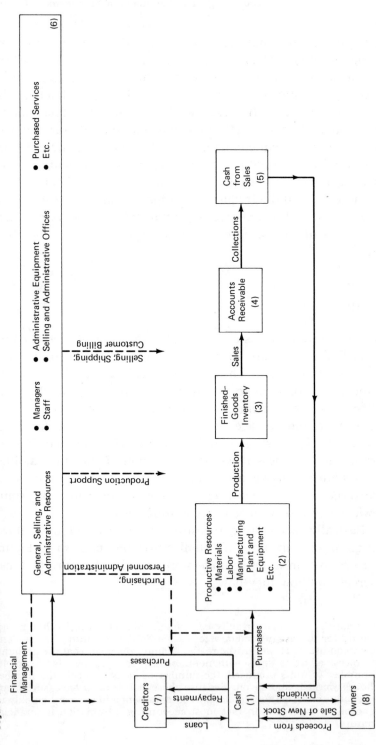

ILLUSTRATION: ESTABLISHING A BUSINESS

Imagine that you are going to begin to operate a small firm that will manufacture and sell a new product you have designed, called a "gismo." Section I of this book should have given you some ways to think about the organization of your new firm, and let us suppose that you have applied those ideas to structure your firm. To get the firm started, it is obvious that you need some cash (Box 1 of Figure 5.1). Fortunately, you are able to raise the money you need (we shall discuss the sources of these funds later), and you open a checking account and begin to spend your money.

Most of your purchases are for "productive resources" (Box 2). In other words, you lease a small plant, on which you make your first rent payment. You buy the machinery and other equipment required to make gismos. You purchase the various materials from which you will produce the gismos. And you hire workers to run the machines and perform other operations needed to turn out a finished gismo. You also arrange for some other necessities in your small factory, including gas to heat the building and electricity for the lights and machinery; these will not require cash payments for about a month, but that is earlier than your first sale of gismos.

A second category of resource purchases, though not directly related to the manufacture of gismos, nevertheless represents resources you must have to run your business. We shall call this category "general, selling, and administrative resources" (Box 6). As president of the firm, you will not be spending your time actually making gismos, but you will be very busy running the firm and you must of course pay yourself a salary to meet your personal needs. You also know that you will have to purchase the services of certain staff people to work full time in your firm: A secretary, an accountant, and an office manager seem to represent the bare minimum of needed employees. You also must buy some desks, a typewriter, an electronic printing calculator, a sign for the roof of the building, and so forth.

Also, you need some purchased services, including a janitorial service, trash-collection service, telephone and electrical service for your offices, and an advertising agency to help you promote your product. Finally, in order to sell the gismos you produce, you must hire a full-time sales manager and arrange to utilize a field sales force that will handle your product along with other noncompeting products sold to potential customers. You will pay these salespersons a commission on each gismo sold, and your sales manager will try to oversee their efforts and help them learn about the qualities and advantages of your product. Again, these resources are not directly related to the production of gismos. But they do have an indirect bearing, because your firm cannot survive without these selling, administrative, and support activities, a few of which are represented by the dashed lines in Figure 5.1.

Before proceeding with the flow suggested in Figure 5.1, we note that at this point you are just ready to begin production. You have not made or sold a single gismo, yet much (if not most) of the cash you began with is gone. The money is not "gone" in the same sense as if you had accidentally lost or destroyed it. Rather, either it is "spent" for goods or services from which you have already received the benefits (e.g., your accountant's wages for all the time that person has spent up to now), or it is "invested" in things that will provide benefits in the future (e.g., the materials you will convert into gismos and the office equipment and factory machinery). In accounting parlance, the dollars you have "spent" for benefits already received are called *expenses*, and the "investments" you have made for the provision of future benefits are called *assets*.

### ACCOUNTING FOR PRODUCTION AND SALES

Production of gismos now commences. Orders have not yet begun coming in from the sales force, but you are confident that they will, and you want to have the gismos ready for shipment when they do. As the gismos are completed, they are inspected, boxed, and stacked near the shipping door of your plant. At this stage, the productive resources your cash purchased are evidenced by these finished gismos, or "finished-goods inventory" (Box 3). This conversion of resources includes not only obvious things such as the material used in the gismos and the labor that was involved in making them. It also includes the less obvious "factory overhead" resources that have in some sense been "consumed" in production: factory supervision; heat, light, and power; rent on the building; and even the production machinery that has been "used up" (depreciated) a little because of the production of your first gismos. It is often said colloquially that at this point your "cash is tied up in inventory."

Soon after your finished-goods inventory began (literally) piling up, some orders from the field sales force began to be received. As each order is filled and leaves the factory, a "sale" is recorded. However, the practice in your industry (i.e., among firms selling products similar to gismos) is to grant customers liberal credit terms. In particular, when you bill a customer for an order of gismos, the customer has up to 60 days from the billing date in which to pay without being charged interest. Actually, because of the various steps in processing an order— beginning with the field salesperson's writing up of the order and ending with your sending a bill to the customer—more than 60 days will have elapsed between the time a customer places an order and pays for it.

Thus, at the time of shipping, you have neither the goods you have just shipped nor the money for them. What you *do* have is called an "account receivable"—an obligation on the part of the purchaser to pay you for the goods within the stipulated time period. At this point, it is often said that your original "cash is tied up in accounts receivable."

Finally, usually as long as from three to six months from the time you began production (and longer in some businesses), cash from your customers' payment of their bills begins flowing in (Box 5). As the arrow pointing back to Box 1 indicates, this cash from sales can be used to begin the cycle again. Excluding purchases of long-lived assets—those productive resources you own that will last more than a year, such as the machinery you bought[4]—the difference between the cash inflows from sales and the cash outflows for purchases is called "net cash from operations." This net cash is closely akin to what we intuitively think of as the "profit" from our business—or "loss" if the outflows exceeded the inflows.

**EXERCISE:** How would Boxes 1–6 change for a nonmanufacturing firm: for example, a department store, a grocery store, or a law firm? Why?

---

[4] Your building does not count as a long-lived asset for you, since you do not own it. It *is* a long-lived asset to whomever leased it to you, however.

FINANCING THE FIRM WITH CREDITORS' FUNDS (DEBT)

So far we have talked primarily about how your new business *used* the cash you raised, rather than where the cash came from. These uses included: purchases of long-lived assets; the materials, labor, and other resources used to produce gismos; and the general, selling, and administrative expenses required to operate your firm. The productive resources were "consumed" by the production process, which transformed them into a new resource, finished-goods inventory. This valuable inventory was then transformed into a new valuable (though essentially intangible) resource, accounts receivable.[5] The final transformation occurred when the receivables were collected, that is, transformed into cash. The cash from sales represents a source of "new" cash that can be used to "finance"—in other words, pay for—continued operations.

We have seen how you had to wait quite a long time for cash from sales to begin flowing into your firm, because your firm was new. Hence you needed some "outside financing" to carry you over this time lag. Also, at some point in the future you may wish to purchase a new long-lived asset—a new machine or the building that you now rent or a delivery truck—and not have enough cash in your firm's checking account to pay for it. Again, you will need outside financing. The concept is the same as when we wish to buy a house or a car but do not have enough money in the bank to pay for it—so we borrow from a bank or other financial institution and pay back the mortgage or car loan over a period of years.

Similarly, though more subtly, unless you can sell gismos at a very large profit, so that you have large positive net cash from operations, any time your firm's sales are increasing rapidly, you will need outside financing to provide the cash you will have to "tie up" in larger inventories and receivables to support the increased sales level. (To test your understanding of this point, retrace the steps in Figure 5.1, assuming that you are expecting a large influx of sales orders in the next few months. And to cement your understanding of the figure, go through it yet another time assuming that you are expecting a sales decline: What are

---

[5] It would be tangible only in the sense of your having pieces of paper such as purchase orders or bills of sale representing promises to pay.

the implications of such a decline on the need for outside financing?)

Boxes 7 and 8 of Figure 5.1 represent the sources of cash needed when you begin to operate your firm, when you buy expensive long-lived assets, or when the firm has a rapid sales increase. Box 7, "creditors," represents parties who have lent your firm[6] money to pay for your purchases while you await adequate cash from sales. Since your new firm has no established reputation, creditors will be hesitant to lend it money unless you promise to pay them back rather quickly, say, within the next six months. A local bank may give you such a "short-term" loan, of course charging you interest on the money you borrow.

Were your firm better established, so that lending it money would not seem so risky to a lender, then a bank might be willing to lend the firm money for a longer period of time. For very large corporations, insurance companies are often a source of long-term loans. Many large firms also let large numbers of individuals lend them money. The piece of paper held by the individual that represents the firm's promise to pay interest on the loan and also to repay the money borrowed (the "principal") is called a "bond."

A more subtle, but very important, source of short-term loans is the firms from which your company buys its raw materials and supplies.[7] Usually these suppliers will give you a "grace period" in which to pay them for your purchases. When a vendor does not require your firm to pay cash for goods (or services) when delivered, in effect that vendor is lending your firm money, just as your firm, in effect, is lending its customers money by giving them 60 days in which to pay for their purchases. A significant advantage of such vendor "loans" to your firm is that, unlike bank loans, there usually is no interest charge for the loan. Thus, in effect, you have free use of the vendor's cash until your bill with the vendor comes due. Thus the vendor has an account receivable from your firm that ties up *his* cash, just as you have accounts receivable from your customers tying up *your* cash.

[6] We say the loan is to "your firm" rather than to you, because normally this legally is the case. If your firm is "incorporated" and cannot repay the loan, the lender cannot force you to repay it out of, say, your personal savings account. This is a primary—though not the only—reason why people incorporate their firms.

[7] Such suppliers are frequently referred to as "vendors."

In sum, we have seen that there are several sources of loans or "debt financing" available to a firm. The arrows in Figure 5.1 between Boxes 1 and 7 represent cash coming into the firm from its creditors, and leaving the firm to repay them. As unfortunately often happens to new businesses, your firm at some point might find itself unable to repay its creditors when such payments are due. In such a case, if the creditors are not willing to give your firm some extra time to make these payments, your firm is said to be "bankrupt." For a small business, what usually happens is that the firm is "liquidated"—that is, all of the firm's owned things of value (its assets), including equipment and inventories, are sold and the proceeds are used to pay the firm's creditors.[8] Thus we see that in a sense the creditors really have claims against the firm's assets. If the asset "cash" is insufficient to settle a creditor's claim on the due date, then the creditor can force settlement by bankruptcy and liquidation of the other assets. These creditors' claims against a company's assets are called "liabilities."

FINANCING THE FIRM WITH OWNERS' FUNDS (EQUITY)

There remains one box in Figure 5.1 to be explained—Box 8, "owners." What does it mean to be an "owner" of a firm? Dictionaries define the verb "to own" as meaning "to have or possess." Although this definition fits our intuitive concept of ownership, it is not precise enough to describe what it means to own a business firm. As Figure 5.1 suggests, owners of a firm "give" money to the firm; this money is called "capital." This money from owners is given not in the sense of a charitable "gift" but in the sense that they expect something in return from the firm for allowing it to use their money. In this sense, owners are no different from creditors: Both allow the firm to use some of their money, and both expect to be "paid" for that use of their

---

[8] A "liquid" asset is one that is readily convertible into cash. Hence to "liquidate" a firm means to turn all of its assets into the form of cash. Not all bankrupt firms are liquidated, however. The firm can ask a bankruptcy court to permit it to continue operations, arguing that "there's a brighter day ahead" when the firm will make enough money to be able to pay off its creditors. The most famous recent case of a bankrupt company continuing its operations is the Penn-Central Railroad.

funds.[9] The lender is paid "interest" on the funds he has lent the firm.[10] In addition, the firm must repay the money borrowed according to some predetermined repayment schedule.

### BENEFITS OF OWNERSHIP

Now what does the owner get in return for the capital he has supplied the firm? First, in a corporation, an owner gets a piece of paper acknowledging his payment; this paper is called a "stock certificate," and it reflects his share of ownership vis-à-vis the other owners. For example, if when you started your firm, you chipped in $4000 and friends and relatives put in another $6000, you would have a 40 percent share of the ownership of your firm. This might be reflected by your firm's issuing 100 shares of stock: 40 shares to yourself and 60 to your contributing friends and relatives. If you are not the only owner of the firm, as in this example, you can see we really should not refer to it as *your* firm, but rather should talk about your *share* of ownership in *the* firm.

But an owner gets more than a piece of paper! He also gets his share of the *profits* of the firm, that is, his share of the excess of revenues from selling goods or services over the expenses incurred to supply those goods or services. However, recall from our earlier discussion that these profits were an important source of funds for the firm, which enabled it to cope with the previously discussed cash lag of operations between Boxes 1 and 5 of Figure 5.1, or to help it finance purchases of long-lived assets (i.e., to help it make investments). Thus the firm may not pay out *all* of its profits to the owners. Those profits that *are* paid to owners, however, are *dividends*, which are paid out by an incorporated firm (or *owners' drawings*, which are paid out by an unincor-

---

[9] The exception, remember, is money "lent" by those vendors who do not charge the firm for the privilege of not having to pay a bill for, say, 30 days after the bill is sent. But even these vendors will levy an extra charge after, say, 30 days, much like a Master Charge or BankAmericard credit arrangement.

[10] Did you ever stop to think that when you have a savings account, you are one of your bank's creditors? It must pay you interest for the privilege of using your money (which it in turn lends to others at a higher interest rate).

porated firm). Any profits not paid to owners, but instead kept in the firm to finance its operations and long-lived purchases, are known as *retained earnings*. But we should remember that even if retained in the firm, these earnings (profits) "belong" to the owners. Taken together, capital plus retained earnings is *owners' equity*, or simply *equity*.

*Liquidation.* How then do the owners ever get back their capital or receive their share of these retained earnings? There are three possibilities. Let us consider the unhappy one first. If the firm is liquidated, the proceeds from the sale of the assets are first used to pay back the creditors. If after these repayments there is money left over, this goes to the owners. For example, suppose the firm you began is liquidated. Assume its assets are sold for a total of $30,000, and the liabilities of $24,000 are paid to the creditors. That leaves $6,000, of which you with a 40 percent ownership would get $2,400; the other owners (your friends and relatives) would split up the other $3,600 in proportion to their shares. Note that you did not get back your total investment in the firm—your original $4,000 plus your share of the retained earnings (if any). This is often the case in a liquidation, because assets sold at forced auction generally bring far less than was paid for them, but the creditors' claims do not get reduced because of this. This is why there is considerable financial risk in being an owner of a firm, particularly a new and unproved one!

*Sale of the Firm.* The second way owners get back their capital and share of retained earnings is when the firm is sold. For example, your gismo firm may have been so successful that some larger company wanted to "buy you out" and offered a price so attractive that you and the other owners decided to sell. The proceeds from the sale would be distributed among you and the other owners in proportion to your ownership (40 percent for you, 60 percent for them). When a successful firm is sold, the price is usually higher than the sum of the owners' capital and retained earnings, and hence you would likely receive substantially more than your original $4000 plus your share of retained earnings. This is the other, "happy" side of the story of investing in (i.e., being an owner of) a firm—you may get a very handsome return on your investment!

*Selling Stock.*  The third way owners may get back their money from their ownership investment is to sell their stock. Unlike the previous case, in which *all* the owners sold their stock (and hence we say the *firm* was sold), in this case only *some* stockholders sell their ownership shares. In a firm having only a few shareholders (owners), finding a buyer for your stock may not be easy, and once you find one, the price you receive will have to be negotiated between you and the party purchasing your stock (ownership share). If a firm has a very large number of share-holders, then there presumably will be many owners wanting to sell their shares, and many people wanting to purchase these shares: In other words, there will be a "market" for the shares. The most familiar example of this phenomenon is the New York Stock Exchange, which "makes a market" in hundreds of com-panies' stocks. Sellers of shares communicate (via "stockbrokers") to "traders" at the New York Stock Exchange that they want to sell their shares, and prospective buyers similarly communicate their interests. Every day you can read in many newspapers the prices at which various stocks were "exchanged" between buyers and sellers. Such a price is a function of the buyers' estimates of the firm's prospective profits. (Beyond that general statement, determination of market prices of stocks is a matter well beyond the scope of this book, and the subject of continuing research and debate.)

### OWNERS AS AN ONGOING SOURCE OF FUNDS

There is one final point to make concerning owners as a source of funds for the firm. So far we have referred to owners as supplying capital only when the firm was organized. However, frequently the firm's management needs additional money to finance increased accounts receivable, increased inventories, the purchase of new long-lived assets, and so on. If profits, even if completely retained in the firm, are not adequate for this financ-ing, then the firm can either borrow the money from creditors (i.e., increase the firm's debt) or solicit additional funds from owners (more equity). In the latter case, the mechanism used by an incorporated firm is to issue and sell *additional* shares of stock —referred to as a "new issue." These shares may be purchased by present owners or by other parties. The decision of whether to raise needed funds through debt or through a new issue is a major topic of the field of studies called "financial management."

> **QUESTION:** Suppose I sell you my shares of XYZ Corporation for $50 a share via the New York Stock Exchange, and I had purchased the shares for $30 each as part of a new issue by XYZ. What was the financial impact on XYZ when I bought the shares? What is the impact on XYZ when I sell the shares to you? When you sell them to someone else?

## Accounting Statements: The Balance Sheet

Using Figure 5.1 as a base, we have now completed an overview of the economics of a firm. We have seen how cash is transformed into various productive and overhead resources and how this cash is tied up in inventories and receivables until the goods are sold. We have differentiated between money spent for things that benefit a firm in the short run (expenses) and for things that provide longer-run benefits to the firm (assets). We have talked about profit, the excess of the prices of goods sold (revenues) over the resources used (expenses) in producing them, including overhead items. Finally, we have considered how a firm uses others' money—both creditors' funds (liabilities or debts) and owners' funds (capital plus retained earnings, or owners' equity). We discussed these things not only to help us understand the economics of a firm but also as a basis for understanding accounting, the language of business in general and of management control in particular.

Now we wish to consider what kinds of measurements of the economics of a firm would interest the firm's "observers"—including managers, owners, and creditors. One thing of interest would be a "snapshot" of the firm at a point in time, showing its financial position: that is, showing (1) how it has used the funds entrusted to it in the financing of receivables, inventories, long-lived assets, and other things that will enable the firm to generate cash in the future; and (2) where the money to finance these things came from—how much from creditors (vendors, short-term lenders, and long-term lenders) and how much from the owners (capital and retained earnings). What would be even better would be two such "snapshots," one at the beginning of the year and another 12 months later. Then we could compare the two to see how the firm's financial position has changed over the year.

The accounting statement that gives us this "snapshot" of financial position, formally called a "statement of financial position," is usually known as a *balance sheet*. Table 5.1 shows two balance sheets for a hypothetical manufacturing firm, one as of the beginning of 1977 (December 31, 1976[11]) and the other as of a year later (December 31, 1977). Let us see what these balance sheets tell us, considering first the amounts shown as of December 31, 1977.

ASSETS

First, the upper portion of the balance sheet shows the firm's *assets*—those things owned by the firm that will provide it with future benefits. These assets are usually listed in order of decreasing liquidity; that is, the ones that will be turned into cash most quickly are listed nearest the top. The first category of assets is *current assets,* those that are expected to be converted into cash within a year or less.[12] Of course *cash* is the most liquid current asset because it is already "converted into cash"; hence it is shown first. The $10,781[13] shown in Table 5.1 represents the balance in the cash account (Box 1 of Figure 5.1) at year-end. Apparently, B.L.M.&R. has more cash than is needed to pay bills in the short run; thus it has invested at least part of the excess in *marketable securities,* probably short-term interest-bearing bonds

[11] You can think of the "snapshots" as being taken at midnight on the last day of the year. Thus the balance sheet as of December 31, 1976, can be thought of either as reflecting the financial position at the very end of 1976 or the very beginning of 1977.

[12] Technically, the definition is "convertible into cash during the normal operating cycle of the business." For most firms, this is less than a year. But, say, for a bourbon distiller, who by law must age its bourbon at least four years, the normal operating cycle is four years. Hence three-year-old casks of bourbon in inventory would be a current asset for the distiller.

[13] The suffix $000—thousands of dollars—will be assumed in the text as it is in Table 5.1.

**Table 5.1  B.L.M.&R., Incorporated, Statement of Financial Position as of December 31, 1976 and 1977**

(Thousands of Dollars)

| Assets | 1977 | 1976 |
|---|---|---|
| *Current Assets* | | |
| Cash | $ 10,781 | $ 21,265 |
| Marketable securities | 1,405 | 1,765 |
| Accounts receivable | 67,518 | 58,621 |
| Inventories | 65,466 | 60,943 |
| Total current assets | $145,170 | $142,594 |
| *Property, Plant, and Equipment (at Cost)* | | |
| Land | 9,093 | 9,093 |
| Buildings | 45,701 | 39,914 |
| Equipment | 149,084 | 130,719 |
| | $203,878 | $179,726 |
| Less: accumulated depreciation on buildings and equipment | 88,112 | 78,116 |
| Net property, plant, and equipment | $115,766 | $101,610 |
| Total assets | $260,936 | $244,204 |

| Liabilities and Owners' Equity | 1977 | 1976 |
|---|---|---|
| *Current Liabilities* | | |
| Accounts payable | $ 38,784 | $ 33,196 |
| Short-term loans | 16,758 | 14,197 |
| Taxes payable | 10,815 | 14,400 |
| Total current liabilities | $ 66,357 | $ 61,793 |
| *Long-Term Debt* | | |
| Bank loans | 34,904 | 32,891 |
| Bonds | 17,327 | 17,327 |
| Total long-term debt | 52,231 | 50,218 |
| Total liabilities | $118,588 | $112,011 |
| *Owners' Equity* | | |
| Capital stock | 25,163 | 25,163 |
| Retained earnings | 117,185 | 107,030 |
| Total owners' equity | $142,348 | $132,193 |
| Total liabilities and owners' equity | $260,936 | $244,204 |

or some similar highly liquid security with virtually a guaranteed return.[14]

The next current asset account is *accounts receivable*. The $67,518 represents sales B.L.M.&R. has made for which it has not yet collected the cash (Box 4 of Figure 5.1). The last current asset shown is *inventories*. The $65,466 would include three types of inventory: raw materials (i.e., materials, parts, and components "in the stockroom"); goods in process (i.e., those partially completed goods at various stages of manufacture "on the factory floor"); and finished goods (i.e., completed goods available for shipment to prospective customers). In our model in Figure 5.1, these three kinds of inventory would be represented by part of Box 2 (raw materials), the arrow between Boxes 2 and 3 (goods in process), and Box 3 (finished goods).

The second major category of assets is "property, plant, and equipment," commonly referred to as *fixed assets*. The accounts in this category are self-explanatory: They represent the long-lived productive resources that comprise part of Box 2 of Figure 5.1. Note that (like all assets) fixed assets are shown "at cost"— what was paid for them. Thus, for example, the $9,093 is what B.L.M.&R. paid for its land whenever that land was purchased. We have no way of telling from the balance sheet what that piece of land is "worth" today, and presumably should not care, since the firm is in the business of *using* its fixed assets, not selling them.

*Depreciation.* Another important aspect of fixed-asset accounting is that, with the exception of land, fixed assets are assumed to be "used up" gradually over the course of their lives. The accounting term that reflects this diminishing value of assets is "depreciation." For example, a machine costing $100,000 and expected to have a useful life of five years is said to be depreciated at the rate of $20,000 per year ($100,000 ÷ 5 years).[15] The difference between the machine's original cost and its accumu-

---

[14] If B.L.M.&R. owned stock in another company that it did not intend to sell in the foreseeable future—as opposed to a short-term investment to earn interest on excess cash—this would *not* be shown as a marketable security, but would be shown as an "investment" below the current asset accounts.

[15] This is an example of "straight-line" depreciation. There are other methods, which are taught in accounting courses.

lated depreciation charges is called its "net book value," or simply "book value."[16] These terms are illustrated in Table 5.2:

For B.L.M.&R. in 1977, the balance sheet shows buildings and equipment with an original cost of $194,785 ($45,701 + $149,084) and an accumulated depreciation (remember, land is assumed not to depreciate) of $88,112. Thus in a rough sense we see that B.L.M.&R.'s buildings and equipment are 45 percent ($88,112 ÷ $194,785) "used up" as of the end of 1977. But remember, we should *not* say that B.L.M.&R.'s buildings and equipment are *worth* $106,673 (their net book value = $194,785 — $88,112), because we really do not know how much cash those assets would bring if they were actually put up for sale.

In sum, Table 5.1 shows that B.L.M.&R. has year-end 1977 assets totaling $260,936. The correct interpretation of this figure is as follows: "As of December 31, 1977, B.L.M.&R. had spent— net of $88,112 accumulated depreciation on buildings and equipment—a total of $260,936 for things that will provide the company with future benefits. Of this total, $145,170 represents assets that are in the form of cash or that are expected to be converted into cash during 1978, and $115,766 represents the net investment in long-lived productive resources that will enable B.L.M.&R. to produce more goods for future sale." In other words, what the asset side of the balance sheet tells us is how B.L.M.&R.

**Table 5.2  Illustration of Depreciation Accounting**

| Year | Beginning-of-Year Book Value | Depreciation Charge | Accumulated Depreciation | End-of-Year Book Value |
|------|------------------------------|---------------------|--------------------------|------------------------|
| 1 | $100,000 | $20,000 | $ 20,000 | $80,000 |
| 2 | 80,000 | 20,000 | 40,000 | 60,000 |
| 3 | 60,000 | 20,000 | 60,000 | 40,000 |
| 4 | 40,000 | 20,000 | 80,000 | 20,000 |
| 5 | 20,000 | 20,000 | 100,000 | 0 |

[16] Remember, "value" here does not mean *market* value. If an asset originally costing $100,000 has a book value of $40,000, this means that the asset has given up 60% of the future benefits anticipated when it was acquired; it does *not* mean that the asset could be sold for $40,000, nor that a similar used asset could be purchased for $40,000. Balance sheets are based on *historical costs,* not current market values.

has *used* $260,936 to purchase or invest in things that will not provide their ultimate benefits until some time in the future.

### LIABILITIES AND OWNERS' EQUITY

Conceptually, the liabilities and owners' equity half of the balance sheet is equally simple. It shows where that $260,936 came from, that is, the *sources* of the money put to the *uses* shown on the asset half. From Table 5.1 we see that, as of the end of 1977, B.L.M.&R. owed vendors $38,784, owed short-term creditors (probably banks) $16,758, and owed taxes of $10,815 to the Internal Revenue Service.[17] These three accounts comprise B.L.M.&R.'s *current liabilities*. As you may have guessed already, current liabilities are those obligations that will become due—and hence will "eat up" cash—within the next 12 months.

> **QUESTION:** You now know what current assets and current liabilities are. "Working capital" is defined to be their difference: Working capital = current assets — current liabilities. What would working capital show? Who might be interested in the amount of a firm's working capital? Why?

The next section of the lower portion of B.L.M.&R.'s balance sheet, "long-term debt," shows amounts owed to outside parties that will become due in more than a year, that is, after December 31, 1978. The firm has an unpaid balance of $34,904 on long-term bank loans and also has borrowed money from many investors by issuing bonds.[18] Altogether, we see that the firm owes its short- and long-term creditors a total of $118,588 as of the end of 1977. (This corresponds to Box 7 in Figure 5.1).

The final section of the balance sheet shows how much the firm's owners have invested in the business—the owners' equity that we discussed earlier. B.L.M.&R.'s owners have paid into the firm a total of $25,163 for their shares of stock (Box 8 in Figure

---

[17] This does not mean B.L.M.&R. was a delinquent taxpayer. For example, each individual "owes" the IRS taxes as of January 1, even though they can be paid as late as April 15 without penalty.

[18] Our accounting statements are intentionally simplified. A firm's "real" statements would include notes disclosing the interest rates on loans and bonds and the dates on which the loans or bonds must be paid back by the firm.

5.1).[19] In addition, over the course of the firm's *entire* life, a cumulative total of $117,185 of its profits have been retained and invested in the firm's assets rather than being paid out to shareholders in the form of dividends.

> **QUESTION:  A few years ago a public-interest group called Campaign G.M. reported that General Motors had $8 billion of cash on deposit in some 380 banks around the world. At the time (1970) G.M.'s balance sheet showed about $323 million in the cash asset account; the $8 billion figure referred to was apparently G.M.'s retained earnings of $8.3 billion. Can you explain why the statement concerning $8 billion cash in banks was in error?**

In sum, as of the end of 1977 the liabilities and owners' equity half of B.L.M.&R.'s balance sheet totaled $260,936, the same as the asset total. The total amounts are equal because the liabilities and owners' equity half shows where the funds have come from whose uses are shown on the assets half. The lower portion shows that the $260,936 in assets (uses of funds) were financed by $66,357 of short-term credit, by $52,231 of long-term credit (debt), and by owners' investing $142,348 via stock purchases and retention of the firm's profits.

> **QUESTION:   The owners' equity amount on the balance sheet is sometimes referred to as the "net worth" of the firm. Reviewing what we have said earlier about liquidating a firm and about the dollar amounts shown on a balance sheet in its asset accounts, why is "net worth" a misleading term for owners' equity?**

## Accounting Statements: Flows

Although in discussing "snapshot" balance sheets we referred explicitly only to B.L.M.&R.'s 1977 figures, we earlier mentioned

---

[19] Remember, the firm receives money from stock sales only when it *issues* stock, and not when existing shares are traded between buyers and sellers on a stock exchange.

the usefulness of two balance sheets (as in Table 5.1)—one for the beginning of the year, the other for the end. It is much like the snapshots friends often send us at the holiday season—this year's family portrait is more interesting when we can compare it with the picture sent the past year to see how people (and sometimes dogs and cats) have changed over the past 12 months. Similarly, figures about a company are most useful when there is some basis of comparison, and seldom can a better basis be found than the same firm's figures for the previous year—hence the side-by-side "snapshots" for B.L.M.&R. in Table 5.1.

However, snapshots cannot tell us much if anything about *why* things have changed, but only that they *have* changed. For example, B.L.M.&R.'s cash account decreased by $10,484 (from $21,265 to $10,781) between the beginning and the end of 1977. We might assume that this lower year-end cash balance reflected better cash management by B.L.M.&R. (remember, "cash in the till" earns no return for the firm), but that is only an assumption on our part. Another possibility is that the company has recently paid back a loan and that the cash balance will soon increase again. The point is, based on the comparative 1976 and 1977 balance sheets alone, we have no way of knowing the *reason* for the change in the cash balance.

What we would like to have, then, is some explanation of why amounts in the balance sheet account have changed. We could ask for such an explanation about any one of the many balance sheet accounts. Such an explanation is called a "flow statement," and, as Figure 5.2 indicates, a flow statement explains "what went on in an account" between the two balance sheet "snapshots."

To go back to our simplified balance sheets presented in Table 5.1, we see that they contain eight asset accounts, five liabilities accounts, and two owners' equity accounts, plus several subtotals and totals. But we do not want to overwhelm ourselves with 15 or more flow statements! Thus we must ask ourselves: For which of these 15 accounts do we *most* wish a flow statement? If the reader finds that question difficult to answer, it may be because it was not specified who "we" are. Assume we are shareholders of the company. For which balance sheet account of the firm would we most like to have an explanation of changes between the beginning-of-the-year and year-end amounts?

Figure 5.2  Flow Statements and the Balance Sheet

If we answered "retained earnings" (or "owners' equity"), that certainly would be a reasonable request for shareholders to make, since, unless a firm issues new stock during the year, the change in the owners' investment in the firm is the increase in the retained-earnings account. That is, the change in owners' investment or equity in the firm is the amount of profits that the firm did *not* pay out as dividends to owners, and this is the amount by which retained earnings will go up. With specific reference to B.L.M.&R., we as owners would like to know more about 1977's $10,155 increase in retained earnings (from $107,030 to $117,185).

### THE INCOME STATEMENT

The flow statement we are seeking is variously called an "income statement," a "profit-and-loss statement," or a "P&L." We should remember that retained earnings in a year change by the amount of the firm's profit (or loss) for the year, less dividends (if any) paid to the owners. Also, official accounting terminology for what a layperson calls "profit" is the word "income." That is why the statement we are seeking is called an "income statement."

Table 5.3 shows B.L.M.&R.'s income statement for 1977, the year between our two balance sheet "snapshots" of financial position. As we did with the balance sheets, we shall explain the income statement in the table and how it relates to the firm's economics as depicted in Figure 5.1.

An income statement utilizes two basic terms that must be explained: "revenues" and "expenses."

*Revenue.* A *revenue* is simply an increase in retained earnings arising from the operations of the firm. By far the most

**Table 5.3  B.L.M.&R., Incorporated, Income Statement for the Year Ended December 31, 1977**

(Thousands of Dollars)

| | |
|---|---:|
| Revenues from sales | $315,492 |
| Expenses: | |
| Cost of goods sold | 229,322 |
| Gross margin | $ 86,170 |
| General, selling, and administrative expenses | 56,797 |
| Total expenses | $286,119 |
| Income before income taxes | $ 29,373 |
| Income tax expense | 14,099 |
| Net income | $ 15,274 |

*Reconciliation of Retained Earnings*

| | |
|---|---:|
| Balance at beginning of year | $107,030 |
| Add: 1977 net income | 15,274 |
| | $122,304 |
| Less: 1977 dividends paid | 5,119 |
| Balance at end of year | $117,185 |

common revenues for a firm come from selling its goods and/or services, that is, from its sales.[20] As an illustration of why a sale is a revenue, look back at Table 5.1 and consider the following. Assume B.L.M.&R. has just received an order for one of its products, and a check for $1,500 is enclosed with the order. Ignoring for the moment the process of filling this order (i.e., getting the goods from inventory and shipping them), what is the impact on B.L.M.&R.'s balance sheet from making this sale? Because we have the $1,500 check in hand, the cash asset account goes up by $1,500. But now our balance sheet is no longer balanced: We increased an asset without changing any other account amount. To bring the balance sheet back into balance, we must find either $1,500 worth of decreases in other asset accounts, or $1,500 of increases in liability or owners' equity accounts. As we examine the balance sheet accounts, we can see

[20] Other revenues might include income from marketable securities or interest-bearing savings accounts, or rentals from land or buildings owned by, but not being used by, the company.

that the only account that it makes sense to change by the $1,500 is the retained-earnings account. (As an exercise, try explaining why you would *not* change any of the other accounts.) Hence, by our definition of revenue—an increase in retained earnings arising from the operations of the firm—the sale of $1,500 was a revenue of $1,500.

*Expense.* An *expense* is the algebraic opposite of a revenue —it is a decrease in retained earnings arising from the operations of the firm. To illustrate this, let us now fill the $1500 order B.L.M.&R. has received. Assume the items ordered cost the firm $1,000 to manufacture. As these items are removed from finished-goods inventory, we must reduce the value of that inventory on B.L.M.&R.'s balance sheet by $1,000. But this again throws the balance sheet out of balance. Now we must find $1,000 in asset account increases or $1,000 in liability or owners' equity account decreases. Again, by a process of elimination, we can see that the change necessary to bring the balance sheet back into balance is to reduce retained earnings by $1,000. By our definition, that means the cost of the goods B.L.M.&R. sold is an expense.

Let us now consider both parts of this transaction: the sale and the filling of the order. The changes we have made on the balance sheet to reflect this transaction are as depicted in Table 5.4.

The balance sheet will still balance, since the effect of receiving and filling the order has been to increase both assets and owners' equity (retained earnings) by $500. But what is most important to note is that this sale has resulted in $500 more

**Table 5.4   Balance Sheet Changes Reflecting a Sale**

| Assets | | Liabilities and Owners' Equity | |
|---|---|---|---|
| Cash | + $1,500 | Retained earnings (sale) | + $1,500 |
| Inventories | − 1,000 | Retained earnings (cost | |
| Total current assets | + $ 500 | of goods sold) | − 1,000 |
| Total assets | + $ 500 | Total owners' equity | + $ 500 |
| | | Total liabilities and | |
| | | owners' equity | + $ 500 |

revenues than expenses; hence it added $500 *income* to retained earnings, and this "belongs" to the owners.

Let us consider another kind of expense. Assume that B.L.M.&R.'s accountant makes out a check for $5,000, representing the president's monthly pay. How does this affect the balance sheet? Clearly, cash will go down by $5,000. What will be the offsetting change that will keep our balance sheet in balance? Again, retained earnings must decrease; hence the president's salary for the month is an expense:

Cash   — $5,000          Retained earnings   — $5,000

Although these examples are hardly enough to permit generalizations, our examples do illustrate what indeed is a fact: Revenues involve an inflow of assets and a simultaneous increase in retained earnings; expenses involve an outflow of assets and a simultaneous decrease in retained earnings. Our examples verify this. On the other hand, suppose B.L.M.&R. makes a $10,000 payment to the bank on its loan. Is this an expense? It is an outflow of assets (cash goes down $10,000). But does the retained-earnings account go down? No, the liability account "bank loans" goes down by $10,000. Hence repaying the bank loan is not an expense. Similarly, suppose B.L.M.&R. spends $600 for two new electric typewriters. Are these expenses? The answer is no, because the retained-earnings account does not change. The transaction decreases cash by $600 but increases equipment by $600; in other words, this transaction is simply an exchange of assets—cash for equipment. Thus you see that expense is *not* the same thing as a cash outflow (called an "expenditure"). As our examples indicate, an expenditure ("writing out a check") may be for a new asset, may reduce a liability, or may reduce retained earnings. Only in this last case is the expenditure also an expense.

In sum, then, revenues and expenses are respectively increases and decreases in retained earnings arising from the firm's operations. These changes were of interest to us as owners (shareholders), since they represent changes in our investment in the firm. Because of our curiosity about these changes, we want a separate statement that explains them in some detail. That statement is the *income statement*.

UNDERSTANDING THE INCOME STATEMENT

Let us now examine B.L.M.&R.'s income statement in Table 5.3. The only revenue item for B.L.M.&R. in 1977 was its sales of $315,492. If, like most other businesses, B.L.M.&R. grants its customers credit—that is, does not require them to pay cash immediately upon receipt of the goods or services purchased— then the amount of 1977 sales revenue may differ from the amount of cash received from customers in 1977. Again, this is because of the time lag illustrated in Figure 5.1: The sale is recorded as the goods are shipped (the "sales" arrow coming out of Box 3), but the cash is not received until later (the "collections" arrow between Boxes 4 and 5).[21]

The first expense shown is "cost of goods sold." As goods are manufactured, their production costs are accumulated and reflected in the inventory account on the balance sheet. Although cash must be spent to pay the costs of producing these goods, the goods are an asset, because the firm will not receive any benefit from producing them until they are sold (in the future). As we saw previously, when items *are* sold, they are removed from inventory, the value of the inventory asset account is appropriately reduced, and an expense called the "cost of the goods sold" is recorded. Table 5.3 shows that the goods that B.L.M.&R. sold for $315,492 had cost them $229,322 to produce. Note how we *match* the production expenses with the sales: We initially treat cash outlays for production as an asset (inventory), since those outlays benefit the firm in the future (when the goods are sold). Only when the sale is made are the production costs removed from the inventory account and treated as an expense (cost of goods sold).

The reason for this matching of revenues and expenses is so that the profitability of the items the firm sells can be identified. This is called either "gross profit" or "gross margin"—$86,170 for B.L.M.&R. in 1977. What this means is that, ignoring the firm's overhead expenses (Box 6 of Figure 5.1), B.L.M.&R. was able to sell its products in 1977 for a total of $86,170 more than it cost

---

[21] If B.L.M.&R. were a grocery store, and hence not offering customers the privilege of paying for their purchases at a later date, then sales and cash inflows from sales *would* be the same; that is, in Figure 5.1, Box 4 and the collections arrow would be eliminated.

the firm to produce[22] those products. As the reader probably can see, this margin figure would also be meaningful if we expressed it as a percentage of sales. Thus, treating sales as 100 percent, we see that B.L.M.&R.'s gross margin was about 27 percent of sales ($86,170 ÷ $315,492). This means that on its average sale in 1977, the firm made 27 cents on every dollar of sales revenue; in other words, it had a "27 percent gross margin."

> **QUESTION:** Perhaps you have heard a merchant or other business person say "my margins are being squeezed." What does this mean, and what could cause it?

The next expenses shown in Table 5.3 are called "general, selling, and administrative expenses." As we described previously (Figure 5.1, Box 6), these are not costs *directly* related to manufacturing products, but they nevertheless are costs that are very necessary to the firm's operations. Often people abbreviate this account name as G,S&A. Even more frequently, these expenses are referred to as "overhead." Presumably, this latter colloquial term developed some time ago among people operating small businesses. They had to pay rent and utilities for "the roof over their heads," quite apart from how profitable their sales were "under that roof" (gross margin). But the term "overhead" is somewhat misleading today, since for most firms the large portion of G,S&A expenses is for *people*, not for occupancy costs such as rent and utilities.

After deducting G,S&A expenses from gross margin, the remainder is called "income before income taxes," or, just as frequently, "profit before taxes" (PBT). In an unincorporated firm, this amount is divided among (though not necessarily distributed to) the owners—called "partners"—and they pay taxes on it at their personal tax rates. A corporation pays taxes on this amount[23] at corporate tax rates, which are 20 percent on the first $25,000 of PBT, 22 percent on the next $25,000, and 48 percent on all

---

[22] If the firm were a retailer, such as a drugstore, "produce" would mean "purchase from suppliers."

[23] Actually, a firm's tax return may differ somewhat from its published income statement, and hence its reported income before taxes may differ from its taxable income as determined by IRS regulations. But the subject of tax-versus-book accounting is well beyond the scope of this introductory treatment of accounting.

income above $50,000. The remainder after income tax expense is called "net income," or, alternatively, "net profit" or "profit after taxes" (PAT).

Now our task of explaining in some detail why the balance in B.L.M.&R.'s retained-earnings account increased by $10,155 during 1977 is almost complete. The simple calculation shown at the bottom of Table 5.3, "Reconciliation of Retained Earnings," completes our task. It reminds us that over the year, the retained-earnings account increases by the amount of the firm's net profits *less* any of those profits paid out as dividends to owners. As can be seen, the net increase of $10,155 ($117,185 — $107,030) that we wished to explain is what was left after paying out $5,119 of the $15,274 profits as dividends. We as owners of B.L.M.&R. now have a much clearer understanding of why "our" balance sheet account—that is, retained earnings—changed during 1977.

### CASH FLOW STATEMENT

Having explained the income statement, which was the flow statement most interesting to us as owners of the firm, we must remember that there are other interested observers of the firm, including its creditors and managers. A second flow statement that is of interest to them, as well as to owners, is the *cash flow* statement. Such a statement for B.L.M.&R. would summarize the transactions during 1977 that accounted for the decrease in the firm's cash balance from $21,265 to $10,781. In other words, it would show where the firm obtained its cash and how it spent its cash. You, the reader, could prepare a cash flow statement for yourself as an individual "enterprise" by looking over your checkbook records for the past year, and categorizing where your cash deposits came from ("sources") and for what purposes you wrote out checks ("uses").

Cash flow statements are particularly important on a *prospective basis*—that is, for looking ahead to see whether a firm's sources of cash are adequate to fund its uses of cash. If there are points where the uses exceed the sources, then the managers of the firm that they must arrange in advance to borrow additional funds to cover those "shortfall" periods, paying back these loans in months when cash inflows exceed outflows. This is completely analogous to your sitting down and trying to predict what your checkbook balances *will* be at various points in the year, being especially watchful for times when your account will be overdrawn if, for instance, a "send-more-money" letter does not reach home in time.

Actually, in the financial statements corporations furnish the public in the firms' annual reports, instead of a cash flow statement they present a "funds flow statement." In this sense, the term "funds" usually means "cash or near-cash."[24] For example, if the firm sells on credit, a revenue dollar is counted, in effect, as a source of near-cash when the sale is made. This is done because at the time of the sale it becomes almost certain that the cash proceeds *will* flow in, even though the actual payment may not be received for, say, 30 days. Similarly, if a vendor delivers goods to the firm on, say, the tenth of the month but does not require payment until the end of the month, our funds flow concept records the near-cash outflow at the time of delivery rather than waiting until the time of actual cash payment. Again, this is done because it is certain that the vendor *will* have to be paid in cash in the near future. If this seems confusing, simply think of "funds" as being essentially the same as cash, and then you will not be seriously misled. If companies never sold on credit, and if their vendors never offered the companies credit, we would be able to avoid much of this confusion.

Table 5.5 is a funds flow or near-cash flow statement for B.L.M.&R. for 1977. You may recall that a balance sheet was formally called a "statement of financial position"; Table 5.5 shows what is formally called a "statement of changes in financial position." The balance sheet, it will be recalled, showed a "snapshot" at a point in time the investments the firm had made (assets) and from where the funds to finance those investments had come (liabilities and owners' equity). The funds flow statement shows from where *during the year* new funds came and how these *incremental* funds were used. Put another way, the funds flow statement is in essence an explanation of how, during 12

---

[24] The usual terminology for these near-cash funds is "working capital," defined as current assets minus current liabilities. But this is a difficult concept to deal with intuitively, since working capital is not tangible in the sense that cash is; hence we shall persist in referring to it as "near-cash." Over 90 percent of major U.S. companies use near-cash (working capital) rather than cash as the concept of funds in their funds flow statements (statements of changes in financial position).

**Table 5.5  B.L.M.&R., Incorporated, Statement of Changes in Financial Position for the Year Ended December 31, 1977**

(Thousands of Dollars)

| | |
|---|---:|
| *Sources of Funds* | |
| Net income | $15,274 |
| Depreciation (a charge to income that did not use funds) | 9,996 |
| Total funds from operations | $25,270 |
| New long-term bank loans | 7,613 |
| Total sources | $32,883 |
| *Uses of Funds* | |
| Payment of cash dividends | $ 5,119 |
| Expenditures for building addition | 5,787 |
| Expenditures for new equipment | 18,365 |
| Repayment of long-term bank loans | 5,600 |
| Total uses | $34,871 |
| Increase (decrease) in funds | ($ 1,988) |

months, the firm raised cash (or near-cash) and how that cash was spent (or very soon will need to be spent).

Table 5.5 shows that during 1977 B.L.M.&R. raised $32,883. The largest source of funds was the $15,274 profit (net income) the firm made by being able to sell its goods for revenues that exceeded the cost of those goods plus 1977's G,S&A expenses. But $15,274 understates how much *near-cash* the firm's operations generated. Remember that in discussing the balance sheet, we said that fixed assets are *not* recorded as expenses when they are acquired—which *is* when they must be paid for and hence when their purchase causes a cash outflow. Instead, these assets are depreciated over their useful lives, resulting in a depreciation expense that is subtracted from revenues in determining income but that is *not* a cash outflow. Thus in arriving at the $15,274 profit shown on B.L.M.&R.'s income statement, we have deducted depreciation that did not represent a near-cash outflow.

To convert profit into a near-cash figure, we have two choices. First, we can rework B.L.M.&R.'s income statement, omitting depreciation as a deduction, since it did not use up funds. If we did this, we would find that operations generated $25,270. Second, we can use a "backdoor" approach by taking our profit figure and adding back those deductions (expenses) that did *not* require an outflow of funds. Table 5.5 utilizes this latter approach: The $9,996 depreciation expense (which was "hidden" in other figures in Table 5.3) is added back to the $15,274 to give a "total funds from operations" of $25,270. This figure is often called "internally generated funds," reflecting the fact that no outsiders—namely, creditors or shareholders—have been involved in providing these funds.

B.L.M.&R. had one other source of the new funds it raised in 1977. The firm took out $7,613 in new long-term loans from banks. Thus, between its internally generated funds and long-term creditors, in all the firm raised $32,883 in 1977.

The next part of Table 5.5 shows how these funds were used by the firm. Cash dividends used $5,119. The firm also added a new wing to its plant at a cost of $5,787, and spent $18,365 for equipment to be used in the new wing and elsewhere in the plant. B.L.M.&R. also had some payments due on long-term bank loans —$5,600.[25] These uses total $34,871; yet the 1977 sources were $32,883, or $1,988 less than the uses. The bottom line of the statement reflects the fact that because uses of near-cash exceeded sources, the company reduced its near-cash (funds) by this $1,988. In other words, the company spent more funds than it raised, and hence its funds balance decreased, just as your checking-account balance would decrease in any period in which your uses (checks written) exceeded your sources (deposits).

In sum, our statement of changes in financial position (funds flow) has shown us how, during 1977, B.L.M.&R. raised new funds and how those funds—plus another $1,988 on hand at the start of 1977—were used. It helped us understand more fully the differences in the two "snapshots" from Table 5.1, the statement of financial position (balance sheet) as of December 31, 1976, and December 31, 1977. In other words, whereas the balance sheet in Table 5.1 shows us from where, as of the beginning and the end of 1977, *all* of the money invested in the firm

---

[25] Note how new long-term loan proceeds and repayments on old loans are shown separately in Table 5.5, respectively as a $7,613 source and a $5,600 use of funds. From the balance sheets in Table 5.1 we know that outstanding long-term loans went up by $2,013 ($34,904 − $32,891). Now we know that this was not caused by one new $2,013 loan but by two loan transactions ($7,613 − $5,600 = $2,013).

had come (liabilities and owners' equity) and how that money had come (liabilities and owners' equity) and how that money had been used (assets), the funds flow in Table 5.5 shows from where the cash or near-cash *added* during 1977 came and how it was used. On the other hand, the income statement in Table 5.3 tells us in detail how much the firm's *operations* during 1977 had increased the *owners' investment* in the firm. It showed that the owners' interest had increased in 1977 because of profit from operations of $15,274. However, $5,119 of this had been paid out to the owners as dividends, leaving a *net* increase in owners' investment of $10,155. This is reflected in the balance sheet in the retained-earnings account: At year-end that account showed a balance of $117,185, which was $10,155 more than the balance of $107,030 at the beginning of the year.

We shall see in later pages how all three of these financial statements—which we have initially approached primarily from the standpoint of an outside observer of the firm such as a shareholder or a creditor—are also vital to managers in the process of planning and controlling the firm's activities. We shall talk about planning the investments in segments of a business—that is, planning for their new assets (uses of funds), while the treasurer and others worry about whether these new assets will be financed by creditors (short- and long-term debt) or by internally generated funds. We shall also talk about projecting near-cash or actual cash flows, and about budgeting revenues, expenses, and/or profits for each part of the business. Thus not only should this brief introduction to accounting help you to become a better observer of a firm, but it should also help you some day to become a better manager or other member of the organization in which you will work.

# Appendix: Basic Cost Concepts

One summer when I was of high-school age, I worked in a music store. The owner and I got along well, and after a few weeks he told me that if there was anything in the store I wanted to buy, he would sell it to me "wholesale"—that is, at the price he had paid for it when he ordered it from the supplier. I was shocked when he told me that wholesale cost on musical instruments such as guitars, saxophones, and so on, was *one-half* the amount shown on the price tag (the so-called retail price). For the rest of the summer I wondered why the music store owner did not wear more expensive clothes, drive a bigger car, and live in a more exclusive part of town: He *must* have made a lot of money if he sold everything for twice what he had paid for it! It was not until I took a business course several years later that I understood why my boss, the owner, was not one of wealthier inhabitants of my town. The purpose of this Appendix is to help you understand in more depth the economics of a business organization before you proceed further in your studies of management.

Figure 5.1 introduced you to the concept of resource flows through a manufacturing firm. There we indicated how cash is used in making purchases for productive resources and for G,S&A expenses, and how cash is generated by selling the things produced (actually, by *collecting* from customers who have been sold these things). We hoped that the cash generated exceeded the cash required: When it did, we called this excess "cash profit." Let us try here to understand more specifically what circumstances will lead to such a profit.

For our purposes here, we will use a somewhat simpler example than that which was used in Figure 5.1. Let us suppose you are the owner of a pizzeria (or, if your tastes dictate otherwise, of a taco stand, hamburger joint, or rib house). We shall assume that your customers pay for their pizzas on the spot; hence the accounts-receivable portion of Figure 5.1 (Box 4) does not apply. Moreover, we shall assume that you do not make a pizza until someone has placed an order for it; thus you will have no finished-goods inventory (Box 3). You will, of course, have an inventory of supplies—flour, tomato puree, cheese, oregano, and so forth—which we will assume you pay for when the supplier delivers them to your pizzeria. (The size of this inventory does not change drastically over time, since deliveries are made frequently; that is, the cash "tied up" in supplies remains about constant.) Also, let us assume that you rent the storefront that your pizzeria occupies, and also the pizza ovens, a mixer, and the other equipment you need. Your pizzeria employs two people full time. (A summary of financial information appears in Table A.1.) The question we want to deal with is this: What must happen in any given month for your pizzeria to make a profit?

**Table A.1   Financial Information for Pizzeria**

| | |
|---|---|
| Selling price of an average pizza | $   2.50 |
| Cost of ingredients for an average pizza | 0.85 |
| | |
| Wage costs (including fringe benefits) | |
| Two full-time employees | $500.00 each per month |
| | |
| Rental payments | |
| Building | $400.00 per month |
| Equipment | 300.00 per month |
| | |
| Other expenses | |
| Utilities | $195.00 per month |
| Supplies (paper goods, soap, floor wax, etc.) | 90.00 per month |
| Bookkeeping services | 85.00 per month |

## Variable and Fixed Costs

To help us answer this question, it is useful first to think about how costs "behave," that is, how (if at all) they change with the level of activity or "volume" of the firm. In our example the best definition of this volume is "the number of pizzas sold." As you can see intuitively from Table A.1, some of our pizzeria's costs will go up if volume goes up. This is clearly the case with pizza ingredients, for if we make, say, twice as many pizzas, we shall use twice as much flour, cheese, and so forth.

Costs that vary in direct proportion to volume are said to be *variable costs*. Were we to draw a graph of the relationship between ingredients' cost and the number of pizzas sold, called a "cost-volume line," it would look like Figure A.1.

QUESTION:   You may recall from algebra that the equation of a straight line has the form $y = mx + b$, where $y$ is the vertical axis ("dependent variable"), $x$ is the horizontal axis ("independent variable"), $m$ is the "slope" of the line $(\Delta y / \Delta x)$, and $b$ is the "y-intercept" (the value of $y$ where the line crosses the y-axis). What is the equation of the cost-volume line for ingredients?

**Figure A.1**

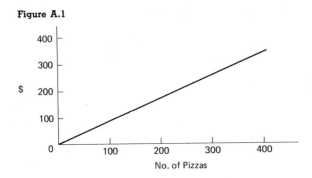

No. of Pizzas

Graphs of variable costs always are similar to Figure A.1. They pass through the origin (that is, where both variables $= 0$) and rise at a constant rate (slope).[1]

Although the cost of pizza ingredients is clearly variable, certain other costs obviously do not change as the number of pizzas sold varies. The clearest examples of this are the rental payments on the building and equipment. Whether we have a high sales volume in the pizzeria or a low one—or even if we shut down for two weeks over the Christmas holidays and sell *no* pizzas for a while—we shall pay $700 per month in rentals. Costs that remain at the same level while volume is changing are called *fixed costs*. A cost-volume graph for the pizzeria's rental costs looks like Figure A.2.

> **QUESTION:** What is the equation of this line? What can you say about the slope of a line representing fixed costs? Variable costs?

Incidentally, it should be pointed out that the word "fixed" in "fixed costs" does not necessarily mean that these costs cannot be changed by management action. For example, we presumably could raise or lower our building rental payments by moving our

---

[1] In practice, there may be some slight differences between a cost-volume graph and a perfectly straight line, often reflecting "economies of scale." For example, our pizzeria might pay less per pound of cheese at a high volume, when lots of cheese is being purchased, than at a low volume. In practice, however, we are not usually so interested in the *entire* line as we are in a segment of it, that segment representing the cost-volume relationship between the lowest and highest anticipated volume. Even if the entire cost-volume line is somewhat curved, a straight line is an adequate approximation of the relevant segment of the curve.

**Figure A.2**

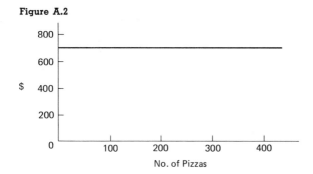

pizzeria to larger or smaller quarters. The point is that our rental costs are fixed in the sense that they do not "automatically" go up and down as the number of pizzas sold goes up and down. On the other hand, the cost of ingredients *does* necessarily change as the volume of pizzas sold varies, and hence is said to be a variable cost.

Now it should be pointed out that not all costs are "purely" variable or "purely" fixed as we have just defined. For example, costs for a firm's wages often vary in steps or "lumps," rather than changing smoothly as did the cost of ingredients.[2] This is true because we cannot add fractions of people; we usually hire people to work full time, and volume can increase for a while before we must hire still another person. Cost-volume lines for lumpy or "step-wise variable" costs look like Figure A.3. In practice, however, lumpy costs can be approximated adequately by a variable-cost line (Figure A.4).

Yet another kind of costs might be called "semivariable," or "semi-fixed." Their cost-volume lines look like Figure A.5. But as the dashed line suggests, semivariable costs can be thought of as being the sum of a fixed cost and a variable cost. This will be clearer to you if you have been answering the questions about equations of cost-volume lines. A variable cost has the equation $y = mx$, where $m$ is the slope. (This is because in the general form $y = mx + b$, $b = 0$ for a variable cost.) Similarly, a fixed cost has the equation $y = b$. (The slope, $m$, equals zero.) A semivariable cost has as its general equation, $y = mx + b$, where

[2] Strictly speaking, even our cost of ingredients was "lumpy": Each "lump" was $0.85, since we either made another whole pizza or we did not. These "lumps" are too tiny to show up on your graph.

**Figure A.3**

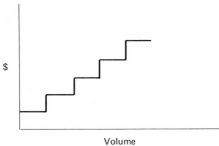

Volume

**Figure A.4**

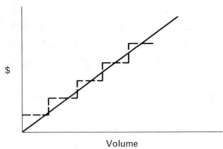

Volume

**Figure A.5**

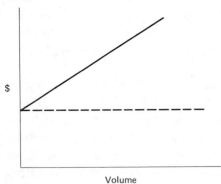

Volume

neither $m$ nor $b$ equals zero: It is the sum of a variable cost, $mx$, and a fixed cost, $b$. A likely example of a semivariable cost for our pizzeria would be supplies. We wish to keep our pizzeria clean, so that we shall wash and wax the floors a certain number of times per month, essentially regardless of how many pizzas we sell. Thus soap and wax expenses are fixed. However, the cost of supplies also includes paper goods, such as napkins and pizza boxes, the cost of which will vary with the number of pizzas sold. Thus the supplies category as a whole is a semivariable cost, having both fixed and variable components.

## Break-even Analysis

Now let us add up the monthly costs in Table A.1 to arrive at a total cost-volume relationship for our pizzeria. Assume we have analyzed each cost category and have determined the cost behavior shown in Table A.2. When graphed, our overall cost-volume line looks like Figure A.6.

The question we wished to answer, however, was not: What will our costs be at different volumes? Rather, it was: What must happen in any given month for the pizzeria to make a profit? We have half (the most difficult half!) of the answer to this latter question, since we do know our costs. What we must build into our analysis is the other half of the answer: information about our revenues. If we think about it, we realize that revenues "behave" exactly as variable costs: If we double the number of pizzas sold, we shall double our revenues. Thus we can graph our revenues just as we did our costs (Figure A.7).

Now, how do we determine the volume (number of pizzas) at which we have neither a profit nor a loss (or have zero profit, if you prefer)? This volume is called the *break-even volume*. We shall "break even" when our revenues just exactly equal our costs.

**Table A.2  Behavior of Pizzeria Costs**

| | |
|---|---|
| Ingredients costs: variable | $0.85 per pizza |
| Wages, rentals, utilities, and bookkeeping: fixed | $1980.00 per month |
| Supplies: semivariable | $45.00 fixed plus $0.03 per pizza[a] |
| Total | $2025.00 fixed plus $0.88 per pizza |

[a] Note how after analysis we have refined our earlier judgment that supplies were $90.00 per month.

**Figure A.6**

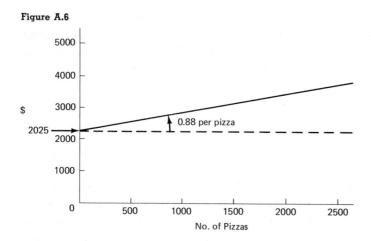

**Figure A.7**

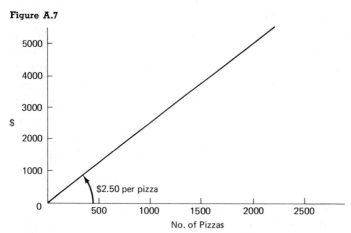

Graphically, if we superimpose our cost and revenue lines, the break-even volume is the number of pizzas sold at the point at which the two lines cross (Figure A.8). From our graph we can see that the break-even volume is at about 1250 pizzas per month. If we sell more than that, we shall make a profit; if we sell fewer, we shall have a loss.

> **QUESTION:** How could you use the graph to approximate the profit or loss at a given volume?

In practice, break-even volumes are usually determined arithmetically rather than by drawing a graph. We have used graphs because they are very helpful in understanding the

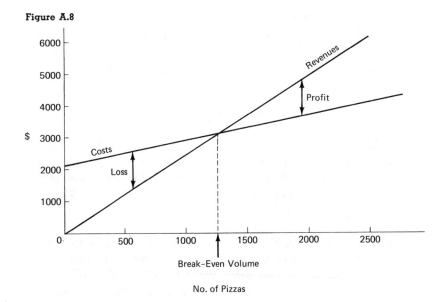

**Figure A.8**

No. of Pizzas

phenomena we are studying. We may recall from algebra that we find the point of intersection of two lines by using their equations:

Costs: $y = 0.88x + 2025$
Revenues: $y = 2.50x$

Costs and revenues will be equal when:

$$0.88x + 2025 = 2.50x$$

Solving this for $x$ (number of pizzas), we have:

$$1.62x = 2025$$
$$x = \frac{2025}{1.62} = 1250 \text{ pizzas}$$

It turns out that our approximation from the graph was a good one!

The solution of our break-even equation is interesting in itself:

$$x = \frac{2025}{1.62}$$

We know that $2025.00 was the amount of fixed costs. Also, we note that $1.62 = $2.50 − $0.88, or the revenue per pizza minus variable costs per pizza. The quantity "price minus variable costs" is known in business as the *unit contribution* from making a sale.

For each pizza we sell, $2.50 goes into our cash register; but, in effect, $0.88 is paid out for the pizza's ingredients and the related paper goods. Thus the *net* "contribution" from our pizza sale is $1.62. In words, then, our break-even volume equation is:

$$\text{Break-even volume} = \frac{\text{Fixed costs}}{\text{Contribution}}$$

**QUESTION:** Assume that it is a year later and that our costs have risen. Accordingly, we have raised our pizza price to $2.75. Our total costs are now $2205.00 fixed plus $0.95 per pizza. What is our new break-even volume? (**Answer:** 1225) Why is it lower than it was before?

**HARDER QUESTION:** Assume everything is as in the previous question, except that this month you have done newspaper advertising, which cost $450. What is the smallest number of **additional** pizza sales your advertising will have to generate for this to have been a wise expenditure? (**Answer:** 250)

Because some people are not particularly comfortable with mathematics, here is a more intuitive way of understanding break-even analysis. Figure A.9 shows a simple "plumbing" diagram for our pizzeria's finances. Pouring in to the top tank are revenues: Every time we sell a pizza, $2.50 flows in. However, everytime we sell a pizza, we must make one, which costs an added $0.88: This is shown as an outflow from the top tank. What remains, the $1.62 contribution, flows into a big pot labeled "fixed costs," with a capacity of $2025. This is why the quantity revenues minus variable costs is called "contribution": The $1.62 is a contribution that goes toward covering (paying) our $2025.00 fixed costs, which will have to be paid whether we sell 200 pizzas or 2000.

Now if (and only if) we sell enough pizzas that we *more* than fill the fixed-cost pot, we shall make a profit; that is, when the fixed-cost pot starts to overflow, the overflow is called "profit." Similarly, if we do *not* succeed in filling the fixed-cost pot, the "underfill" is called "loss." The break-even point is when the fixed-cost pot is full but has not yet overflowed. If the fixed-cost pot "holds" $2025.00, and if every time we make and sell a pizza we throw $1.62 into the fixed-cost pot, then we want to know how

**Figure A.9**

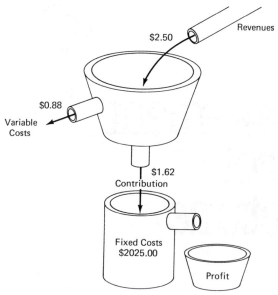

many times we must throw $1.62 into the fixed-cost pot just to fill it. Arithmetically, this question is answered by dividing the size of the pot ($2025.00 fixed costs) by the size of each contribution we throw in ($1.62):

$$\text{Break-even volume} = \frac{\text{Fixed costs}}{\text{Contribution}} = \frac{2025}{1.62} = 1250 \text{ pizzas}$$

## Summary

Costs that increase in proportion to a firm's volume are variable costs; those costs whose level is independent of volume are fixed costs. Each cost item can be analyzed to determine its fixed and variable components; these can then be added to arrive at the firm's total cost-volume relationship.

Combining the cost-volume equation with revenue data enables us to calculate the break-even volume, which is the volume above which the firm will make a profit. This volume can be found by dividing the fixed costs by the unit contribution (unit revenue minus unit variable costs).

# The Management Control Structure

Chapters 4 and 5 have given us an overview of the management control process. In them we have related accounting statements, which constitute an important form of communication in that process, to the basic economics of a firm. In this chapter we shall examine the structural aspects of management control before viewing the management control process in more detail in the following chapter.

Any system consists of both a *structure* and a *process*, that is, what the system "looks like" and how it operates. For example, in biology an organism, or one organ in it, is described in terms of its anatomy—what the structure is—and in terms of its physiology—how it operates.[1] To understand a system, one must understand both its structure and its process; but in learning about systems, including management control systems, it is useful first to study structure, and then to focus on process.

## Responsibility Centers

The structure of a company's management control system is tied closely to the company's *responsibility centers*. A responsibility center is an organizational unit with a person (manager) designated as being responsible for the unit's activities. Thus each of the various organizational units you studied in Section I of this book, which units together comprise the hierarchical organization structure, is a responsibility center. In Section I we were concerned with how to think about developing an organizational structure that would provide both an efficient division of work and the necessary coordination of these divided activities. For our purposes here, we take the company's organizational structure as a given and consider how to think about each responsibility center—be it a group, a section, a department, a division, or whatever—for purposes of planning and control.

In Chapter 4 we discussed activities, which had both inputs —resources the activities consumed—and outputs—work resulting from the activities. Responsibility centers correspond to this concept of activities, with one important additional provision: a responsibility center has a person responsible for the center's activity or activities; in other words, this person is held accountable in some way for the activity's inputs and outputs. Thus, for example, an unattended machine into which raw materials are fed, and out of which automatically (without human intervention) comes some item transformed from those materials, cannot be a responsibility center, even though it *is* an activity. However, suppose the machine were not so automatic: a human operator's judgment is involved in how much raw material to feed into the

---

[1] This useful distinction was made in Robert N. Anthony, *Planning and Control Systems: A Framework for Analysis* (Boston: Division of Research, Harvard Business School, 1965).

machine; and there are dials on the machine that the operator monitors that lead him to move controls or turn valves if the dials indicate an out-of-bounds situation with respect to the machine's functioning or its output. Then the machine-operator team *could* be thought of as a responsibility center. If, in fact, the operator is held accountable for the machine's output, and/or for the materials consumed in producing that output, then the machine-operator team definitely *is* a responsibility center.

For purposes of management control, an organization's responsibility centers are classified according to how these centers' inputs, assets, and outputs are measured by the organization's accounting system. As mentioned earlier, accounting measures resources in terms of money, since money is the most feasible and useful common denominator for items as varied as buildings, kilograms of material, and hours of labor. Accounting measures a responsibility center's inputs (resources consumed) in terms of dollars of *cost*.[2] Outputs are measured in terms of *revenues,* either "real" revenues, if the responsibility center is selling to outside customers, or "imputed" revenues—or *transfer prices*—if the center is transferring its goods or supplying its services to another responsibility center within the company. The set of assets— material inventories, machines, tools, and so on (but *not* the people)—a responsibility center must have to produce its outputs is known as its *investment base* and is also measured in the monetary common denominator. Thus the classification of responsibility centers revolves around accounting measurements of costs, revenues, and investment base.

### EXPENSE CENTERS

If the management control system monetarily measures a responsibility center's inputs, that is, its costs, but does not measure the monetary value of its outputs, then the responsibility center is an *expense center*.[3] This is not to say that expense centers do not *have* outputs; every responsibility center has in-

---

[2] In strict financial accounting parlance, "cost" and "expense" are not synonymous. For our purposes here, however, we shall use these two terms interchangeably.

[3] Some people refer to expense centers as "cost centers." Although technically there is a difference, we are not concerned with that difference in this introductory text.

puts, outputs, and assets employed. Rather, expense-center outputs are not measured in *monetary* terms, because it is either not feasible or not useful to do so.

> **EXAMPLE:** A corporation's legal department has outputs; however, it is not feasible to measure these outputs in monetary terms (and for most of these outputs, it is not feasible to measure them quantitatively at all). The assembly department in an electronics firm clearly has measurable outputs, and it is feasible to measure these outputs monetarily (e.g., retail sales value of the products assembled); however, it may be more useful to measure the department's outputs in terms of the number of units assembled, instead of the selling value of these units.

Actually, we can think of there being two different kinds of expense centers, depending on whether or not we can a priori state how many dollars' worth of inputs *should* be consumed in producing the center's outputs. For example, in many factory departments we can make quasi-scientific determinations of the "right" amount of resources to be used in producing a unit of output—for instance, we can determine that the labor, leather, and other resources used to make a given pair of shoes *should* cost $14.73. These determinations are often made by industrial engineers, and hence these "should-cost" amounts are called "engineered costs," or "standard costs." Responsibility centers in which most of the costs incurred are engineered costs are known as either *engineered-expense centers* or *standard-cost centers* (both have exactly the same meaning). Thus in an engineered-expense center we can examine the center's apparent *efficiency* by comparing the center's actual costs—inputs consumed in producing the center's outputs—with what the costs in the center *should* have been, given what its outputs are.[4]

In many other expense centers, it is not possible to say with any degree of confidence what amount of resources should be used to produce the center's outputs. Management, for example, cannot say how much the corporation *should* spend for activities such as research and development, advertising, donations, em-

---

[4] We say "apparent" efficiency, because an expense center that is truly efficient may appear to be inefficient if the engineered costs are incorrectly determined or are out of date.

ployee parties, legal work, and so on. These, therefore, are called "discretionary expenses." Accordingly, there is no way to determine scientifically what *should* be the expense budgets for personnel, legal, accounting, and research departments. Hence these responsibility centers, and others where most of the costs are discretionary, are known as *discretionary-expense centers.* Clearly, these centers do not lend themselves to quantitative measures of efficiency, as did engineered-expense centers. Neither do their outputs, which often defy *any* quantitative measurement, lend themselves to monetary measures.

### REVENUE CENTERS

If a responsibility center's outputs are measured monetarily (i.e., as revenues), but there is no attempt made to combine these revenues with a monetary measurement of the center's inputs (costs), then the center is known as a *revenue center.* Revenue centers are usually found in a company's sales organization. Not only may the entire sales organization, headed by the sales manager, be measured as a revenue center, but so may regional sales districts[5] and even individual salespersons' territories be treated as revenue centers. Thus whenever a selling organization unit is expected to meet a sales budget expressed in *monetary* terms, that unit is a revenue center.[6] Revenue centers are both conceptually and operationally easy to deal with, since determining the numbers of units of products a revenue center has sold and multiplying these numbers by the products' prices is a rather straightforward procedure.

### PROFIT CENTERS

We have said that revenues measure a responsibility center's outputs, and expenses (costs) measure its inputs (resources consumed). If expenses are subtracted from revenues to deter-

---

[5] This is true provided there is a district sales manager responsible for sales performance in the district; otherwise, the district is not a *responsibility* center.
[6] Revenue centers usually have budgets for selling expenses. From this standpoint the revenue center is *also* a discretionary-expense center. These budgets do *not* include the cost of the goods sold by the unit; if they did, the unit would be a profit center, not a revenue center.

mine the center's profitability, then (not surprisingly) the responsibility center is known as a *profit center*. It should be quickly pointed out, however, that the "profit" thus calculated is not quite the same as the profit we talked about in the preceding chapter. In financial accounting statements (those issued to shareholders and other outsiders), revenue from an item is not recognized until that item is shipped to a customer outside the company; at that point, the cost of the item is "matched" against the revenue, and the gross margin from the sale is calculated. For management control purposes, however, "revenue" measures a responsibility center's outputs, and "expense," its inputs, regardless of when the outputs are sold to an outside customer. For example, a factory is a profit center when it "sells" its output during a given period to the sales department, and subtracts from these revenues the costs incurred in producing this output, *whether or not* the output is sold by the sales department to outside customers during the same period.

*Transfer Prices.*   The fact that a responsibility center can "sell" its output to another responsibility center, even though this does not constitute revenue in the same sense as sales to outside customers, makes it clear that there are two kinds of prices or revenues involved in measuring profit centers. If the center is selling to outside customers, then the prices and revenues are the same as those used in the company's income statement. However, if the center is "selling" to another responsibility center within the company, then the revenue is based on a *transfer price* and is not reflected in the company's income statement. The fact that these latter revenues in some sense are "phony" should not lead one to believe that they are unimportant or irrelevant. Indeed, from the standpoint of the factory manager whose plant is treated as a profit center, this person's "sale" is made and "profit" earned when the goods produced in the plant are transferred to the selling department, not at some later time. Thus to this manager the "real" revenue to the company is irrelevant, and the transfer-price-based revenue figure is the relevant one for measuring the *plant's* performance.

Although a treatment of how transfer prices are determined is appropriately left to advanced accounting texts, we should mention in passing that setting transfer prices is by no means a trivial matter. The manager of the "selling" responsibility center (the plant manager in our previous example) tends to want the transfer price to be as high as defensible, since the higher the transfer price, the higher the profitability of the plant. For the same reason, the head of the "buying" responsibility center, for instance, a sales manager, will want a lower transfer price so that this person's operation—sales—appears to produce a larger portion of the company's profits. These opposite feelings regarding what is the "right" transfer price can lead to much emotion-laden negotiation between the selling and buying responsibility centers, and it is not unusual for these centers not to be able to agree on a transfer price, forcing arbitration or a decision by the common boss (or sometimes even the president of the firm) of the two centers' managers. These time-consuming hassles are avoided only when the transferred good or service has an essentially identical counterpart readily available outside the company at a market price.

Given that we have said that transfer-price revenues are "not real" as far as the company's published financial statements are concerned, and that setting these prices is time consuming and emotion laden, the reader may well wonder why companies bother with treating a responsibility center as a profit center. The answer is that many heads of companies believe that if a responsibility center is in effect a "mini-business" within the company as a whole, this center's manager will be better motivated and will make better decisions if the manager and the center are measured as though the center *were* an independent business. This treatment for management control purposes assumes, of course, that the company's top management has delegated most of the decision-making authority for the profit center to its manager, so that that person can manage the center, in effect, as a separate business entity. It is clearly unfair for the top management of a company to treat a responsibility center as a profit center while at the same time making all of the important decisions about the center's operations at corporate headquarters.

It should also be noted that although decisions that improve a profit center's profits for an accounting period may not be reflected in the corporation's published income statement in *that* period, these decisions will be reflected in the published statement of some *later* period.

**EXAMPLE: Plant X of ABC Corporation is treated as a profit center. Near the end of 1977 Plant X increased its efficiency, resulting in higher profit-center profits as this plant's products were transferred to the sales department. However, as of December 31, 1977, these goods were in the sales department's inventory, so that the savings did not appear as a reduction in the cost-of-goods-sold figure on the 1977 ABC Corporation income statement. But if these goods are sold in 1978, the 1978 income statement will reflect the lower costs, and hence higher profits.**

Finally, we should point out that many profit centers sell some—often, most—of their goods and services to outside customers. If only a minor portion of a responsibility center's products are sold in-house to other responsibility centers, then clearly it makes sense to treat the center as a profit center. However, many company presidents feel that they obtain better performance from responsibility-center managers if the center is treated as a profit center, even though *all* of the center's output is "sold" to other responsibility centers within the company.

**EXAMPLE: Some automobile companies treat their engine plants as profit centers, even though all of these engines are "sold" to other parts of the company (primarily to assembly plants), and none of the engines is sold directly to outside customers.**

INVESTMENT CENTERS

To understand the rationale for treating a responsibility center as an investment center, we must first understand the overall objective of a business organization. Although we tend to think of companies as profit seekers, the notion that a business's primary economic goal is earning profits per se is an oversimplified one.[7] A more realistic generalization is: The overall economic objective of a business is to *earn a satisfactory return on the funds invested in it.* In other words, businesses do not focus on the absolute dollar level of their profits, but rather focus on the

---

[7] Of course, businesses also have noneconomic goals, such as being viewed as a desirable employer and a good corporate citizen in the community.

level of profits in comparison with the amount of investment required to generate those profits:

$$\text{Return on Investment} = \frac{\text{Profits}}{\text{Investment}}$$

The preceding ROI formula is deceptively simple. For example, we mentioned earlier how "profit" for a profit center is not determined in the same way as profit (net income) on the company's published income statement. Similarly, it is not a simple matter to decide what constitutes the "investment" in a company, let alone the investment in a given responsibility center within the company. For our purposes in this introductory treatment, let us think of investment as being collectively all of the items shown on the right-hand (liabilities and owners' equity) side of the balance sheet: We previously pointed out that this side shows the *sources* of the funds entrusted to the company by its creditors and owners.

Also, we explained earlier that balance sheets balance because the company has invested (used) all of these funds (sources) in its assets, the left-hand side of the balance sheet. Thus we can actually think of investment as being *either* all liabilities and owners' equity *or* total assets, since the two are numerically equal. For purposes of management control, it is easier to think of investment in terms of assets, since for the most part we can physically identify the assets assigned to a given responsibility center, whereas it is not feasible (nor useful) to identify the specific sources of funds used to finance the assets in the responsibility center.

Given that a firm's objective is to earn an adequate ROI, we can see that it might be desirable to translate this overall objective to specific responsibility centers in the company, so that, in effect, managers below the level of the president are concerned about the company's ROI. A responsibility center in which *both* profits (outputs minus inputs) and investment (assets employed) are measured, *and* in which these two amounts are compared (as, for example, in the preceding ROI formula[8]), is known as an *investment center*. From this definition, it is clear that invest-

---

[8] There are ways other than the ROI formula to make this comparison, but we will not mention them here.

ment centers are really just "special" profit centers; that is, profit is always measured for investment centers. Thus all of the preceding comments about profit centers apply also to investment centers. However, the measurement of assets employed in an investment center poses a new set of problems not found in other profit centers. These complex problems involve questions such as: Should fixed assets be valued at cost, at net book value, or at market value? Should the corporation's cash balance be allocated to investment centers, even though cash is managed centrally at corporate headquarters? Because of the difficulties involved in resolving questions such as these, investment centers normally are used only for large and relatively autonomous divisions in a company, such as the appliance division of General Motors (Frigidaire) or the phonograph records and tape division of Radio Corporation of America.

## Choosing Types of Responsibility Centers

We said at the beginning of this chapter that a company usually designs its organizational hierarchy according to its resolution of the "balancing act" issues described in Section I, and then decides how to treat each organization unit (responsibility center) in that hierarchy for purposes of management control. Given these responsibility centers in the organization structure, then, how does one decide whether a specific responsibility center should be treated as an engineered-expense center, a discretionary-expense center, a revenue center, a profit center, or an investment center?

The answer to this question centers on the notion of *controllability*. For each responsibility center, we must ask: To what extent does the manager of this center have control over the center's inputs, outputs, and investment base (assets)? By "control" we do not mean absolute control, for seldom does a given manager have complete control over any aspect of a responsibility center's operations: Forces external to the company, higher levels of management, union work rules, and so on, will always "conspire" to remove some degree of controllability from the manager. Rather, by "control" we mean *significant influence*.

**EXAMPLE:** Foremen do not have complete control over labor costs in their departments, because they do not determine the workers' hourly wages. However, if the foremen do exercise significant influence over how the workers spend their time, then we can say that labor costs are controllable by the foremen, because they do significantly influence these costs.

To apply this concept, consider Organization A, a simple organization depicted in Figure 6.1. This organization chart could represent either a small company or an autonomous product division in a larger one. Our task is to determine the appropriate measurement—that is, the type of responsibility center—for each unit of Organization A.

Without any other specific knowledge about the organization except its organization chart, it seems likely that we shall wish to measure the overall organization and its head, the general manager (or the president, if this were a separate company), on the basis of profits. This is the case because the heads of all of the resource-consuming and revenue-generating operations and services report to this person. What is not so obvious, however, is whether we also should include investment in measuring the organization's performance. If this were an independent company, then the president would certainly exercise significant influence over the level of assets employed, and thus an investment-center approach would be appropriate. This approach would also make sense if Organization A were part of a larger organization, but with the general manager still having significant influence over investment in Organization A. However, if the general manager has little or no influence over the level of assets in the organization, then evaluation of *his* performance should be based on a profit-center approach rather than treating his organization as an investment center.

This does not mean, however, that the company of which Organization A is a part should not evaluate Organization A's return on investment. Organization A's ROI should be monitored regardless of the degree of influence A's general manager has on the level of investment in A, since the overall company cannot control its ROI without evaluating the ROI in each of its divisions. Thus we are drawing a distinction between the measurement of Organization A as an *economic entity* and the measurement of

Figure 6.1   Organization A

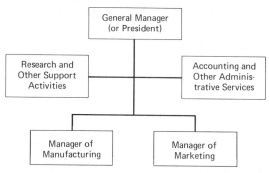

the performance of A's general manager as a *responsibility-center manager*. In the latter case, it is inequitable to consider ROI if the general manager does not control investment, even though the company may evaluate Organization A's economic viability in terms of its ROI. Some companies confuse evaluations of an entity and of the entity's manager, which can lead to frustration and hostility if the manager cannot control all of the factors included in the entity's measurement scheme.

Turning now to lower-level units in Figure 6.1, we see that all of the staff departments—research, accounting, and so on— report to the general manager. These units' performance, to the extent that it can be measured quantitatively, is "captured" in the general manager's measurement scheme, be it profits or ROI. In terms of the measurement of each of these support/administrative units, it seems that treating each as a discretionary expense center is appropriate. As we saw earlier, there is usually no way to measure monetarily (or, often, in any quantitative terms) the output of these units, so that they must be treated as expense centers. Moreover, since we cannot determine scientifically the "right" amount these units should spend to produce their outputs, these units must be *discretionary* expense centers (rather than engineered-expense centers).

As for Organization A's manufacturing operations, it is not immediately clear whether these should be regarded as an engineered expense center, a profit center, or perhaps even an investment center. If the manufacturing manager is told what must be produced and when it must be delivered, if he is "given" a set of assets with which to produce the output, and if all goods manufactured are transferred to the marketing department for sale, then manufacturing should *probably* be treated as an engineered-expense center. This would be the case because all the manager of manufacturing apparently can control are his production costs. We qualified that conclusion with "probably," because, despite the manager's lack of influence over revenues, some companies treat such units as profit centers (or, more correctly, as *quasi*-profit centers) in the belief that the manufacturing manager will be better motivated if measured on profits rather than only on costs. Other companies treat manufacturing operations as profit centers because product quality is controlled in the factory, and quality in turn has an impact on sales volume and hence revenues. Finally, in some companies the manufacturing managers exercise significant influence over the level of their operations' assets, and hence an investment-center approach may be appropriate.

A similar choice faces us with regard to the marketing manager. If marketing Organization A's products is only a passive, order-taking task, then it may be appropriate to treat the marketing department as a discretionary expense center. If, on the other hand, the sales force does have an impact on sales volume through personal selling, supported by the marketing department's advertising and other promotional activities, then treating the marketing department as a revenue center seems appropriate.[9] If it is felt that the marketing people in general, and their manager in particular, will be more highly motivated if they feel they are generating profits rather than "just" revenues, then we could charge marketing for goods it "buys" from the factory and treat marketing as a quasi-profit center. Finally, if marketing sets its own credit policies, collects its own receivables, and determines its own inventory levels, then some kind of investment-center approach would be appropriate.

From our consideration of Organization A and Figure 6.1, we see that one cannot easily determine appropriate management control measures without knowing more about resource controllability than is conveyed by the simplistic organization chart.

---

[9] Remember, revenue centers usually also have discretionary-expense budgets for their activities.

Nevertheless, our efforts have revealed the kinds of questions that must be raised and answered in deciding whether to treat a responsibility center as a discretionary-expense, engineered-expense, revenue, profit, or investment center. Again, these questions revolve around the issue of controllability.

## Goal Congruence

So far we have discussed choosing from among control-structure design alternatives in terms of the responsibility-center manager's degree of controllability of the center's inputs, outputs, and investment base. The concern was essentially one of fairness to the manager: It does not seem equitable to include noncontrollable factors when measuring the performance of a responsibility-center manager. Now we shall add another criterion for deciding on how to measure a responsibility center. This criterion is needed for two reasons. First, as mentioned earlier in the discussion of quasi-profit centers, some organizations consciously and successfully use performance measures that *do* include some noncontrollable factors. Second, because there are *degrees* of controllability between the extremes of completely controllable and entirely noncontrollable, it is not always apparent which alternative measure of a responsibility center will be the most appropriate. This additional criterion is known as *goal congruence*. We can say that goal congruence exists when managers, acting in their perceived self-interest, are motivated to take actions that are also in the best interests of the company.

There are two important aspects of this definition. First, it is assumed that a member of an organization is more concerned about satisfying personal needs than about the organization's meeting whatever goals its top management has enunciated. Second, implicit in the definition is the possibility that the person's self-interest and the organization's goals may conflict. It is assumed that if a manager can take an action that he perceives will protect or enhance his self-interest, even though the action is contrary to the organization's goals, the manager will take the action.

**EXAMPLE:** The Division X sales manager was told that she could expect a promotion to a better job in another division if she exceeded her 1977 sales budget. In early December 1977 she had not exceeded the budget; thus she persuaded a regular customer of one of Division X's products to take early delivery of a large order originally scheduled for delivery in January 1978. This enabled the manager to exceed her 1977 budget, but the customer insisted on a 5 percent discount for agreeing to accept the delivery earlier than it was needed. The sales manager was promoted. However, the next time the customer ordered more of the product, he insisted on the lower price, saying that if Division X would not sell to him at the December 1977 price, he would buy from another company. Thus the sales manager hurt <u>both</u> 1977 <u>and</u> 1978 Division X profits as a result of taking an action that helped her get promoted.

Perfect congruence between individual and organizational goals does not exist. However, the control system should not be designed in a way that *encourages* the manager to act contrary to the organization's best interests, as in the foregoing example. In designing control systems, managers should use this goal-congruence criterion by asking (and answering) the following two questions about any proposed management control practice:

1.  What action does it motivate people to take in their own perceived self-interest?
2.  Is this action in the best interests of the organization?

To illustrate the application of the goal-congruence criterion, consider again Organization A in Figure 6.1. Assume that reporting to the manufacturing manager are the several plants that produce Organization A's product line, glass bottles; and reporting to the marketing manager are the managers of the several sales districts that sell these bottles. (Neither the plants nor the sales districts are shown in Figure 6.1.) Bottles are not produced until the plant receives a customer's order, and competition in the industry centers on the quality of the bottles (how well they work in the customers' automated bottling machines) and meeting the customers' delivery requirements. All competitors charge the same prices for comparable bottles. One aspect of the business is that customers sometimes underestimate their needs and hence place special orders for rush deliveries. The sales districts are treated as revenue centers. The general manager is trying to decide whether to treat the plants as profit centers or as engineered-expense centers. This question is problematical, because both the sales force and the plants influence volume—the sales force through its selling efforts, and the plants through controlling product quality and production schedules (hence delivery schedules). Whatever decision is made—profit centers or expense centers—the general manager knows that the plant managers will try very earnestly to maximize their performance on this financial measure, in part because the general manager intends to base the plant managers' bonus system on the same measure.

In thinking about this decision, the general manager tries to imagine how *he* would behave if he were a plant manager under each of the proposed measures. He concludes that the following plant manager behavior is likely under each alternative:

*Engineered-Expense Center*

- Minimize production costs through efficient scheduling and wastage controls: This will help the plant meet or beat its expense budget.
- Other than minimizing in-plant spoilage, do not spend money for quality controls, since the benefits of good quality control accrue to the marketing department (increased revenues), not to the plants.
- Resist requests from the sales districts for filling special orders, since these will interrupt the efficient production schedule and thereby increase production costs.

*Profit Center*

- Minimize production costs through efficient scheduling and wastage controls: This helps the plant, since lower costs mean higher profits.
- Maintain product quality, since lost sales due to poor quality will make it harder to meet or beat the profit target.
- Fill requests for special orders if the customer's need seems genuine and if not filling the special order on time may cause the customer to shift business (revenues) to another bottle supplier.

The general manager concludes that, although the expense-center approach may lead to lower costs and higher profits in the short run, in the longer run profits will be hurt because the plants' cost consciousness will result in driving customers to buy from competitors. In other words, the expense-center approach would not lead to plant-manager decisions that are congruent with corporate goals, whereas the profit-center approach would.

An interesting and a useful way of looking at problems like this is to think of the proposed management control practice as defining rules of a "game." We assume that the "players" will play to win, and ask whether the tactics they are likely to adopt in order to win are desirable from the standpoint of the organization's best interests. In the illustration, the two proposed "games" were the "expense-center game" and the "profit-center game." When the "players," the plant managers, play these games to win, the tactics of the profit-center game are more desirable to Organization A than those of the expense-center game.

In effect, then, since the president of a company cannot personally make the hundreds of daily decisions involved in operating a company, one of the president's jobs is (with expert assistance) to design a "game," so that the "players" in trying to win this game will take the same actions that the president would if he had the time to make all these decisions himself. If a company chooses to treat a responsibility center as, say, a profit center, even though the center has no significant influence over the cost of the goods sold, it is because the president likes the way the center's manager plays this game, the "quasi-profit center game," better than the way the same manager would play, say, the "revenue-center game."

## Structural Changes

We should also point out that in practice it is not always assumed that the organization structure is "frozen" when deciding how to measure responsibility centers. After considering alternative measurement approaches for an organizational unit, a company may not be pleased with any of the alternatives, and thus may conclude that the structure needs to be changed.

EXAMPLE: College Automobiles had three departments: new cars, used cars, and service. Each department was treated as a profit center, and each of the three department managers received a substantial bonus based on his or her department's profits. The new- and used-car department managers reported to the president, whereas the service manager reported to the head of the new-car department. This resulted in conflicts between the service manager and the new- and used-car managers. The service manager ran her department like an independent garage, keeping the department so busy that recent purchasers of cars had to wait as long as four weeks for warranty work, which was less profitable to the service department than other work. These customers complained vociferously to the new- and used-car managers. The used-car manager also claimed that the service manager gave preference to new-car owners over those who had bought used cars. The president of the dealership concluded that the same thing was likely to happen if the service department was changed to an expense center, since the service manager would still report to the new-car manager and would still be motivated to keep the shop always full so that there would be no idle labor costs.

The president decided to change the organizational structure so that the service manager reported directly to the president: This structural change was intended to eliminate any favoritism toward one type of customer. The president also changed the service department to an expense center, so that the service manager would be indifferent between performing low-profit warranty work or other, higher-profit, work. Finally, the service manager's bonus scheme was changed, so that her bonus was based half on meeting the department's expense budget and half on <u>overall</u> dealership profits. The president felt that this would help control service department costs, but at the same time would motivate the service manager to run her department in a way that would enhance <u>repeat purchases</u> of cars by both the dealership's new- and used-car customers because of the customer goodwill created in the service department.

Thus this particular problem was addressed (and largely solved, incidentally) by a combination organizational structure change and a control system change.

## Implications

Most of you will not be in a position in the next few years to decide how all of an organization's responsibility centers should be measured. However, you will probably be working in a responsibility center, in either a managerial or a nonmanagerial role. As a manager, you will certainly be cognizant of whether you feel higher management is using an equitable measurement scheme for your unit. If you are displeased with this scheme, you will want to think of alternatives that may fit better with the aspects of the unit's activities that you feel are controllable by you as the responsibility center's manager. You may conclude that your company is confusing how they should evaluate you as a manager with how they should appraise your department's performance as an economic entity.

Even for those of you who are not managers, this chapter should nevertheless help you understand some of the things going on in your responsibility center. For example, you might not otherwise understand why your boss, a sales manager, is always worrying about profits, instead of simply revenues; or you might not otherwise understand pressures put on you and your co-workers to help keep inventories (part of investment) as low as practicable; or you might not otherwise understand why your boss is concerned about prices of your unit's product, even though all of that product is transferred to another unit and none is sold directly to outside customers.

Similarly, in the next chapter we shall examine the management control process, not solely to train you as a manager, but primarily to help you understand what is going on around you when you begin full-time organizational work.

# The Management Control Process

In Chapter 4 we described briefly the nature of management control and the four steps in the control cycle (see Figure 4.1). In this final chapter of the section, we shall consider in more detail the organizational activities involved in each of these four steps.

## Programming

We previously defined programming as the process of deciding what activities an organization will undertake. This involves planning the *outputs* that are to be produced, and either establishing or continuing the activities needed to produce these outputs. Examples of programs include: each of the various product lines made by a manufacturing firm or sold by a merchandising firm; research-and-development programs; employee-training programs; in a social welfare organization, programs for child health, drug abuse, legal aid for the elderly, and so on; and those for a television station or network—news, sports, situation-comedy, and other programs. Note that the focus of a program is on the goods or services (i.e., the outputs) that the organization will be providing to some "constituency," be it customers, the local community, employees, or some other activities within the organization (e.g., a company's successful product-development programs become production and sales programs for the company's plants and marketing department.)

Like organizational structures, programs often are hierarchical. For example, General Electric Company has as one of its major corporate programs a "consumer products program." A subprogram within it would be the "home appliances program." A subprogram of home appliances is the "refrigerator program." Within the refrigerator program are the "G.E." and "Hotpoint" brand-name subprograms. For Hotpoint there would be an "advertising program," which in turn would include (among others) a "print media program."[1] This program hierarchy does not necessarily correspond in a one-to-one fashion with units in an organizational hierarchy, however. For example, Plant X might produce both G.E. and Hotpoint refrigerators; Plant Y might produce both refrigerators and freezers; or there might be a Hotpoint advertising department that works with advertising agencies in developing advertising for all Hotpoint appliances (not only refrigerators). Thus a program at any level in a program hierarchy is not necessarily tied uniquely to a responsibility center which is responsible for that, and only that, program. Rather, a given responsibility center often performs tasks related to several of the organization's programs.

This noncorrespondence of programs and organizational

---

[1] General Electric Company does not necessarily employ the names used here for these programs, but the names we have used are certainly descriptive of programs existing within General Electric.

units suggests that we might think of an organization's activities in terms of a grid or matrix, as illustrated in Figure 7.1. Each $x$ in a square or "cell" of the matrix represents an activity; the activity is performed by the responsibility center shown for the row of the matrix in which the $x$ appears, and relates to the program shown for the column in which the $x$ appears.

**EXAMPLE: Suppose that in Figure 7.1 Department 6 is a General Motors automobile assembly plant, and Program A is the Chevrolet Nova product line. Then the x in the Department 6 row and Program A column represents that plant's assembly tasks related to Nova cars. The x for the Department 6-Program C combination represents the plant's assembly tasks on another G.M. car, say, the Pontiac Phoenix model line, and the x for Department 6-Program E represents assembly of still another G.M. model line.**

To reiterate, the programming process focuses primarily on what the organization's programs (columns of the matrix) will be, and only secondarily on which organizational units (matrix rows) will perform the tasks related to the program. The concern with organizational units in programming is one of whether or not the organization already has units that can perform the tasks necessary to carry out the programs.[2]

**QUESTION: How would you label the rows and columns of Figure 7.1 to describe the organizational units and programs of your college or university? Does your school have a matrix organization, as described in footnote 2?**

ADDING OR DROPPING A PROGRAM

Our discussion of programming thus far has not made clear when or how often program decisions are made. Figure 4.1 would imply that programming is a regular, repetitive process, much

[2] In some organizations a person called a *program manager* is held responsible for the results of a program, even though that manager does not directly control any of the various departments working on the program. In that instance, in effect the program is treated as a responsibility center, and the organization is said to have a "matrix" structure, as mentioned in Section I of this book.

Figure 7.1  Program-Responsibility Center Matrix

| | Program A | Program B | Program C | Program D | Program E | Program F |
|---|---|---|---|---|---|---|
| Department * 1 | x | | | x | x | |
| Department 2 | x | x | x | | | x |
| Department 3 | | x | | | x | |
| Department 4 | x | | x | | | x |
| Department 5 | | x | | x | | x |
| Department 6 | x | | x | | x | |
| Department 7 | x | | | x | | x |
| Department 8 | | | x | x | | |

*The term "department" is used here generically to mean any responsibility center, whether it is called a section, department, division, or whatever.

like annual budget preparation. In some instances this is true: For example, television networks make explicit programming decisions three times a year—for the fall "season," winter/spring season, and summer. Each season every existing television program is reviewed (especially its ratings), and a decision is made whether to drop it at the end of the season, continue it, or (especially for the summer season) show reruns of it. "Pilot" films of possible new programs are reviewed, and decisions are made as to which of these should be made new series in the upcoming season.

In most organizations, however, the programming process is not as regularized and explicit as in the example of network television programming. Typically, most of an organization's programs are "silently" approved for continuation; that is, at no specified point in time is the question of whether to continue them explicitly asked, and therefore these programs are continued without being carefully reviewed. However, if a program begins "to get into trouble"—for instance, if the sales of a certain product drop significantly—then it is subjected to a review. In this review, a judgment would be made as to whether certain program modifications could be made to correct the problem (e.g., adding a new feature to a product or promoting the product more aggressively) or whether the program should be dropped. Such reviews are not made according to some predetermined schedule, but rather when the program somehow catches management's attention as "being a problem program."

Similarly, in most organizations new program ideas are introduced whenever the idea strikes management as being worth serious consideration. In some instances the implementation of the idea—that is, the introduction of a new program—may have to wait until some specific time (e.g., the next model-year for a new model automobile), but the *decision* to add the program may be made at any time during the year.

In recent years, some organizations have begun thoroughly reviewing their programs according to some specific schedule, even though the programs are not perceived as being "in trouble." This is particularly true of companies' administrative-support programs—accounting services, personnel programs, legal services, and other programs with substantial amounts of *discretionary* costs. These prescheduled in-depth reviews are referred to as *zero-base reviews*,[3] because the company starts at "ground zero" by asking the question, "Why should we have this program at all?" If the answer to that question indicates that the program should exist, then questions are asked as to whether the program tasks are being performed effectively, whether the program's quality level is appropriate, whether too much or not enough money is being spent on the program, and so forth. In sum, a zero-base review puts an existing program to the same kind of tests to which a new-program proposal would be subjected.

## Budgeting

Once an organization has determined what its programs for the coming year will be, the budgeting process can begin. The process of *budgeting* involves expressing the organization's planned ac-

---

[3] They are also called "zero-base budgeting," but this is misleading because the reviews are really part of the programming process, not the budgeting process.

tivities for the coming year[4] in terms of dollars. Before describing this process, we should first understand why organizations prepare budgets. The reasons can be categorized as: coordination, communication, control, and evaluation.

1. *Coordination.* As we have seen, literally hundreds of tasks are performed in an organization, and many of these tasks have interrelationships. Perhaps the most obvious is the linkage between the number of units of a product a company's marketing department plans to sell and the number that the factories will have to produce. In turn, the company's plans for purchasing materials and supplies must be coordinated with the production output plans, as must be personnel-hiring plans. Production planning must also be coordinated with the purchase and installation of new equipment, and so forth. The annual budgeting cycle is a significant mechanism in coordinating many of an organization's interrelated tasks.

2. *Communication.* The managers of an organization's responsibility centers both want and need to know what is expected of their centers during the coming year. Sales offices need to know what volume the company is expecting them to sell; that is, each office needs a sales budget. Administrative offices, such as the controller's office or the personnel department, need to know how much they are permitted to spend; in other words, each needs an expense budget. Similar statements can be made for every responsibility center in the organization. The budgeting process results in an approved budget for each responsibility center; that budget communicates to the center's manager the performance expected of that center for the coming year.

3. *Control.* The budgeting process results in a set of baselines or targets for the coming year against which actual performance can be compared at various points during the year. Without these targets, it would be much more difficult to answer the question, "How have we done so far this year?" Accordingly, without these targets companies or organizational units within them would be much slower to recognize "out-of-bounds" or "out-of-control" situations. Since

---

[4] Although we say the "coming year," in most instances a responsibility center's annual budget totals are also subdivided into quarterly, monthly, or even weekly amounts.

past performance obviously cannot be changed, it is important to be able to identify problem situations as they are beginning to develop, rather than after a major problem has been allowed to develop. Budgets provide guidance as to the possible emergence of problem situations by identifying "off-target" performance. This is sometimes referred to as the *attention-getting* role that budgets play.

4. *Evaluation.* In most instances it is difficult to evaluate the performance of a manager or of that manager's responsibility center without knowledge of what was expected of that person or of the responsibility center.[5] Budget figures provide the starting point—the performance evaluation "baseline"—for judging performance. This is not to say that meeting or "beating" a budget automatically constitutes good performance, nor that missing a budget target necessarily signals poor performance. However, it is much more difficult to make any performance evaluation without knowledge of what performance was expected—that is, without knowing the targets or budget figures. Similarly, although judgment is important in rewarding or penalizing a manager for his performance, such rewards or penalties tend to be viewed as more fair when they are based in part on actual performance relative to a predetermined target, rather than being based solely on the evaluator's judgment.

### THE BUDGETING CYCLE

Now that we have some insights into *why* organizations budget, let us now look at *how* these budgets are prepared. The description that follows is based on the process used in an actual company, which we shall call the Empire Glass Company.[6] This company's glass products division was referred to (though not by name) in the "goal congruence" section of the preceding chapter. Figure 7.2 is a partial organization chart for Empire, showing the organizational units involved in the budgeting process. The following description focuses on the glass products

[5] As has been pointed out in the preceding chapter, evaluating the manager of a unit and evaluating the performance of that unit are not necessarily synonymous.
[6] This description is based on Harvard Business School's *Empire Glass Company* case study, case number ICH 9-109-043.

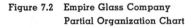

Figure 7.2   Empire Glass Company
            Partial Organization Chart

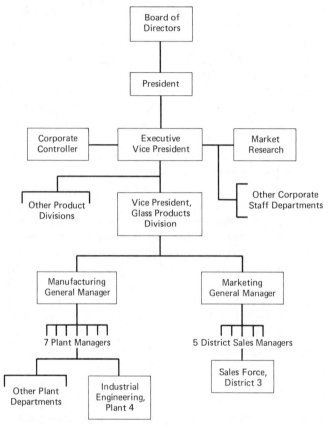

division of Empire; other divisions' budgeting procedures are similar.

Empire's budgeting cycle begins on May 15 of the year preceding the budget year, at which time each product division's vice president submits to headquarters preliminary estimates of the next three years' sales, profits, and plant and equipment expenditures for his division. After these vice presidents' opinions are received, the headquarters market research staff develops a formal statement of the marketing climate in detail for the coming budget year and in general terms for the subsequent two years. These general factors are used by market research as the basis for constructing a sales forecast for the company broken down by division. In preparing this forecast, consideration is given to general economic conditions, total industry market growth, product development trends, and Empire's share of each market. The completed forecasts are then sent to the appropriate divisions for review, criticism, and adjustments.

Empire's aim in preparing these sales forecasts at corporate headquarters is to assure uniformity among the divisions with respect to assumptions about business conditions and pricing. The forecasts also provide a rough indication to the divisions of what the home office, based on information available at that level, feels is a reasonable and an obtainable sales level.

The next step is for the division's general manager of marketing to ask each district sales manager what the expected sales of the district are for the coming year. In turn, the district manager asks all members of the sales force to submit a sales target for their territories. The district manager then discusses with the appropriate salesperson any target that appears to be overly optimistic or unduly pessimistic. When the district manager is satisfied with the sales budgets for each territory, the combined total for the district is submitted to the division's marketing manager. This person goes through a process similar to that undertaken by the district manager—any district budget that appears out of line is discussed with the district manager responsible for it. When the marketing manager is satisfied with the districts' budgets, they are sent to the division vice president for approval, and then sent on to headquarters, where corporate management reviews and approves them.

In Empire the policy is that at each level in the marketing organizational "chain" the sales budget is to be *negotiated* between the superior and subordinate; no number is to be accepted without question by a superior, nor can a superior change a subordinate's budget without the latter's concurrence. Thus these pairs of managers negotiate their budgets; salesperson–district manager; district manager–marketing manager; marketing manager–division vice president; and division vice president– corporate management. Note that with the exception of the sales force and corporate top management, each person in the chain at some point during the process will be a "budgetee" (subordinate), as well as a "budgeter" (superior).

**QUESTION:** In your opinion, why does Empire take the time
and trouble to allow these superior-subordinate negotiations of
sales figures, rather than simply using the numbers developed
by the headquarters market research department as the sales
budgets?

After the division's sales budget has been approved, it is
then determined how many bottles each of the seven plants will
need to produce in order that the five sales districts will have
available the bottles they have agreed to sell.[7] These plant "sales"
(output) budgets are further refined to the point that, in effect,
they represent tentative monthly production schedules for the
coming year. These figures are then sent to the respective plants.

Empire treats each of its seven plants as a profit center.
(Each sales district is a revenue center, and the division as a
whole is an investment center.) Accordingly, when a plant ships
bottles to an Empire customer, the revenue is credited both to
the plant and to the sales district that wrote the order. Thus the
monthly sales figures for the coming year that the plants receive
constitute *both a* production schedule *and* a plant sales budget.[8]

With their monthly sales figures in hand, the plants proceed
to develop budgets for the costs that will be incurred in making
the required bottles. These manufacturing costs are divided into
two groups: variable costs (those costs, such as raw materials,
which in total vary in proportion to volume),[9] and nonvariable
or "fixed" costs, whose amount does not automatically vary with
volume changes. In budgeting the variable costs, the plant industrial engineering department plays a major role. They determine
unit "standards," that is, how many pounds of raw materials
should be used to make a gross (12 dozen) of each type of bottle,

[7] Empire does not maintain inventories of bottles, but rather produces to
customer order, delivering the bottles two to three weeks after an order has
been placed. In a company that does maintain finished-goods inventories,
the plants' outputs and districts' sales would not be equal if the company
desired either to build up or reduce finished-goods inventories.
[8] Empire's plants ship bottles directly to customers, rather than to inter-
mediary warehouses in the sales districts; thus the sales revenue credited
to plants is based on the amount paid by the customer. If Empire instead
"sold" its output to sales district warehouses, the plant revenue would be
based on a "transfer price," as described in the preceding chapter: A plant
would record its revenue *before* the company had done so, since shipment
to the warehouse would precede shipment to an outside customer.
[9] See the Appendix to Chapter 5.

and how many labor hours should be used. These per-unit "physical" amounts (i.e., pounds and hours) are then multiplied by input cost rates (i.e., price per pound or wage rate per hour) to arrive at unit standards expressed in monetary terms. Then the variable cost per unit for each type of bottle is multiplied by the number of units to be produced to arrive at the total variable manufacturing costs for that type. Figure 7.3 shows how the unit standard variable cost per bottle would be developed, and how this amount would be used to arrive at the monthly variable manufacturing cost budgets for each type of bottle.

Each plant also budgets its fixed costs. These costs include depreciation on plant and equipment, plant maintenance, property taxes and insurance, nonvariable utilities costs, and—most importantly—the cost of the *people* who are supervisors and those in the plant's support departments: industrial engineering, personnel, accounting, purchasing, scheduling, tooling, and quality control.[10] As pointed out in the preceding chapter, many of the costs of these support departments are discretionary; that is, there is no "scientific" way to determine the "right" amounts for these budgets, unlike the case of variable manufacturing costs shown in Figure 7.3, which are "engineered" costs.

The end result of these plant budgeting activities is a budgeted plant income statement for the coming year. This statement would have this format (details omitted):

Plant No. 4 Operating Budget for 197_

| | |
|---|---|
| Sales | $XXX |
| Less: variable manufacturing costs | XXX |
| Contribution margin | $XXX |
| Less: fixed costs | XXX |
| Income (pretax) | $XXX |

[10] Many people who are not familiar with business operations mistakenly believe that fixed overhead is usually made up primarily of *non*people items such as depreciation, utilities, and insurance, when in fact these items tend to be less significant than the "people costs" in fixed overhead. Similarly, to many persons' surprise, overhead costs (both variable and fixed components) often exceed the sum of material and productive labor costs. These statements apply both to manufacturing firms and to many kinds of service businesses.

**Figure 7.3   Empire Glass Company**
**Developing Variable-Cost Budgets***

Ketchup Bottles
(one "unit" = one gross = 144 bottles)

Materials:

| Sand | Soda Ash | Limestone |
|---|---|---|
| 50 lbs. per unit | 10 lbs. per unit | 15 lbs. per unit |
| × $0.0046 per lb. | × $0.0068 per lb. | × $0.0072 per lb. |
| = $0.230 per unit | = $0.068 per unit | = $0.108 per unit |

$0.406 per unit

Labor:  0.1 hr. per unit × $4.85 per hr. = $0.485 per unit

Variable Overhead (e.g., power) :          $0.012 per unit       This unit standard
                                                                  cost was used for
        Total Unit Variable Costs:          $0.903 per unit       all months of the
                                                                  year, not only
        January Output Budget:              × 17,350 units        January.

Total budgeted variable manufacturing
costs of ketchup bottles in              = $15,667.05
January

*The numbers used here are illustrative only and are not intended to
 reflect accurately the real costs of making bottles.

Since Empire treats its plants as profit centers, it is the "bottom line" of this budget—pretax income—that is the baseline against which the plant's operations will be controlled in the coming year and evaluated at the end of the year. Of course, in the coming year the *plant's* managers will be concerned about every item *above* the bottom line, in order to help keep operations under control so as to meet the income target. However, the division vice president and corporate top management will tend to monitor the income figure, rather than the details leading to that figure: Empire has told its plant managers that they are responsible for profits, and hence top management's focus on the income figure is consistent with the delegation of day-to-day operating decisions to the plant managers and their subordinates.

The plant profit budgets are completed in September and are then reviewed successively by the manufacturing general manager, the division vice president, and corporate top management. As was true with the sales budgets, each of these reviews may result in the superior's questioning some aspect of the subordinate's (budgetee's) budget, in which case a revision is negotiated. By December, all of the budgets have been consolidated and approved up through the president. This final corporate-wide operating budget is then approved by the board of directors at its December meeting. Thus the budgeting cycle in Empire spans a period of about seven months.

TYPES OF BUDGETS

The budgeting process just described for Empire Glass actually focuses on only one portion of the company's "master budget" or "budget package." This package is made up of three separate but interrelated budgets:

1. *The Operating Budget:* This budget shows in monetary terms the planned operations for the coming year. (This was the budget we described for Empire Glass.) Essentially, this budget is a projected income statement for the coming year.
2. *The Capital Expenditures Budget:* This budget shows planned purchases of equipment and other noncurrent assets, such as buildings or land. The analytical techniques for deciding on which proposed capital expenditures should be approved for purchase are beyond the scope of this introductory text; they can be learned in a finance or management accounting course.
3. *The Cash Flow Budget:* This budget shows anticipated receipts of cash and expected expenditures of this cash. Cash receipts come from the collection of sales revenues, new borrowings, issuance of additional shares of stock, and the sale of fixed assets. Disbursements are required for paying expenses, repaying debts, purchasing new fixed assets (i.e., capital expenditures), and paying dividends to the company's owners (shareholders).

These three descriptions of budget components suggest the interrelationships among these budgets. For example, sales revenues are related to collections, but revenues and collections are not equal if the amount of accounts receivable is not constant.

(Refer back to Figure 5.1.) Similarly, the descriptions suggest another way in which the budget process is a coordinating mechanism. For example, the company treasurer must be certain that the cash generated by operations (collections minus payment of expenses), plus cash from other sources, is adequate to finance new plant and equipment purchases, debt repayment, and anticipated dividend payments.

Another way to classify budgets is in terms of whether the budget relates to a program, a responsibility center, or an item of expenditure:

1. *Program budgets* describe the operating plans, capital expenditures, and cash flows relating to a company's programs. In terms of Figure 7.1 a budget "subpackage" can be developed for each column of the matrix. These budgets have been prepared in business organizations for many years. Only in recent years has the concept of program budgeting or "PPBS" been seen in governmental agencies and other not-for-profit organizations.
2. *Responsibility-center budgets* reflect the planned activities for an organization's responsibility centers, the rows of the matrix in Figure 7.1. These budgets are key in the control and performance evaluation functions of management, since these budgets are identified with specific managers who have been given responsibility for their organizational units' performance.
3. *Item-of-expenditure budgets* show what kinds of resources will be purchased—for example, the services of productive workers, raw materials, supplies, equipment, the services of support personnel and managers, and so on. Unlike program and responsibility-center budgets, which simply slice the *entire* organizational budget "pie" in two different ways, item-of-expenditure budgets focus only on purchases or cash outflows (not on revenues or cash inflows). In terms of Figure 7.1, each $x$ in a square of the matrix represents, in part, a line-item budget for a given program's tasks in a given responsibility center.[11]

---

[11] Until recent years, the U.S. Congress focused solely on item-of-expenditure or "line-item" budgets when appropriating funds to the various federal government agencies. Many other not-for-profit organizations still focus solely on line-item budgets.

This second classification of budgets enables an organization to think of an expenditure in any of three ways, each of which answers a different question:

1. For what purpose (in terms of the organization's planned outputs) is the expenditure to be made? (Program budgets deal with this question.)
2. What organizational unit is to use the resource that is to be purchased? (Responsibility-center budgets enter the picture here.)
3. What kinds of resources are going to be purchased? (This is the domain of item-of-expenditure budgets.)

Similarly, many organizations construct their accounting records so that *actual* expenditures (and also revenues or cash inflows in the case of programs and responsibility centers) can be identified with a given program, responsibility center, and line item.

**EXAMPLE:** Huron Corporation's accounting structure uses account numbers that enable the aforementioned three-way identification. For example, account number 17-85-31 identifies supervisory costs (line-item code 31) in the product development group (department code 85) for the automobile parts product line (program code 17). This structure permits Huron to determine corporate-wide supervisory costs (by adding the amounts in all accounts whose last two digits are 31), total corporate product development efforts (all accounts with middle two digits 85), and total auto parts costs (all cost accounts with first two digits 17).

The kind of three-dimensional account summarizations described in the example are easily made in most organizations, because all but very small organizations now use computer systems to store and process their accounting data.

*Nonmonetary "Budgets."* The budgets we have discussed so far are plans expressed in financial or monetary terms. However, to the extent that a budget represents a target to be attained, budgets can also be expressed in nonmonetary terms. These nonmonetary budget figures are found generally at lower levels of the organization, rather than in the overall organizational budget package. For example, a factory department's output budget could be expressed as the number of units of product that are to be worked on; or the budget for an architectural design task could be expressed in hours of architects' time to be expended, rather than in dollars. These nonmonetary budgets can be very useful for control purposes, since it is more natural for a first-level supervisor to think in terms of units worked on, pounds of materials consumed, hours worked, and so forth, than to think of these factors in terms of dollars. However, when we begin to aggregate these lower-level nonmonetary budgets, for them to be most useful we must use the monetary common denominator for the aggregate budgets.

> **EXAMPLE:** Referring back to Figure 7.3, we see that it would be easier for the foreman of the department making a run of ketchup bottles to think in terms of 50 lbs. of sand and 6 minutes (0.1 hr.) per gross of ketchup bottles than to think of these factors respectively as $0.23 per gross and $0.485 per gross. Similarly, to that foreman, the January output target for ketchup bottles is more meaningfully thought of as 17,350 gross rather than as $15,667.05 of production costs. But to the factory manager, thinking of production volume in terms of dollars is more meaningful, since different types of bottles (e.g., ketchup bottles and gallon cider jugs) are not easily comparable in any terms except dollars.

A second type of nonmonetary "budget" relates to targets or objectives that *cannot* be expressed in monetary terms. For example, an objective for a supervisor might be to reduce the number of grievances filed by the unionized employees or to reduce the percent of defective work in the department. Similarly, an organization's personnel director may have the objective of increasing the proportions of minority and female employees, or the controller may be expected to revise the budgeting procedures and to prepare a manual describing the revised procedures. In some companies formal procedures exist for setting these nonmonetary targets, and for determining whether these nonfinancial objectives have been attained; such companies often refer to these procedures as a *management-by-objectives* system, or MBO.[12]

---

[12] MBO was described in greater detail in Section I.

## Operating/Accounting

As in Empire Glass, the budget preparation cycle typically is completed only shortly before the beginning of the year for which the budget package has been prepared. The start of that year begins the *operating/accounting* phase of the management control cycle: The year's activities commence, and the inputs to, and outputs of, those activities are measured in monetary terms in the organization's accounting system.

These monetary measurements of operations constitute a vast number of accounting transactions, which would be overwhelming to an individual observer. They are not so bewildering, however, when we think of them in terms of a few "streams" of operating information. These streams are:[13]

1. *Payroll:* These records show how much each employee has earned, how much he has been paid, and how much has been withheld from his pay for federal and state taxes, health insurance premiums, and so forth.
2. *Purchasing and Materials:* These records show orders placed for services or materials, receipts of these items, amounts owed to the suppliers (accounts payable), materials held in inventory, and issuance of materials to production departments.
3. *Production:* These records show what has been ordered by customers, manufacturing schedules for filling these orders (or for replenishing finished goods inventory if the orders will be filled from inventory), and production schedules for parts and subassemblies that will not be assembled into finished products until some later time.
4. *Plant and Equipment:* These records show the original cost and purchase date of each building and each significant piece of equipment, the cost of "pools" of less significant items such as tools or desks, the location of these items, in many cases the appraised value for insurance purposes, and the related depreciation information for all of these noncurrent assets.
5. *Sales:* These records show for each cash sale the amount

[13] This classification is based on pp. 291–292 of Anthony and Reece, *Management Accounting Principles*, 3rd ed. (Homewood, Ill.: Richard D. Irwin, Inc., 1975).

of the sale and, in most instances, what was sold.[14] For credit sales, the date when payment is due and the identification of the customer who owes for the sale are also recorded: These are *accounts-receivable* records.

6. *Finance:* These records include not only the organization's bank balances in checking and savings accounts, but also information on amounts owed to financial institutions (*debts*) and the payment dates for these debts. Also included are records showing who owns a corporation's shares of stock, how many shares each party owns, and dividend payments made or soon to be made to these shareholders.

7. *Cost:* In a manufacturing firm, these records show the costs incurred in making each item that the firm sells. In a service organization, these records show the costs incurred in rendering the organization's services (e.g., the cost incurred by an architectural firm in designing a certain building).

8. *Responsibility Centers:* These records show revenues, expenses, and assets classified by responsibility center, rather than by products or services, which are programs. (See Figure 7.1.)

These streams vary in relative importance, depending on the nature of the organization. For example, a retailing firm has relatively few employees for the amount of its sales, so the payroll stream is of lesser importance and the purchasing stream is of major importance. On the other hand, in a service organization such as a hospital or university the payroll stream is the dominant one. Similarly, although the organizations just mentioned do not have a production stream, this stream is of major importance for firms such as automobile manufacturers, producers of phonograph records, or food-processing companies.

Referring back to Figure 5.1, it is also clear that these streams are interrelated. For example, the sales and finance streams are related by the act of a customer's paying for his purchase; the purchasing stream is tied with the production stream as materials enter the production process; and the payroll

---

[14] Until the advent of electronic cash registers, many retailing firms such as grocery, department, and drugstores did not attempt to identify the specific items that had been sold to a given customer. Rather, the total sales of a given item for a given period were deduced from inventory records for that item.

stream is related to the cost stream, which is the basis of valuing finished-goods inventory, since employees work to produce the organization's products.

An important aspect of the operating/accounting phase is the reporting of the information that is being gathered. Clearly, no one person in an organization has the need to see all of the data being gathered in the aforementioned eight streams—and, of course, that person probably would not have the time or mental facility to read and comprehend all of this information, even if he did have the need. What people in organizations do need is information in a summarized form that relates to the activities for which they are responsible. Thus the focus of reporting in any organization is the activities in each of the organization's *responsibility centers,* and the recipients of these reports are the centers' *managers.* In other words, the basis of reporting information is the responsibility-center stream, and the criterion for determining a report's contents is the *usefulness* of the report to the manager who will receive it.[15]

We have seen previously that an organization's responsibility centers are hierarchical. Therefore, management reports reflect this hierarchical structure, with each report in the hierarchy encompassing a broader array of activities, but containing a greater degree of summarization, than the reports at the next lower level. This report structure is best understood by considering an example, such as that shown in Figure 7.4, which shows a report hierarchy for a hypothetical grocery store chain. The reports in Table 7.1 are called *control reports,* since they contain both actual and budgeted data, and an actual versus a budget comparison is a key step in the final step of the management control process (described in the next section of this chapter).

The top report in Table 7.1 is an income statement for North-Central Markets, Incorporated, for the month of April. With the exception of breaking down total sales by region, the "actual"

---

[15] Because today's computers can produce reports at a very low cost, in some organizations this criterion of usefulness seems to be overlooked, and managers are inundated with stacks of that familiar green-and-white-striped computer output paper. Too much information can be worse than too little, because the manager may feel overwhelmed and not look at *any* of the computer output piled up on his desk.

**Table 7.1  Management Report Hierarchy  North-Central Markets, Incorporated**

1. Top-Level Report—Corporation (dollar amounts are thousands)

| Month of April | Actual | Budget | Variance |
|---|---|---|---|
| Sales (no. of stores) | | | |
|   Michigan (18) | $ 5,619 | $ 5,700 | $ (81) |
|   Ohio (21) | 6,639 | 5,940 | 699 |
|   Indiana (11) | 3,321 | 3,480 | (159) |
|   Illinois (23) | 7,149 | 6,900 | 249 |
|   Wisconsin (9) | 2,808 | 2,730 | 78 |
|     Total (82) | $25,536 | $24,750 | $ 786 |
| Cost of sales | 20,811 | 20,040 | 771 |
| Gross margin | $ 4,725 | $ 4,710 | $ 15 |
| Operating and administrative expense | 4,341 | 4,300 | 41 |
| Income before taxes | $ 384 | $ 410 | $ (26) |
| Tax expense | 183 | 195 | (12) |
| Net income | $ 201 | $ 215 | $ (14) |

2. Second-Level Report—Wisconsin Region (dollar amounts are thousands)

| Month of April | Actual (%) | Budget (%) | Variance |
|---|---|---|---|
| Store No. 1: | | | |
|   Sales | $ 349 | $ 340 | $ 9 |
|   Gross margin (%) | $ 68 (19.5) | $ 65 (19.1) | $ 3 |
| Store No. 2: | | | |
|   Sales | $ 284 | $ 295 | $(11) |
|   Gross margin (%) | $ 51 (18.0) | $ 56 (19.0) | $ (5) |
| Store No. 3: | | | |
|   Sales | $ 306 | $ 300 | $ 6 |
|   Gross margin (%) | $ 57 (18.6) | $ 57 (19.0) | $ 0 |
| (Stores 4–9 are omitted from this illustration.) | | | |
| Region Totals: | | | |
|   Sales | $2,808 | $2,730 | $ 78 |
|   Gross margin | $ 521 | $ 520 | $ 1 |
|   Operating expenses* | 380 | 355 | 25 |
|   Regional income | $ 141 | $ 165 | $(24) |

* Expenses incurred by the nine stores in this region; does not include any allocation of corporate home office administrative expenses. The sum of the five regions' operating expenses plus the home office expenses equals the amount shown on the "operating and administrative expense" line of the top-level report.

3.  Third-Level Report—Store No. 2 of the Wisconsin Region

| Month of April | Actual (%) | | Budget (%) | | Variance |
|---|---|---|---|---|---|
| Sales:* | | | | | |
| Grocery | $140,502 | (49.4) | $143,000 | (48.5) | $ (2,498) |
| Meat | 56,264 | (19.8) | 59,000 | (20.0) | (2,736) |
| Produce | 14,377 | (5.1) | 15,000 | (5.1) | (623) |
| Dairy | 28,773 | (10.1) | 29,000 | (9.8) | (227) |
| Bakery | 5,952 | (2.1) | 6,000 | (2.0) | (48) |
| Deli | 8,409 | (3.0) | 9,000 | (3.1) | (591) |
| Nonfoods | 29,886 | (10.5) | 34,000 | (11.5) | (4,114) |
| Total | $284,163 | (100.0) | $295,000 | (100.0) | $(10,837) |
| Gross Margin:† | | | | | |
| Grocery | $ 20,513 | (14.6) | $ 20,400 | (14.3) | $ 113 |
| Meat | 9,115 | (16.2) | 12,000 | (20.3) | (2,885) |
| Produce | 3,422 | (23.8) | 4,500 | (30.0) | (1,078) |
| Dairy | 5,064 | (17.6) | 5,800 | (20.0) | (736) |
| Bakery | 2,869 | (48.2) | 2,400 | (40.0) | 469 |
| Deli | 2,304 | (27.4) | 3,000 | (33.3) | (696) |
| Nonfoods | 7,983 | (26.7) | 7,900 | (23.2) | 83 |
| Total | $ 51,270 | (18.0) | $ 56,000 | (19.0) | $ (4,630) |
| Operating Expenses:‡ | | | | | |
| Payroll | $ 20,685 | (7.3) | $ 22,000 | (7.5) | $ (1,315) |
| Other | 15,240 | (5.4) | 16,000 | (5.4) | (760) |
| Store Income | $ 15,345 | (5.4) | $ 18,000 | (6.1) | $ (2,655) |

* Percentage figures for sales show portion of total sales accounted for by each product category.

† Gross margin percentages are gross margin divided by sales for each category.

‡ Percentages show operating expenses as a percent of sales. Store income percentages are income as a percent of store sales.

column of this income statement is in the same format as the annual income statement issued to North-Central's shareholders. However, the "budget" and "variance" columns are for management's use, and are not generally shown to people who are not employees of North-Central—nor even to employees who are not in management positions. Note that this top-level report shows that net income is $14,000 under budget, even though sales exceed budget by $786,000. This situation—rising sales accompanied by falling profits—indicates that a problem exists, but the top-level report is of only limited usefulness in trying to trace the sources of the problem.

Section 2 of Table 7.1, the regional report, contains two key figures for each store, sales and gross margin, as well as a summarization of regional results. Note that the sales total in this second-level report, $2,808,000, is the same as that shown in the Wisconsin line of the top-level report; this illustrates the hierarchical nature of management reports. (Of course, top management would have available to it all five of the second-level [regional] reports, as well as the top-level summary report.) Note also that the Wisconsin region reflects the overall corporate pattern of over-budget sales but under-budget income.

The third section of Table 7.1 shows the lowest-level report prepared by North-Central, a partial income statement for a specific store. This statement is "partial" in the sense that it does not include any allocation of "home office" administrative expense, nor a tax expense figure. Thus the sum of the 82 stores' income figures would be more than the income before taxes amount on the top-level report. Omitting some corporate expenses from individual store statements is justifiable on the grounds that a store manager cannot influence home office or tax expenses.

The information in this third-level (store) report is useful to the store manager, who can see results by individual product category in the store. For example, the manager can see that although April's grocery product sales were $2498 below budget, the actual grocery product gross margin was $113 over budget, because the average gross margin on these grocery products was 14.6 percent instead of the budgeted 14.3 percent. Also note that the Store No. 2 totals for sales and gross margin on this third-level report appear (rounded to the nearest thousand) on the second-level (regional) report, again reflecting the hierarchical reporting structure.

> QUESTION: Suppose you were trying to sell some mechanical cash registers to North-Central. What are the implications of Figure 7.4 for the requirements these registers would have to fulfill? Now suppose instead that you were trying to sell North-Central a new electronic cash register system, which identifies each item sold from a bar code printed on the item's label. What would this electronic system (which includes the registers,

**bar-code reading devices, a small computer, and computer programs) need to be able to do so that North-Central could continue producing the report package described in Figure 7.4?**

It is important to realize that Figure 7.4 does not *constitute* the entire April performance report "package," but only illustrates portions of that package. The entire package would consist of 88 reports: the top-level summary, five regional reports, and 82 individual store reports. Moreover, the reports in Figure 7.4 have been simplified somewhat from the actual reports used by North-Central's managers. For example, in addition to the data shown in Section 3 of Figure 7.4, an actual North-Central individual store report for the month of April also shows: each variance as a percentage of the budget; the actual, budget, and variance figures for the year to date (i.e., January through April); and some additional indicators of performance, including a breakdown of payroll costs by store department (grocery, meat, etc.), the number of manhours worked, the number of customers, and the average sales per customer. The omission of these additional data does not affect the "message" of the illustration, however: Off-budget conditions noted on the top level report can be traced first to regions, and then to individual stores, in order better to understand—and thus be able to correct—the causes of the below-standard performance.

## Evaluation

In describing the hierarchy of management reports, we have already gained some insight into the final step of the four-phase control cycle—*evaluation*.[16] In this step management first evaluates overall organizational performance, and then the performance of each responsibility center in the organization. This latter

[16] Because of the close relationship between the design of management reports and their use, some authors classify the preparation of these reports as part of the evaluation step, rather than the operating/accounting step, of the control cycle. This difference is not important; what is important is the notion that these reports are the linkage between the vast quantity of "raw" accounting data and the use of management reports to help evaluate organizational performance.

evaluation is based in part on the *management-by-exception* principle: Any responsibility center whose performance has not varied significantly from its budget is usually deemed to have done a satisfactory job, and attention is focused on those responsibility centers who have substantially missed or exceeded their budget targets. These off-budget situations are explored to see: (1) whether they constitute problems that need to be corrected; (2) whether they represent the results of superior effort that should be especially rewarded; or (3) whether they simply reflect the fact that the budget was not appropriate for the conditions actually experienced. This third possibility relates to the "re-budgeting" arrow in Figure 4.1.

The major problem in the evaluation step is that, if it is done properly, it is not as simple a process as the preceding paragraph might suggest. The key to evaluating "properly" is to address *first* the third possibility mentioned previously: Is there a variance—a difference between actual and budgeted results—because the conditions assumed beforehand when the budget was prepared are quite different from the conditions actually experienced? Unfortunately, too often this question does not get asked, and performance is labeled "excellent" or "bad" depending on whether the variance is "favorable" (revenues above budget, or expenses below budget) or "unfavorable" (revenues under budget, or expenses over budget). Moreover, even if the budget is felt to be appropriate for the actual conditions experienced, a "favorable" variance in a responsibility center may not reflect praiseworthy performance by the center's manager, nor does an "unfavorable" variance necessarily signal poor managerial performance. These points are best understood by considering the following series of examples.

**EXAMPLE 1:** The upholstery department of the Gibbs Reclining Chair Company was budgeted to use $50,000 worth of vinyl upholstery material in July. In fact, $58,000 worth of vinyl material was used in July. Thus there was an "unfavorable" materials variance of $8,000.

Investigation of this variance revealed that the July budget had assumed that 1,000 chairs would be upholstered at a materials cost of $50 per chair. In fact, in July 1,200 chairs were upholstered; had this been known in advance, the July budget would have been $60,000. The upholstery department had been able to save this $2,000 ($60,000 "after-the-fact" budget minus $58,000 actual expense) for two reasons: (1) the department's purchasing agent had negotiated a better price from Gibbs' vinyl supplier; and (2) the workers had made special efforts to cut down on material wastage. Thus the department's performance in July was commendable, even though a management report had showed an "unfavorable" variance.

EXAMPLE 2: The Taste-Treat Ice Cream Company had budgeted August ice cream sales in a certain sales territory at $250,000, the same as sales had been the previous August. Actual August sales in this territory were $275,000. Thus there was a "favorable" revenue variance of $25,000, or 10 percent over budgeted sales.

In late September, Taste-Treat received a report from an association of ice cream companies which showed total August ice cream sales in various territories. In the territory mentioned previously, unusually hot weather had caused ice cream sales to be 23 percent higher than the previous year. Since total sales were up 23 percent, but Taste-Treat's were up only 10 percent, Taste-Treat had lost market share to its competitors, which certainly was not a "favorable" outcome. (If Taste-Treat had retained its market share, its August sales would have been $250,000 $\times$ 123% = $307,500; this is $32,500 more than the $275,000 sales it actually made.)

EXAMPLE 3: The Comfy Clothing Company had several divisions, each of which manufactured and marketed a different type of apparel. The marketing manager of the sweater division had a September marketing budget of $350,000. Even though September sweater sales were above the budgeted amount (a "favorable" variance), the actual marketing expenses were only $300,000 (a $50,000 "favorable" variance). In part because of this September performance, in late October the sweater division marketing manager was promoted to a more responsible job in the corporate-marketing department.

October and November sales of the sweater division were well below budget, more than offsetting the September over-budget sales level. This problem was attributed to the new sweater division marketing manager's "learning his new job." In fact, the sales drop occurred primarily because the former marketing manager had canceled a $70,000 advertising campaign in September. The new division marketing manager did not reveal this, since the former manager was now the new manager's "boss" at corporate headquarters.

EXAMPLE 4: The machining department of the Apex Valve Company had a November machine maintenance budget of $15,000. However, machine maintenance in November totaled $22,000, creating an "unfavorable" variance of $7,000.

Investigation revealed that the machining department manager had spent $8,000 in November for an unanticipated major machine overhaul. Had this not been done, the maintenance expenses would have been $14,000, or $1,000 under budget. However, had the department kept using the machine without its being overhauled, within a few months it would have been worn beyond repair, and a replacement machine costing about $50,000 would have been needed. After understanding the situation, top management praised the department manager for the foresight shown by the manager in overhauling the machine.

These four examples illustrate the fact that variance figures in control reports *raise* questions about performance rather than *answer* questions. In Example 1 the apparently unfavorable variance occurred because the volume of activity assumed in the budget (1,000 chairs) was below the volume actually experienced (1,200); in other words, when the budget was adjusted for actual conditions, in fact performance was favorable. Conversely, in Example 2, a "favorable" $25,000 increase in sales was in fact insufficient, since sales *should* have increased by $57,500 given the actual conditions prevailing in August (industry sales up 23 percent).

Examples 3 and 4 point out the importance of the *time dimension* in performance evaluation. In Example 3 a manager took an action (cutting out a $70,000 advertising campaign) that made him "look good" in September, just before his promotion; yet his decision hurt the company and made his successor "look bad" in succeeding months. Similarly, in Example 4, the manager made a decision which was in the best longer-run interests of the company, even though in the short run (November) this decision caused an unfavorable variance. Fortunately, the management in Apex Valve Company had the good sense to investigate the situation that had been "flagged" by the variance before making a judgment on performance.

We should not infer from the four examples, however, that "unfavorable" variances *usually* turn out upon investigation to reflect favorable situations, nor that "favorable" variances *usually* really hide unfavorable situations. In fact, in most instances the budget *does* constitute a reasonable standard for the actual conditions experienced, and a manager *does* consider the longer-run as well as the shorter-run implications of his decisions (since usually the *same* manager will be there to "live with" these longer-run implications). The point is that because the variance *usually* gives a meaningful signal about performance, top managers sometimes forget that this signal is *not always* a meaningful one, and these managers thus make some unfair performance judgments. These latter instances, though few in number, can cause a great deal of employee resentment and discontent.

We now have seen the first three steps of the evaluation process: (1) identifying "out-of-bounds" situations from control report variance figures; (2) investigating these situations; and (3) evaluating whether the situation is favorable or unfavorable. The fourth step is to take *appropriate action*. If investigation has revealed good managerial performance (as in Examples 1 and 4), the responsible manager is exhorted to "keep up the good work," and he may be given some special reward for his performance. (These rewards will be discussed shortly.) On the other hand, if the situation is an unfavorable one, the responsible manager is encouraged to understand the causes, so that the problem can be corrected as soon as possible. This is the "corrective-action" arrow in Figure 4.1. If the causes included such things as poor judgment, lack of effort, or improper decisions on the part of the responsible manager, the manager may be reprimanded or, in extreme cases, demoted or even fired.

The rewards for noteworthy managerial performance can take several forms. One reward is praise received from a superior. This may be informal, where the superior simply tells the subordinate that he has done an excellent job with respect to some time period or some specific task. Somewhat more formal is the praise given in a letter to the subordinate, with a copy for his personnel file and perhaps a copy to some very high-level manager, such as the president. Praise of a manager can also be more widely disseminated by putting an article describing the praise-worthy performance in a company's employee newspaper, or by giving a party for the manager and his colleagues.

Another form of reward involves monetary payments. A person may be given a "one-shot" bonus because of some note-worthy achievement, or he may be given an increase in salary. Higher-level managers' rewards may take the form of shares of the company's common stock, or "options" to buy shares of the company's stock over the next few years at *today's* market price.[17] Still another monetary reward is a "formula-based" bonus, where the manager receives a bonus, the amount of which is related to performance in his department and perhaps also to company performance.

> **EXAMPLE:** **The factory superintendent in the Fraser Company will receive a year-end bonus, the amount of which is to be determined as follows:**
>
> (1) **One percent of the amount by which actual production costs are below budgeted production costs, after adjusting the budget to reflect actual production volume; PLUS**
>
> (2) **One-half percent of the Fraser Company's after-tax profits.**
>
> **In 1977 this bonus amounted to $30,000 for the factory superintendent.**

Some companies are hesitant to use such formula-based bonuses, however, in part because of the problems we discussed earlier in deciding whether a "favorable" variance really reflects good mana-gerial performance. These companies argue that while a formula-based reward may appear to more *objective,* that does not mean that it is in fact more *equitable* than a bonus whose amount is determined more judgmentally.

Despite the prevalence of monetary rewards in businesses,

---

[17] If the stock price does not rise during the option period, this reward is monetarily worthless. However, if the stock does rise, the option holder can buy from the company the promised shares at the promised price (called "exercising the option"), and then sell them at a gain. Thus an option gives the benefit of potential gain from owning common stock without the manager's having to tie up his money for several years by actually owning the stock.

one should not assume that a monetary reward is always as satisfying to a person as a nonmonetary one. For example, a manager who is already receiving a substantial salary that enables his family to live comfortably may be more gratified by a newspaper photograph showing him receiving a "Certificate of Distinguished Performance" from the company president than he would be by receiving a $10,000 bonus. Nevertheless, the timing and amounts of bonuses or the amounts of salaries are carefully watched by a manager as signals of how top management views him in comparison with his peers. For example, a manager receiving a $10,000 bonus may be disgruntled if a colleague whom he believes is not superior to him receives a $12,000 bonus. Also, monetary rewards are focused upon by employees if there is very little other feedback to them about how their superiors view their performance.

> EXAMPLE: In a certain business school, on July 1 each year the dean informed each faculty member by letter of the member's salary increase for the coming school year. These were viewed as cost-of-living increases, since persons of the same age and rank received identical increases. However, the dean awarded a few of these increases the preceding January 1, so that these persons got an extra six months' raise. (If a person received his raise on January 1, he did not receive another raise on July 1 of the same year.) What was important to the faculty members was not whether they got the increased paycheck for an extra six months, but rather whether the dean had signaled to them by giving them their raise early that they were superior performers. This was felt to be an important signal, since normally the dean did not discuss with a faculty member how the member's performance was viewed by the school's administration.

Managerial rewards—especially those that are formula based—carry with them a risk to the organization. That risk is that the reward will be based on some short-run factor that in fact is not in the long-run best interests of the company. While a manager usually will be motivated to try to "look good" on whatever measurement scale his superiors are evaluating him, that motivation may be greatly intensified if short-run rewards (or the fear of short-run penalties) are tied to the measure.

**EXAMPLE:** In the early 1960s, 45 executives from several electrical equipment manufacturers were indicted for conspiring to fix prices. Trial testimony and interviews with some of these executives indicated that they had been rewarded by their companies for the annual profits their operations achieved as a result of the price-fixing. Similarly, some of them said they were told they would be fired if their operations did not attain each year's profit budget, and because of industry overcapacity the only apparent way to achieve these profits was for the companies to take turns winning "competitive" bids. The trial did <u>not</u> prove that top management of these companies had told these executives to <u>fix prices</u>; but top management had based substantial rewards for these executives on their meeting annual profit levels which the executives perceived to be attainable only if the conspiracy were maintained. When the conspiracy was revealed and the trial completed, substantial fines were levied on many of the executives and their companies, and some of the individuals involved served jail sentences.

To address this problem of a manager's focusing on short-run profit to the detriment of the company's other short-run goals and long-term interests, some companies have introduced "multiple-measures" systems of performance evaluation. For example, a division manager's performance might include evaluation of profit performance, change in market share, community activities, employee relations, and short-run versus long-run considerations. The problems with this approach are twofold. First, the easily measurable factors tend to "drive out" the ones that are difficult to measure: For example, market share is given more emphasis than employee relations, because the former is easier to quantify. Second, the performance measures that *investors* in the company feel are important tend to eclipse the factors these investors do not usually concern themselves with; for instance, the profit measure is emphasized far more than community activities. One major company that uses *eight* measures in its evaluation scheme has found that one of the eight, profitability, gets almost all of the attention at *all* levels of management. This company was one of those involved in the aforementioned price-fixing conspiracy.

In sum, performance evaluation is fraught with difficulties, most of them surrounding the inherent conflicts between an evaluation's objectivity and equitability. The desire for objectivity tends to result in evaluations based on measurable factors, usually accounting-related numbers; but these evaluations can be attacked as being inflexible, arbitrary, impersonal, and hence unfair. The desire for equitability tends to introduce more judgment into the evaluation; but this judgment can lead to charges of "playing favorites" or "ignoring the facts" (i.e., the quantitative facts). Thus, like the issues described in Section I of this book, effective performance evaluation requires a "balancing act," this time between objectivity and equitability in the evaluation.

# III

# THE MANAGER'S JOB

G RADUALLY, we have focused on the management process in this book. We began in Chapter 1 with a look at the broad perspective of business—the issues surrounding the firm as a social institution in society. Then in Sections I and II, we began to look inside at the functioning of the business firm—how it structures itself to do work and how it designs its planning-and-control systems to ensure that this work in fact gets done. Throughout, references have been made to the manager. But actually the manager has remained a kind of black box, some important but mysterious element that somehow holds the business together. It is the purpose of Section III to focus on this famous element in every business, the manager. Here we open up the black box to find out what is inside, to learn how the manager works.

Who is the manager anyway? We can define the manager as that person formally in charge of the whole firm or one of its units—its divisions, departments, branches, shops, or whatever. In other words, the manager is distinguished by the formal authority he is granted. Managers do not typically make the firm's products or provide its services directly to its customers, but they do take responsibility for the actions associated with those processes.

Thus managers, by definition, have formal authority, purely and simply. Who, then, does this definition describe? If we stop to think about it for a moment, the answer is: a wide group indeed. In business firms, it includes presidents in charge of the whole organization, vice presidents in charge of divisions, sales managers in charge of branches, foremen in charge of shops, and many others. In fact, although this is not our focus in this book, it is evident that our definition includes prime ministers, archbishops, hospital chiefs, university deans, and even hockey coaches. (It is no coincidence that the operating chief of a baseball team is called a "manager.") All are in charge of an organization or one of its units. (To simplify matters, we shall use the term "organization" throughout this section to refer to both whole businesses and the units within them.)

## Why Do Businesses Need Managers?

Why must a group of people who have come together to do a
job have a manager? It turns out that sometimes in small,
face-to-face groups, work can get done without a manager. When
we go on a canoe trip with friends, we do not designate someone
as being formally in charge of our "organization." But although
this may be the case with the smallest and least formal of
groups, it hardly applies to a giant corporation (or even, for
that matter, to a small business firm with bankers, clients, and
owners to respond to). Formal organizations like businesses, and
even some informal ones (we shall repeatedly see examples
of the "managing" of street gangs), apparently need managers.
Why? We can delineate at least four purposes of the manager:

1. *The prime purpose of the manager is to ensure that his
   organization serve its basic purpose, namely, the
   efficient production of its goods and services.* The manager,
   as the definition implies, is in charge. To him falls the
   praise or blame when performance results come in; to him
   falls the responsibility for the organization. Ultimately,
   there is no doubt about who is in charge, who is responsible.
   The first purpose gives rise to the next two.
2. *The manager must design and maintain the stability of
   his organization's operations.* Now we can begin to see the
   linking together of the different themes in this book.
   To the manager ultimately falls the responsibility for the
   design of the work system (the structure described in
   Section I) and for the operations of the maintenance system
   (the planning-and-control system described in Section II).
   Through these systems, managers ensure that their
   organizations maintain stable and efficient operations.
3. *The manager must, through the process of strategy
   formulation, ensure that his organization adapt in a
   controlled way to its changing environment.* In Section I, we
   saw the critical need for balance between stability and
   change. Here we see that managers take prime responsibility
   for maintaining this balance. It is they who see to it that
   the organization adapt itself in a careful way to its
   environment. It is they who walk the tightrope between
   stability and change. *Strategy formulation* is the process by
   which important (or precedent-setting) decisions are made

and interrelated. Thus it is through the formulation of strategies that the manager adapts his organization to its environment.

4. *The manager must ensure that the organization serve those people who control it.* Now we can see the link to Chapter 1. It is the managers who must balance the needs of those who, like the owners, want something from the organization. The manager must ensure that each remains sufficiently happy so that no one will disrupt the operations of the organization.

These then are the prime reasons why organizations need managers—to focus ultimate responsibility for performance on a single individual, that responsibility involving the need to design and stabilize the operations and adapt them to a changing environment, and to ensure that the organization serves those who control it.

> **EXERCISE:** Select an organization that you know—the less ordinary the better (say, the corner "greasy spoon" restaurant, a ski hill, the student newspaper, etc.). Make a list of all the managers who work there. Then, one at a time, imagine how this organization would function without them. What would happen? Would the organization be viable?

So far we have talked in terms of generalities. What interests us here is *how* rather than *what,* not the purposes of the black box we have called the manager, but rather how it functions. Let us now open up the box.

## The Manager's Roles

We can describe the manager's work in terms of *roles,* organized sets of behavior belonging to an identifiable office or position. The word has come to the field of management from the theater, where it has essentially the same meaning. When on the stage, actors adopt organized patterns of behavior identifiable with the characters they are playing. Similarly, when an individual becomes a manager, he adopts certain patterns of behavior

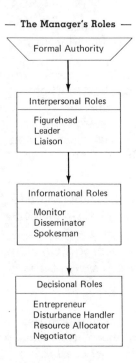

simply because he is in the position of manager. It is these patterns of behavior around which this section of this book is built.

Our description will proceed in three parts. We shall argue that directly as a result of formal authority, the manager is led into interpersonal relationships. These will be described in terms of three *interpersonal* roles. These interpersonal relationships in turn provide the manager with access to information. How he collects and what he does directly with the information will be discussed in terms of three *informational* roles. And finally authority, interpersonal relationships, and information allow the manager (and require him as well) to play four key *decisional* roles in the organization's decision-making system. The figure above shows these relationships among the ten roles we shall be describing.

Before proceeding, however, some characteristics of this role set should be noted. First, we shall be discussing tangible behaviors, those that can be observed. Each role relates to some activities that we can watch managers performing. In fact, this set of ten roles was derived from a study of the work of five

American chief executives (of three large business firms, a large hospital, and a middle-sized school system). Virtually every activity these people performed during five weeks (368 verbal contacts, including meetings and telephone calls, and 890 pieces of incoming and outgoing mail) can be explained in terms of one or more of the ten roles.

Second, these ten roles seem to explain the behavior of all managers, not only chief executives (and not only managers of business firms). These roles relate to managing in general; as such, they help to describe the work of all managers. (That is not to say, of course, that special managers do not perform additional, special roles.) As we shall see, this contention is supported by studies of managers as diverse as presidents of the United States and leaders of street gangs.

Third, while the roles will be discussed one by one, in the manager's job they cannot be separated. They are tightly linked together in what the psychologist would call a "gestalt," an integrated whole. The manager's job is not simply the algebraic sum of these ten roles, but much more—the whole that results when these roles are linked together in the managerial job.

# 8

# The Manager's Interpersonal Roles

The first set of roles derives directly from the manager's formal authority. In essence, formal authority provides the manager with status, and status enables him to play the three interpersonal roles. The interpersonal roles are distinguished by the fact that they have as their prime purpose the development of relationships between the manager and other people; it is the interpersonal contact that is of key importance, not the passing of information or the making of decisions per se.

## The Manager as Figurehead

The first role of the manager, and perhaps the simplest, is that of *figurehead*. In essence, because of his formal authority, the manager is the symbol of his organization, obliged to perform a number of related duties. All involve interpersonal relationships. The company president gives out a gold watch to a retiring employee; the foreman attends the wedding of his machine operator; the Pope presides at midnight mass.

Being a figurehead appears to be the simplest of managerial roles, involving duties that almost anyone can do. Can we say, therefore, that the figurehead role is an unimportant one, perhaps not worthy of the busy manager, with lots of demands on his time? Why should he not delegate these tasks to someone else? The answer is evident in our examples. Imagine a papal representative appearing in St. Peter's to announce that the Pope is far too busy for midnight mass this year, that he has sent an archbishop in his place who, after all, has a stronger voice. Imagine the retiring employee being presented his gold watch by the secretary to the president. Imagine the sales manager refusing to see the firm's biggest and most important customer, telling him to deal instead, like everyone else, with the salesmen. Davis, who studied the work of field sales managers, found:

> Some customers . . . refuse to have any dealings with anyone but the field manager. A small New York State brewer insisted upon purchasing his entire supply of cans from the manufacturer's branch manager even though the local salesman was qualified and authorized to render identical service. The brewer argued that his account deserved the attention of management. Whether the attitude is warranted or not, the fact remains that in this instance the title and prestige of the local manager were needed to maintain customer relations.[1]

Thus there is no escape for the manager. If he is to hold office, he must play the role of figurehead.

Of course, not all managers carry the same burdens. It stands to reason that in small organizations, less in the public

[1] R. T. Davis, *Performance and Development of Field Sales Managers* (Boston: Harvard Business School, Division of Research, 1957), p. 43–44.

eye—say, a manufacturer of pens as opposed to IBM—the figure-head load for managers would be lighter. And within organizations, the senior managers, having to act as official representatives of the organization, would have more of these duties to perform than those lower down. The president must do more of the ceremonial work than the foreman. In some cases, at senior levels of the largest organizations, the figurehead load becomes so heavy that a special leader is designated to do only that kind of work (but without the formal authority to make decisions, that person is not really the organization's manager). Governments are, of course, the largest "organizations" we know; in Great Britain, for example, we find that the Queen is designated as the figurehead of state. In this way, she takes on a good part—never all—of the figurehead duties that would otherwise fall to the Prime Minister. He in turn has more time to manage the government. (Unfortunately for the President of the United States, no such arrangement exists there. The full weight of the figurehead burden falls squarely on his shoulders.)

## The Manager as Leader

The leader role encompasses the manager's activities and inter-personal relationships with his own employees, that is, with the people who constitute his own organizational unit. The essence of the leader role is to integrate the needs of the individual employee with the goals or purposes of the organization. We discussed this issue at length in Section I, noting various ways in which organizations achieve this—through the compensation system and fringe benefits, by promotional practices and performance-appraisal systems. Here our primary interest is in what activities managers engage in to carry out their role as leader.

There are a series of tangible leadership activities all managers perform, such as hiring their employees, training them, judging their performance, rewarding them, and perhaps also promoting and dismissing them.

Other leadership activities involve encouraging or motivating employees. These may sometimes constitute distinct and separate activities, as when a president stops by the office of an employee to tell him how pleased he is with the latter's report on the possibilities for a new product. But often motivational activities are blended in with others, for example, in the preceding case, the president might simply have made his during a meeting designed for some other purpose (such as to discuss the report).

In fact, subordinates are typically very sensitive to such leadership clues and look for them everywhere. Thus in virtually everything he does, the manager's actions may be screened by subordinates looking for messages. And thus we find that it is here in the leader role that managerial power most clearly manifests itself. Formal authority vests the manager with great potential power; leadership activity determines how much of it will be realized. William F. Whyte, in his study of the street gang, provides an apt illustration of the extent of this power:

> The leader is the focal point for the organization of his group. In his absence, the members of the gang are divided into a number of small groups. There is no common activity or general conversation. When the leader appears, the situation changes strikingly. The small units form into one large group. The conversation becomes general, and unified action frequently follows. The leader becomes the central point in the discussion. A follower starts to say something, pauses when he notices that the leader is not listening, and begins again when he has the leader's attention. When the leader leaves the group, unity gives way to the divisions that existed before his appearance.[2]

Earlier, we mentioned that the leader role has been the subject of considerable study by management researchers. In fact, relatively little of this research has been on the actual behavior of leaders—what they do in the leader role. Most has focused on trying to identify *traits* of successful leaders. The question these researchers posed, in essence, was: What are the personal characteristics (or traits) that distinguish men and women who successfully lead others? Are they more intelligent, taller, friendlier, etc.? Can we identify that certain something that distinguishes them? Particular attention was given to the notion of involvement of subordinates in decision-making. The

[2] W. F. Whyte, *Street Corner Society,* 2d ed. (Chicago: University of Chicago Press, 1955), p. 258.

question posed by these researchers was almost rhetorical: Do successful leaders elicit participation from their employees, or do they make decisions autocratically?

Ironically, the answer to this question, and to the others, turned out to be different from what one might think at first glance. First, despite all the research, few traits could be identified that were characteristic of all kinds of effective leaders. And the ones that were isolated (such as self-confidence) were so general as to be of almost no use in predicting who would turn out to be a successful leader. Even the studies of autocratic and participative leaders produced their surprises. It turned out that sometimes the autocratic leaders were more effective!

What are we to make of these findings? Apparently, in leadership much depends on the situation. There may be certain personal characteristics that disqualify some people from exercising leadership, no matter what the situation, but the same individual is not suited for all leadership situations. The classic example of situational leadership is encountered in a play in which a British aristocrat and his butler are marooned on a desert island. In England, the aristocrat was well suited to the role of leader. His training and education gave him all the necessary qualities of a gentleman that a sophisticated (and aristocratic) society required. But this was not the case on the island. There, survival depended not on one's accent or how one held a spoon, but on one's ability to deal with a threatening physical situation. And the butler was far better suited to the situation. In time, therefore, he emerged as the leader, and the aristocrat became, in effect, his servant. By the time they were found, the two had completely reversed their original roles. But the moment they were discovered, they reverted back. In effect, they returned immediately to the former situation requiring the former pattern of leadership.

> **QUESTION:** What personal characteristics would you look for in the leader of: a hockey team, a research laboratory, the Roman Catholic Church, an army squad (in peacetime vs. wartime in the jungle), a factory foreman, the president of a high-powered consulting firm, a student project team?

To conclude, much of the leader role remains in the realm of darkness. Despite great research efforts, leadership still seems to depend on that mysterious chemistry (called "charisma") that causes some individuals to be followed and others to follow. Every freshman class of business students contains some people who will no doubt rise to high positions in industry. And although every member of that class thinks he knows who they will be, no one can say for sure.

## The Manager as Liaison

If interpersonal relationships between the manager and his employees have been the focus of considerable research attention, then those between the manager and people outside the organizational chain of command (that is, neither employees nor bosses, but people outside the unit, though perhaps inside the larger organization) have hardly been studied at all. This is the case despite the evidence from many studies that managers spend as much time with people outside their units as with their employees: presidents with other presidents and government officials, and so on; foremen with other foremen, with suppliers and personnel specialists; and so on. For example, one study of 160 British senior and middle managers found that they averaged 41 percent of their contact time with employees, 12 percent with their own bosses, and 47 percent with other people outside the organizational chain of command (19 percent with their colleagues, 13 percent with fellow specialists, 8 percent with people inside their own organizations but outside their own units, and 8 percent with people wholly outside their organizations). In another study, factory foremen were found to spend 46 percent of their time with their subordinates, 10 percent with their bosses, and 44 percent with people outside their chain of command. In the study of 5 chief executives, the respective figures were 48 percent, 7 percent (in this case, with directors of their organizations, since chief executives have no bosses per se), and 44 percent.[3] Hence we can see the crucial importance of *liaison* contacts for the manager.

[3] These figures come respectively from the studies of R. Stewart *Managers and Their Jobs* (London: Macmillan, 1967), F. J. Jasinski "Foremen Relationships Outside the Work Group" *Personnel* (1956: 130–136), and H. Mintzberg, *The Nature of Managerial Work* (New York: Harper & Row, 1973).

**QUESTION: Before reading on, ask yourself: Why do managers spend so much time with people outside their own units?**

How can we explain these figures? The answer, again, lies in formal authority. By virtue of the office he occupies, the manager is able to (and obliged to) maintain high-level contacts for his organization. As one observer of the managerial scene has written:

> First, a manager has status. He is set apart from nonmanagerial employees, and he is accepted in the managerial class. He stops eating lunch with nonmanagerial associates and starts eating lunch with other managers, often in a private dining room. Many of his nonmanagerial friendships dissolve and are replaced by friendships within the managerial group. He is admitted to membership in social clubs which were formerly closed to him, by convention if not by fiat. He is invited to be an officer in charitable and professional organizations.[4]

How exactly do these status contacts serve the manager? Are they merely ego boosters or ways of showing off? There may be a grain of truth in these explanations, but they do not justify the great amount of time managers spend on these activities. Clearly, these status contacts must serve the needs of the organization, not merely the personal needs of the individuals who happen to occupy the position of manager.

It turns out, as we shall see more clearly in the next chapter, that these status contacts serve a most important purpose: They establish a web or network of contacts by which the manager informs himself about his environment.

How does the manager build this network? We can see a variety of activities all related to the liaison role: the manager joins a golf club, attends an industry conference, makes a television appearance, seeks a position in the local chamber of commerce, writes to congratulate an old friend whose promotion has been announced in the newspaper, cultivates an old-boy network, and acknowledges a favor by letter. In all cases, the manager's prime motive is the same—to establish, maintain, and

---

[4] W. H. Starbuck, "Organizational Growth and Development" in J. G. March (ed.) *Handbook of Organizations* (Chicago: Rand McNally, 1965), p. 512.

extend a network of personal contacts that can feed him with information external to his own unit or organization.

Research on managerial work suggests that all managers devote a good deal of attention to developing such networks of contacts. Consider these two extremes. Our first quotation comes from Richard Neustadt's study of President Franklin D. Roosevelt:

> His personal sources were the product of a sociability and curiosity that reached back to the other Roosevelt's time. He had an enormous acquaintance in various phases of national life and at various levels of government; he also had his wife and her variety of contacts. He extended his acquaintanceships abroad; in the war years Winston Churchill, among others, became a "personal source." Roosevelt quite deliberately exploited these relationships and mixed them up to widen his own range of information. He changed his sources as his interests changed, but no one who had ever interested him was quite forgotten or immune to sudden use.[5]

And at the other extreme, we have William F. Whyte's views on the liaison role of the leader of a street gang:

> The leader is better known and more respected outside his group than are any of his followers. His capacity for social movement is greater. One of the most important functions he performs is that of relating his group to other groups in the district. Whether the relationship is one of conflict, competition, or cooperation, he is expected to represent the interests of his fellows. The politician and the racketeer must deal with the leader in order to win the support of his followers. The leader's reputation outside the group tends to support his standing within the group, and his position in the group supports his reputation among outsiders.[6]

Not only do managers spend considerable time in these networks of contacts, but also they ensure that their networks are wide. The contacts of chief executives have been found to include

[5] R. E. Neustadt, *Presidential Power: The Politics of Leadership* (New York: Wiley, 1960), pp. 156–157.
[6] Whyte, op. cit., pp. 259–260.

clients, business associates and suppliers, peers who manage their own organizations, government and trade organization officials, codirectors, and independents (those with no relevant organizational affiliation). Figure 8.1 shows the results of one study[7], with the upper figures representing the proportion of total contact time the chief executives had with each group and the lower figures representing the proportion of mail from each group. Many of these contacts had relatively formal relationships with the chief executive. They made occasional status requests and engaged in ceremonial activities with him. Peers asked him to speak; consultants sought contracts; politicians requested advice; and consumers wrote for free merchandise.

To gain access to outside information, the chief executives in these studies developed networks of informers—self-designed external information systems. Some informers were personal contacts—friends, peers, and codirectors—who sent various reports and told of the latest events and opportunities. In addition, the chief executives retained numbers of experts—consultants, lawyers, underwriters—to provide specialized advice. Trade organizations kept them up to date on events in the trade—the unionization of a competitor, the state of impending legislation in Washington, the promotion of a peer. Finally, stemming from their personal reputations and that of their organizations, these managers were fed with unsolicited information and ideas—a suggestion for a contract, a comment on a product, a reaction to an advertisement.

Foremen also deal with complex networks of outsiders. In a study by Guest, it was found that "The average foreman talked with many different individuals, rarely fewer than 25 and often more than 50. He dealt with a wide variety of persons in the operating and service departments and on different levels"[8] Jasinski (discussing the same study as Guest), has noted foreman-to-foreman relationships, in which the foremen must "get along" rather than exert authority over one another, and diagonal relationships, in which "foremen advised and made suggestions to, rather than directed, these non-subordinate operators."[9]

[7] Mintzberg, op. cit., p. 46.
[8] R. H. Guest, "Of Time and the Foreman," *Personnel* (1955–56: p. 483).
[9] Jasinski, op. cit., p. 132.

Figure 8.1 The Chief Executives' Contacts*

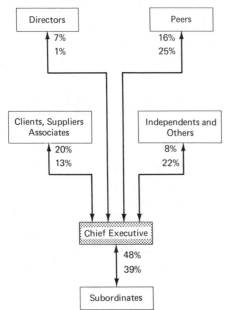

* Figures indicate, respectively, proportion of total contact time spent
with each group and proportion of
mail from each group.

> **EXERCISE:** Return to the list you made earlier of managers in
> organizations that are <u>extraordinary</u> but familiar to you (res-
> taurant, ski hill, student newspaper, etc.) and list the liaison
> contacts you think these managers should make. Check out
> your findings with these kinds of managers.

To sum up, in the liaison role the manager, by virtue of his
authority and associated status, is able to develop a special kind of
external linkage system. And in the leader role he creates the
linkages to all of his own employees. Now let us see what he does
with these interpersonal relationships.

# 9

# The Manager's Informational Roles

Obviously, interpersonal contacts are not ends in themselves (except in the sense that they satisfy the managers' social needs). One important use of them is in getting information for the manager. To begin, let us consider some accounts of the manager's role in information processing. First we have an anecdote from the study of five chief executives, in this case related to the work of the president of a large company in the field of advanced technology:

A company vice-president must leave a meeting on the west coast early. He and some colleagues were in the process of negotiating an acquisition. Shortly after the meeting ends, the vice-president, anxious to know the result, calls across the country to the president at headquarters in Boston. The president, who has just spoken to the other negotiators, describes the outcome. Later, in reply to the observer's comment, "So you are in Boston, they are both out west, yet you are in a better position to tell the vice-president what went on," the president comments, "I usually am!"

Our second illustration comes from Richard Neustadt's study of President Franklin Delano Roosevelt:

The essence of Roosevelt's technique for information-gathering was competition. "He would call you in," one of his aides once told me, "and he'd ask you to get the story on some complicated business, and you'd come back after a couple of days of hard labor and present the juicy morsel you'd uncovered under a stone somewhere, and *then* you'd find out he knew all about it, along with something else you *didn't* know. Where he got his information from he wouldn't mention, usually, but after he had done this to you once or twice you got damn careful about *your* information."[1]

What do these accounts tell us about managerial work? They indicate that, to his subordinates, to the observer, and to the person himself, the manager clearly occupies the central position in the movement of a certain kind of information within his organization. In effect, the manager is his organization's nerve center. The flow of nonroutine information in an organization focuses on its manager.

This reflects two features of the manager's job—his unique access to external information and his all-embracing access to internal information. Consider, first, the manager's access to internal information. In all but the least-structured organizations, each person below the manager is a specialist, and the manager, relatively speaking, is a generalist. At the top of the corporate

[1] R. E. Neustadt, *Presidential Power: The Politics of Leadership* (New York: Wiley, 1960), p. 157.

hierarchy, the president oversees vice presidents charged with specialist functions such as marketing, production, and finance. And reporting to the foreman are lathe operators, milling machine operators, and so on. With formal lines of communication to each of these specialists, the manager develops a broad base of information, and emerges as a nerve center of internal information. He may not know as much about any one function as the specialist charged with it, but he is the only one to know a significant amount about all functions. As a result, various outsiders turn to the manager when the information that they need from his organization involves more than one function, or when they do not know which specialist can answer their questions.

Second is his access to external information. Because of his status and its manifestation in the *liaison* role, the manager has unique access to other managers, who are themselves nerve centers. These sources ensure that he is best informed about events in his organization's environment. The result is that the manager becomes the focal point in his organization for special external information.

For illustration of this in another context, let us turn again to the study of street gangs. George Homans, who reviews the study by Whyte, has stressed both the internal and external aspects of nerve-center information, as follows:

> Since interaction flowed toward [the leaders], they were better informed about the problems and desires of group members than were any of the followers and therefore better able to decide on an appropriate course of action. Since they were in close touch with other gang leaders, they were also better informed than their followers about conditions in Cornerville at large. Moreover, in their position at the focus of the chains of interaction, they were better able than any follower to pass on to the group the decisions that had been reached.[2]

Three roles characterize managers as nerve centers. In the *monitor* role, managers inform themselves about their organizations and environments, and in the *disseminator* and *spokesman* roles, they transmit their information to others.

[2] G. C. Homans, *The Human Group* (New York: Harcourt Brace Jovanovich, 1950), p. 187.

## The Manager as Monitor

The monitor role describes the manager's behavior as he collects information, building up a data base on the operations of his own organization and the trends and events in its environment. To understand the monitor role, we must first consider the manager's *media,* the channels through which his information comes. Five media can be distinguished:

- *Mail:* documented information (reports, magazines, letters, memos, etc.)
- *Telephone:* verbal information
- *Unscheduled meetings:* verbal, face-to-face information
- *Scheduled meetings:* verbal, face-to-face information through preplanned encounters
- *Tours:* direct observation of activities

One of the interesting results of virtually every study of managers' work—no matter what the industry, the level in the organization, or the function supervised—is that managers rely heavily on verbal media of communication, namely, the telephone and, especially, meetings. Generally, managers have been found to spend 60 to 80 percent of their time in verbal communication, as, for example, 66 percent in a study of 160 British senior and middle managers, and 75 percent in a study of 5 American chief executives. Figure 9.1 shows the specific distribution in this second study—6 percent in telephone calls, 10 percent in unscheduled meetings, and 59 percent in scheduled meetings. Only 3 percent was spent in tours, leaving a grand total of only 22 percent for desk work (namely, in that place where managers handle their mail and do their office reading).

We should reflect on this finding for a moment, because it is a very important one. It tells us that managers spend little of their time working alone quietly, that most of the time they are involved in verbal communication. Why? Well, to get some explanation, the incoming mail of these five chief executives was analyzed. Some interesting things turned up. A full 36 percent of the mail turned out to be rather inconsequential—status requests (such as documents to sign), and the like, related to the

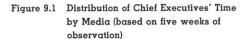

Figure 9.1  Distribution of Chief Executives' Time
by Media (based on five weeks of
observation)

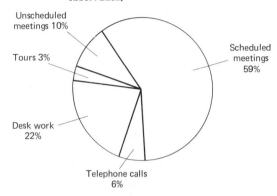

figurehead role, or general information for reference only. Another 51 percent informed the chief executives in general ways about their organizations and environments. This consisted of reports of various kinds, magazines and newspapers, special information on events and ideas. The chief executives skimmed much of this information and did little with it directly. For example, during five weeks of study, the chief executives received 104 magazines and newspapers. Most of these were skimmed very quickly, almost ritualistically (sometimes at the rate of two per minute), and only four elicited immediate action of some kind (such as making a telephone call, writing a letter, or forwarding a clipping to someone). Even some of the accounting reports were given rather cursory attention. This left only 13 percent for a third category of mail, namely, that of specific and immediate concern to the manager (for example, related to important decisions to be approved and advice on current situations and problems).

Therefore, we can explain the manager's treatment of mail as a medium by the fact that little of it contains issues of live action. (We shall see repeatedly that the job of manager is one of action, not reflection.) Thus mail-processing turns out to be, in large part, a chore for the manager, something that must be done. And during one week of observation, one chief executive repeatedly sifted through his mail, hesitant to process it, yet searching for items that could not be left unattended. From Monday to Friday, he found 32 pieces of mail worthy of attention. Then he came in for a period of three hours on Saturday to process the rest, to "get rid of all this stuff." This activity reflects a general concern: No matter how inconsequential the contents, the flow of mail cannot be impeded or the manager will be swamped with paper.

Even outgoing mail seems not to be very important to managers. In one study of nine managing directors (presidents) of Swedish companies, the researcher concluded:

> One of the most noticeable characteristic features in common between the different executives was the limited use of letters as a means of communication. There were chief executives who signed not more than one or two letters a week, and the maximum was two or three letters a day. The picture of the chief executive as a man who is busy dictating and signing letters was not borne out by any of our studies.[3]

A similar result was found in the study of American chief executives. One commented, "I don't like to write memos, as you can probably tell. I much prefer face-to-face contact." Another repeated the same sentiments. "I try to write as few letters as possible. I happen to be immeasurably better with the spoken word than with the written word." Their reasons are clear. Contrasted with verbal communication, letter-writing is time consuming, primarily since words to be documented must be chosen carefully. Furthermore, the information moves slowly to the target, and much time elapses before there is feedback. This presents no difficulty for formal documents, for lengthy or routine reports, or for general information. But for much of their important information, managers must use other media. Mail as a medium does not fit well with managers who prefer live action.

We would think that tours would be used extensively by managers, since this exposes them to activities taking place in their organizations. But in fact tours are little used (3 percent in the study of U.S. chief executives, 10 percent for the Swedish managing directors, 6 percent for the British senior and middle

[3] S. Carlson, *Executive Behavior* (Stockholm: Strombergs, 1951), p. 83.

managers). Again, tours do not count as live action. Managers appear reluctant to engage in open-ended activities such as tours; they prefer, instead, activities of specific and immediate use to them.

This leaves the verbal media. They are the action media; they provide immediate feedback (for example, you can ask the woman on the telephone or the man in front of you, "What did you mean by that?"), and they tend to bring a richer input of data (tone of voice, inflection, facial expression, mood, as well as the message conveyed by the actual words).

**EXERCISE:** Write to a friend trying to explain something you have done, say, something you have fixed or a party you have attended or whatever. When you finish, tell him or her the same thing verbally. Compare the results for the two media. In which did your thought flow more easily? Were you able to convey some messages in your verbal account that you could not convey in your written account? But what if you had to tell 20 friends? Might it not have been easier to record your thoughts and reproduce them for distribution? And what if you wished to recall your reaction to these things three years from now? Could you retain the memory of them without recording them?

What kind of information does the manager seek? Traditionally, it was thought that he needed, above all, aggregated, historical information, such as the accumulated results of the operations of his organization (such as cost and sales reports). But our findings about the emphasis on verbal media suggest otherwise. In fact, research has shown that managers favor a rather different kind of information.

First of all, it turns out that managers like their information to be current. As a result, their informational diet inevitably contains much rumor and hearsay. "Is this any way to run an airline" (or other organization)? The answer seems to be yes. Managers need current information because they must often react quickly to events taking place around them. Today's rumor may be tomorrow's fact. But tomorrow may be too late. A football coach who is gearing his team up for the title game and who hears a rumor that the opposing team has developed a new series of plays can try to find out what the plays are and in turn develop a defensive strategy. Otherwise he may wait till game time, and then perhaps find out—too late—that the rumor was fact. Similarly, the company president who hears the rumor that a competitor is about to introduce a new product may be able to get the full information and preempt the competitor with a sales push. Thus managers have good reason to prefer current information and to favor the verbal channels through which this tends to flow.

Second, research indicates that managers prefer *tangible* rather than aggregated information (for example, the fact that Fickle Incorporated canceled its contract rather than that sales were down last month). Why? H. Edward Wrapp has explained clearly in an excellent article entitled "Good Managers Don't Make Policy Decisions":

> Top-level managers are frequently criticized by writers, consultants, and lower levels of management for continuing to enmesh themselves in operating problems, after promotion to the top, rather than withdrawing to the "big picture." Without any doubt, some managers do get lost in a welter of detail and insist on making too many decisions. Superficially, the good manager may seem to make the same mistake—but his purposes are different. He knows that only by keeping well informed about the decisions being made can he avoid the sterility so often found in those who isolate themselves from operations. If he follows the advice to free himself from operations, he may soon find himself subsisting on a diet of abstractions, leaving the choice of what he eats in the hands of his subordinates.[4]

Hence managers need tangible information to avoid the sterility of abstractions. Richard Neustadt, in analyzing the behavior of President Roosevelt, has noted the same point, explaining that tangible information helps the manager to understand issues. Neustadt further links the tangible with the current nature of the manager's information:

> It is not information of a general sort that helps a President see personal stakes; not summaries, not surveys, not the *bland*

[4] H. E. Wrapp, "Good Managers Don't Make Policy Decisions," *Harvard Business Review* (September–October, 1967), p. 92.

*amalgams*. Rather . . . it is the odds and ends of *tangible detail* that pieced together in his mind illuminate the underside of issues put before him. To help himself he must reach out as widely as he can for every scrap of fact, opinion, gossip, bearing on his interests and relationships as President. He must become his own director of his own central intelligence.[5]

Now, how can we reconcile the point in Section II about the importance of the formal reporting system (the accounting reports, budgets, and the like) with the point in this section about the kinds of information managers apparently prefer? For, while the formal systems give largely historical and aggregated information, we have seen that the manager seeks largely current and tangible information. Managers, of course, use the former too, but it seems that the formal reports are designed to serve, in large part, the staff specialists of the organization, the non-managers who are charged with advising the managers on problems that are encountered. When a problem—an "exception"—is detected, in many cases it is then conveyed to the manager as a tangible piece of evidence (as likely as not in verbal form, perhaps by means of a phone call).

One final point requires mention. If the formal system (sometimes called a Management Information System, or, more simply, an MIS) is not the manager's prime source of information, then what is? We saw the answer in our discussion of the manager as liaison (and also in Neustadt's words that the manager becomes "his own director of his own central intelligence"). In effect, the manager builds his own information system through the network of verbal contacts that he establishes with outsiders and with his own employees.

To conclude our discussion of the manager as monitor, it should be noted that unlike other workers, the manager does not leave the telephone or the meeting to get back to work. Rather, these contacts *are* his work. The ordinary work of the organization—producing a product, undertaking research, or conducting a study or writing a report—is seldom undertaken by its manager. The manager's productive output can be measured primarily in terms of verbally transmitted information.

[5] Neustadt, op. cit., pp. 153–154; italics added.

## The Manager as Disseminator

What does the manager do with his information? Well, for one thing, if he does in fact have access to special information because of his high-status liaison contacts and his role of leader, and if he does in fact emerge as an informational nerve center of his own organization, then it stands to reason that the manager has "privileged" information that his employees need. Thus he must transmit it to them directly. This he does in the context of the *disseminator* role. In one good illustration of this, a chief executive of a consulting firm attended a meeting of an outside board of directors on which he sat. There he heard some information from a fellow board member (another nerve center) about a contract on which his firm was bidding. Upon his return to his own organization, the manager immediately went to the office of a subordinate who was working on the bid and told him about what he had learned at the board meeting.

This illustrates our point perfectly. The manager is able to get the information by virtue of his status; that is, only as chief executive would he sit on the outside board of directors. In his liaison role, he establishes the contact with the fellow board members; this in turn leads to his picking up the privileged bit of information (in his role as monitor); in his role as disseminator, he shares his new information with an employee.

In managerial work such sharing of privileged information happens all the time. But there is one fly in the ointment. Most of the manager's privileged information is verbal. If it were documented, dissemination would be an easy matter. "Miss Secours, please make a copy of this document for Messrs. Besoin, Manque, and Cherche." But when the information is verbal, dissemination is a time-consuming matter, for verbal information exists in "natural" memory, that is, in the brain of the manager. He must sit down with each individual (or in a group) and "dump memory," so to speak, that is, take the time to tell all. Hence the disseminator role can be a time-consuming one, and, as we shall soon see, can lead to some rather serious problems for the manager.

One special aspect of the disseminator role should be mentioned here. Earlier we noted as one of the manager's prime purposes the reconciliation of the values of those who control and influence the organization. In effect, the manager must somehow take their different needs and aspirations and combine them into some overall goals for the organization. Should it emphasize profit or growth? Is product quality important? How much emphasis should be placed on employee welfare, especially when it conflicts with profit? One important aspect of the disseminator role, therefore, is to pass into the organization some indication of the goals that should be pursued.

Andreas Papandreou, a well-known economist and manager as well (leader of the Greek socialist party) has referred to the top manager of the firm as its "peak coordinator," that person who combines all its values into some kind of preference function that can guide decision-making. Managers serve in this capacity, although not to the point of expressing preference functions. There is no evidence from the studies of managers that such functions exist (that is, that a manager can tell exactly what the preferences of his organization would be for any hypothetical issue). The expression of values or goals is a much more fluid phenomenon than that, always changing and best expressed when tangible decisions must be made. Value statements are made by the manager not in terms of global preferences but as specific answers to specific questions. For example, it is unlikely that we would find a manager saying, "Here we prefer profit to growth." More commonly, we hear, "I like the second option; it has a better return on investment even though it's smaller." Furthermore, there is no reason to believe that the manager enters all situations with well-defined preferences. Sometimes the preferences develop as issues develop, as new information and new alternatives appear. We want what we get just as often as we get what we want. But no matter how goals and values are expressed, the determination of them for the organization is one important aspect of managerial work.

## The Manager as Spokesman

The manager's role in the organization's information system does not end with being a disseminator. Just as he must pass some of his information to employees, so also must he pass some of it to people outside the organization. In effect, as his organization's formal authority and its nerve center, the manager must serve as its official *spokesman*. This can entail a variety of activities. For a company president, it may mean speaking on behalf of the organization to a congressional committee, being interviewed by a stock analyst who wishes to know the firm's future plans, or conferring with stockholders about annual results. For the foreman, it can mean keeping the plant manager informed, telling the personnel department about problems with new employees, or informing the assembly department about when to expect the machined parts.

One of the reasons managers so enthusiastically seek out current and tangible information can be found in the spokesman role. How can the manager speak for his organization when his own information is out of date? A few years ago, when General Motors was embroiled in its early problems with Ralph Nader, the president of the company was forced to appear before a congressional committee and admit that he had no knowledge of his company's having hired private detectives to pry into the private life of Mr. Nader. This manager could have saved himself serious embarrassment had he been exposed to this tangible bit of information a bit earlier, in time to stop the action. Managers need up-to-the-minute information, and tangible information too, if they are to play the spokesman role effiectively.

Thus we have seen in this chapter that managers spend a great deal of their time in activities that are informational in nature. They devote considerable attention to getting information in their monitor role and to passing it along to others in their disseminator and spokesman roles. But, of course, that is not the end of the line. Information serves a fundamental purpose in the organization, namely, in the making of decisions.

# 10

# The Manager's Decisional Roles

Authority, interpersonal contacts, and information—all are necessary for an organization to function, but none accomplishes anything per se. It is only when the organization takes action—when it produces a product or provides a service—that it serves its primary purpose. And a prerequisite to action is decision—the determination of what actions are to be taken. Thus we see in the manager's job a natural flow: Authority leads to information, and both enable the manager to make decisions that in turn lead to organizational action.

Let us extend our notion of decision with another, related

term: "strategy." Strategy describes the consistencies in an organization's decisions. Thus if all a company's products are purple (that is, every time a new product is introduced, a decision is made to paint it purple), we say that the company has a "purple product strategy." Similarly, if a farmer decides every year to increase the number of animals he has, we might talk of an "expansion strategy," and if he decides to increase the range of animals every year—adding pigs, then cows, then goats, and so on—then we might talk of a "diversification strategy." Thus strategy implies some consistency in streams of decisions. (Sometimes the term "strategy" is used for what the firm *intends* to do, in effect, for the consistent decisions it intends to make. But we should be careful to distinguish *intended* strategies from *realized* strategies, those that actually get put into practice.)

> **EXERCISE:** Describe your own strategies in the things you do, not your intended strategies but those you actually realize. Go back over a recent period of your life and make a chronology, or list by date, of the different decisions you have made (in summer jobs taken, social, athletic, and entertainment activities engaged in, and so on). Is there any consistency? That is, do you have some strategy? Are you surprised by what you see? Do your realized strategies differ from your intended ones? Or even from those that you thought were your realized strategies?

If strategy relates to decision streams, then strategy *formulation* describes how organizations develop their decision streams.

## Strategy Formulation in Three Modes

Before we discuss the manager's roles in strategy formulation, we should ask how organizations make their strategies, that is, how they make their many decisions and interrelate them to form strategies. In fact, we are only now beginning to research systematically this important and fascinating process. But for years people have been writing about it, and they have described it in three essentially different ways, which we shall call "modes" (approaches) to strategy formulation. We shall see that in each of these the manager's involvement is quite different. Before proceeding, it should be noted that the existence of three different modes does not imply that two are wrong and one is right. Rather, it suggests that organizations can under different circumstances or conditions approach the making of their strategies in different ways. (Theories that suggest different ways of going about doing things under different conditions are known as *contingency theories*. Earlier, we had another example of contingency theory —that different managers succeed when they are autocratic or when they encourage the participation of their employees, depending on the circumstances.)

### THE ENTREPRENEURIAL MODE OF STRATEGY FORMULATION

First is the *entrepreneurial* mode. Here, the manager is the central participant in strategy formulation; in fact he is the only one. In the entrepreneurial mode, everything focuses on the chief executive, the "entrepreneur." It is he who makes all key decisions and interrelates them. Therefore, the organization's strategy really emerges as an extension of his own vision of where the organization should go. One brain makes and interrelates all the decisions. In effect, he charts some general course, and then makes decisions to move the organization in that direction. And because the entrepreneur need answer to no one else, he can move in that direction in big, bold steps; that is, his decisions are ambitious ones.

Obviously, not all organizations can follow the entrepreneurial mode. Which ones can? The most evident case is the little company in which the owner is the manager and can do more or less what he wishes. Also, if the organization is young, this helps too, since the organization can (perhaps must) move boldly to establish itself. It does not have the momentum that comes with age. But sometimes we find the entrepreneurial mode in other cases too, especially when a powerful (charismatic) leader emerges. Napoleon might have been thought of as an entrepreneur at the head of the French Government, as was De Gaulle a century and a half later. In both cases, charismatic individuals held the reins of power firmly.

### THE ADAPTIVE MODE OF STRATEGY FORMULATION

The second mode of strategy formulation, the *adaptive* mode, is very different from the entrepreneurial one. Here, the organization faces a difficult environment, not one where a single entrepreneur can move at will. Furthermore, the power of decision-making in the organization is divided among different people with different goals. As a result, the organization cannot move quickly or boldly. Nor can it pursue a single vision of where to go, for the different strategy-makers have different visions. Thus the process of strategy formulation becomes one of continual bargaining, with each of the strategy-makers trying to get his own needs satisfied. The organization cannot follow any single goal, but rather, in the words of Cyert and March, it must attend to different goals sequentially.[1] For example, if there is a goal conflict over long-term growth versus short-term profit, the organization may make a decision to favor short-term profit one day (by, say, cutting back advertising expenditures), and three weeks later it may make another decision to favor long-term growth (by, say, introducing a new product with great potential, which might take years to become profitable).

In general, in the adaptive mode the organization must move in small, disjointed steps, constantly meandering along according to the pressures that it encounters in its complex environment and the needs of the different strategy-makers. Decisions cannot be tightly integrated to form clearly defined strategies.

Who are these different strategy-makers and what is the role of the manager in the adaptive mode? First of all, in the organization using the adaptive mode, there is not *the* manager as in the entrepreneurial mode, but there are many, and they may bargain among themselves as to which decisions should be made. For example, when the president of a company is weak, the vice presidents of manufacturing, marketing, and engineering may be in a perpetual state of bargaining over the outcome of every decision process. (If the president is strong, however, the organization may revert to the entrepreneurial mode.) Also others get involved in the strategy formulation process—the operators and staff specialists inside the organization and a host of outside influencers.

In effect, using the adaptive mode are those organizations most influenced by outside groups and least controlled by their

[1] C. M. Cyert and J. G. March, *A Behavioral Theory of the Firm* (Englewood Cliffs, N.J.: Prentice-Hall, 1963).

chief executives. Also organizations in complex environments tend to use the adaptive mode. Typical organizations fitting these conditions are universities (where the power is divided among trustees, administrators, faculty, students, and governments) and hospitals (where trustees, administrators, doctors, and nurses share the power). But even in business firms, particularly large ones very much in the public eye, such as giant automobile-manufacturing firms, the adaptive mode of strategy formulation may be used.

### THE PLANNING MODE OF STRATEGY FORMULATION

The third mode is very different again. This is the *planning* mode, in which the organization relies heavily on the systematic analysis of those staff specialists called "planners." Here, decisions are tightly integrated to form clearly defined strategies. In effect, periodically the planners and managers sit down with the necessary information and systematically develop strategic plans —intended strategies set down on paper to be implemented.

In the planning mode, the manager's participation in strategy-making is somewhat diminished in favor of the planner. This does not mean that the manager has nothing to do; what it means is that much of his burden is taken over by those staff specialists who have more time to probe deeply into the issues. In discussing strategy formulation in the government context (generally referred to as policy-making), one U.S. senator has commented:

> I am convinced that we never will get the kind of policy planning we need if we expect the top-level officers to participate actively in the planning process. They simply do not have the time, and in any event they rarely have the outlook or the talents of the good planner. They cannot argue the advantages and disadvantages at length in the kind of give-and-take essential if one is to reach a solid understanding with others on points of agreement and disagreement.[2]

---

[2] Quoted in R. N. Anthony, *Planning and Control Systems: A Framework for Analysis* (Boston: Harvard Business School, Division of Research, 1965), pp. 46–47.

Where do we find organizations that favor the planning mode? Generally, they can be found where the following conditions prevail: The organization is large enough to afford strategic planning (which tends to be expensive), and the environment is sufficiently stable so that the plans made today will have some meaning tomorrow. (Can a company plan its future product lines when consumer tastes are in a state of flux and cannot be predicted? Can a public university plan for next year if the government will not tell it what its budget will be?) Also, planning is easiest when power is not divided in the organization; otherwise the experience may be useless, since the different influencers may never be able to agree on a specific plan for the future. Hence we tend to find planning in large organizations in stable environments and with few contentious issues to attract influencers. Electric utilities and telephone companies are perhaps the best examples of organizations able to rely on the planning mode.

Figure 10.1 summarizes our discussion of the three modes in symbolic form. Hence we see the entrepreneurial organization taking big, bold steps toward the general vision of its entrepreneur; the adaptive organization taking small, disjointed steps with no real sense of direction; and the planning organization developing one clearly defined line of strategic action from the day the plans are made to the day they are realized.

> **EXERCISE:** Go back to the organizations you listed earlier and list for each the conditions we have been discussing: the stability and complexity of their environments, the nature of power division in the organizations, each organization's age and size, the influence or charisma of the chief executive, and so on. Then try to predict which mode of strategy formulation each organization uses. Then go back to the organization and try to find out through interviews and your own observation which mode in fact seems to be used.

Of course, despite the neat separation of these three modes, real organizations never fit one or the other exactly. There will always be some mixture in every organization: power can never be as centralized as described in the entrepreneurial mode; environment can never be as stable as described in the planning mode; and direction can never be as ill defined as described in

Figure 10.1 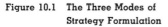The Three Modes of
Strategy Formulation

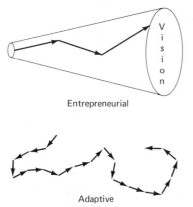

the adaptive mode; and so on. Nevertheless, many organizations
do lean toward one mode or the other, and thus this trichotomy
helps us to understand how organizations function.

Now we can return to a closer look at the manager's roles
in the formulation of strategy for his organizational unit. One
point is clear. No matter what the favored mode, the manager is
a key individual in strategy formulation. This is so for two reasons, which relate directly to our discussion of the other roles.
First, the manager (by definition) has formal authority in his
organization, so that only he can commit the organization to
important decisions. Therefore, no matter who else gets involved
in strategy formulation, ultimately the manager must decide (or
at least approve) all major actions that the organization intends
to take. Second, if the manager is the nerve center of his organization, then he has the key information that must be used in the
strategy formulation process.

The manager may be described as playing four key roles in
strategy formulation. Two of these are suggested by the modes
we have just discussed. In effect, the organization through its
leaders may be considered to make decisions along a range,
from opportunities at one end (most characteristic of the en-

trepreneurial mode, in which the organization moves freely and boldly) to disturbances or crises at the other end (more characteristic of the adaptive mode, in which the organization moves because it is pushed, because it must). Thus our first two roles describe the manager as entrepreneur and as disturbance handler. The others view him as a resource allocator and a negotiator.

## The Manager as Entrepreneur

Even in the nonentrepreneurial organization, there is always an entrepreneurial role for the manager to play. That is, he must initiate projects to explore the opportunities—to improve the organization voluntarily—and he must see these projects through to completion. This is the notion of change that we discussed in Section I. The manager uses his information system to identify opportunities in his organization's environment. Perhaps there is a chance to introduce a new product and seize an important part of the market; perhaps an employee has left a competitive firm and would fit nicely into the manager's organization; or perhaps a new market can be opened.

What does the manager do once he has found that opportunity? In some cases, he can act quickly and decisively, and that is that (for instance, hire the new employee). But other opportunities, such as introducing new products or tapping new markets, are rather more involved. They cannot be decided all at once but must be split into steps and dealt with bit by bit over long periods of time. This is not unlike the adaptive mode, in which decisions are also made step by step. In effect, when issues are complex, the manager must react to them a little at a time. Thus a single decision (for example, to introduce a new product) actually becomes a multiplicity of decisions sequenced over time (to investigate the opportunity, to design the product, to test-market it, to modify the product, to determine the channels of distribution, to mount an advertising campaign, etc.). In this way, a complex issue can gradually come to be comprehended. As an analogy, imagine being taught an algebra course in one session of ten hours as opposed to ten sessions of one hour each spread over ten weeks.

Another reason why managers split complex decisions into series of mini-decisions is that they are busy people. This is the way they can cope with pressure. The difficult issues are tackled with many little nibbles rather than one big bite. It is far easier for the busy person to spend one-half hour on a complex issue once a week than to have to stop everything else for three days simply to work on that issue. The other demands on the manager's time—the mail piling up, the callers at the door, and so on—simply preclude such intense and extended concentration on any one issue.

Thus, for each complex issue, the manager initiates an *improvement project* to study and, if necessary, develop it. The project will continue for perhaps a month, possibly even for years. Here is a typical example from the study of the work of a school superintendent. We can see in this example both the initiation of the project and its development in steps, with one step described in detail:

> **In reaction to vigorous public debate, a committee of eight people was formed, including the superintendent, a school committee member, and assistant superintendents and principals, to investigate the issue of serving lunches to school children. In the last meeting, the decision was made to begin a pilot program. At this meeting, one of the participants is leading the discussion on methods of measuring the appropriate factors in the pilot program. After some time, the talk shifts to what appears to be the issue at hand—choosing a committee of citizens to oversee the pilot program. Leading the discussion, the superintendent begins to recommend the types of people required and the specific people who seem to fit. Each participant generates more suggestions, until the superintendent announces that enough acceptable names have been suggested. It is decided that the superintendent will write letters inviting these people to join the committee. When the replies are received, the group will meet again. The superintendent comments, "I think we've gone as far as we can go," and the participants prepare to leave.**

One author has described this process as being analogous to a stranded rope:

> The manager's job can usefully be pictured as a stranded rope made of fibres of different lengths—where length represents time—each fibre coming to the surface one or more times in observable "episodes" and representing a single issue. The higher the level of manager the longer the average length of the fibre, the more intertwined the issues become, and the greater the number of episodes per issue. A prime managerial skill may be the capacity to keep a number of "issues" in play over a large number of episodes, and long periods of time.[3]

What is the manager's involvement in these improvement projects? Essentially, he can approach each in two ways. He can delegate responsibility for the project to someone in his organization, and only approve (or *authorize*) it when it is ready to go. Or he may supervise the project himself. Typically, a great many projects are delegated, but many are also kept under the manager's supervision. In the study of the five American chief executives, each was found to supervise a great number of projects, of a wide variety, in one case ranging from acquiring new firms to reorienting salesmen to new product lines.

In effect, each manager maintains an inventory of these improvement projects. The inventory of active projects appears to change continually, as new ones are added, old ones reach completion, and others wait in storage until the manager is able to find time to begin work on them. Furthermore, projects in active inventory are subject to frequent delays between successive steps. A particular project may be held in limbo while the manager waits for information, or a project may be delayed for purposes of timing, as the manager awaits some development before going on to the next step (the retirement of someone blocking progress, the easing of funds, the solution of an engineering difficulty). The overall effect of delays is that the manager is able to maintain a very large inventory of active improvement projects, perhaps as many as 50 in the case of chief executives.

The manager as supervisor of improvement projects may be likened to a juggler. At any one point in time he has a number of balls in the air. Periodically, one comes down, receives a short

---

[3] D. L. Marples, "Studies of Managers—A Fresh Start" *The Journal of Management Studies* (1967), p. 287.

burst of energy, and goes up again. Meanwhile, new balls wait on the sidelines, and, at random intervals, old balls are discarded and new ones added.

To summarize, in the entrepreneur role the manager functions both as initiator and as designer of important controlled change in his organization. This change takes place in the form of improvement projects, many of which are supervised directly by the manager and all of which come under his control in one way or another.

## The Manager as Disturbance Handler

If the entrepreneurial role describes the opportunity end of the scale, the manager as an initiator of voluntary change, then the *disturbance handler* role describes the other end of the scale, the manager as an initiator of involuntary change, change because the pressures on the organization force it to change. Of course, reactive change is most characteristic of the adaptive mode. Nevertheless, just as there is some entrepreneurship even in the most adaptive organization, so also there are disturbances and crises even in the most entrepreneurial organization (In fact, the more an organization innovates, that is, the more it ventures boldly into the unknown, the more it is likely to encounter the unexpected, namely, disturbances and crises.)

Why should the manager have to play the key role in the handling of disturbances in his organization? The best answer probably is: Who else will? The very notion of a disturbance or a crisis is that something is not working normally. Perhaps something has fallen between the cracks (between existing departments), perhaps two employees are in dispute over an issue. In effect, in the organization all the people below the manager are, as noted earlier, specialists charged with some specific aspect of the work. (Some years ago, Tom Lehrer, a satirical folk singer, did a parody of Wernher von Braun, the German World War II rocket designer who later worked for NASA. Referring to von Braun's wartime activities and his claim to being apolitical, Lehrer sang "'Once the rockets are up, who cares where they come down; that's not my department' says Wernher von Braun.")

The manager oversees all the specialists who report to him. Hence the manager always understands something of the work of each; he is the generalist. When a dispute arises or something falls between the cracks, who can attend to it? Obviously, not the specialist. It is the generalist who understands the whole organization, the manager, who must see to it.

The types of disturbances in organizations are many—the sudden departure of a subordinate, fire in a facility, the loss of an important customer, a feud between two subordinates. Consider these three illustrations, drawn from the study of chief executives:

A particular professional staffer schedules an appointment with the chief executive for the first time in several years. There is an "explosive situation" in his department, he claims, and he and his colleagues will walk out if their boss is not fired. After the meeting, the chief executive's first action is to open information channels, advising the board chairman and seeking his advice, asking his deputy to watch for signs of the trouble. Every opportunity during the next few days is used to gain more information, while contact is maintained with the dissidents. Eventually it is decided that their concern is a real one, and a strategy is worked out—to confront the executive with the problem at a social function and to point out his need to change.

During a meeting in progress, the deputy comes in quickly and leaves a message. "Harry Jamison will call . . . Elwood man . . . feels that Mr. Flagdale was forced out . . . wishes to object . . . wants a hearing." The issue relates to the ratification of a new executive at the open board meeting to be held that evening. A group associated with the organization, people who favor the previous office holder, are pressuring the directors and the chief executive. That evening, in an informal meeting of the directors preceding the board meeting, the extent of the lobby becomes clear. As each director enters, he tells of pressuring telephone calls, usually from close contacts. They try to develop a picture of the situation—who are the dissidents, what is their exact complaint, what actions might they take? Once the issue is clear, the chief executive immediately takes charge, developing an approach, and acting to have it carried out. One board member will find the dissidents before the meeting, attempt to understand their position, and explain the possible embarrassment to the resigning executive if the issue is raised at the meeting. If necessary, the resignation can be delayed. At the board meeting there is no incident.

While the chief executive and two of his vice presidents are meeting informally, the secretary receives a telephone call from a purchasing agent in one of the plants. She immediately conveys the message to the chief executive. The note reads, "Heard from grapevine—will ship 2000 [parts to competitor]." To the executives, this means that a supplier who signed an agreement to develop a certain part for the firm, and who has since been bought by a competitor, may be reneging on his commitment, supplying the competitor instead. Discussion of other issues ceases and the office begins to take on the appearance of the headquarters of an army under siege. One executive searches for a copy of the contract with the supplier, while the other is on the telephone finding out how many of these parts are called for in the sales plan, and at what times. After intensive discussion a tentative strategy evolves. The firm will attempt to force the supplier to honor the agreement immediately, despite extra holding costs. This will delay the competitor. However, as calmness begins to prevail again, the executives reconsider their position and agree to limit action to a written request to the supplier asking for clarification.

What these illustrations show is that managers play key roles in handling disturbances in their own organizations. We can also see here another reason why managers find current information so important: They need it to deal with high-pressure disturbances.

To conclude, all managers must spend a great part of their time in handling disturbances. (Some, of course, spend more time on this than others. Foremen, for example, because they must keep the production facilities running smoothly, seem to spend more time handling disturbances than do most other managers.) Although it is fashionable to write about the long-range perspective of high-level executives and to depict them as reflective planners, it seems evident that even these high-level managers must spend much of their time reacting very quickly to high-pressure disturbance situations. These arise not only because "poor" managers ignore situations until they reach crisis proportions but also because "good" managers cannot anticipate the consequences of all actions taken by their organizations.

Many have written of the manager as a kind of orchestra conductor, standing on a platform removed from the details of operations and leading all the employees in a well-coordinated, harmonious effort. Leonard Sayles, an insightful researcher on managerial work, has turned this famous analogy around and put it into a more realistic perspective:

> The achievement of . . . stability, which is the manager's objective, is a never-to-be-attained ideal. He is like a symphony orchestra conductor, endeavoring to maintain a melodious performance in which the contributions of the various instruments are coordinated and sequenced, patterned and paced, while the orchestra members are having various personal difficulties, stage hands are moving music stands, alternating excessive heat and cold are creating audience and instrument problems, and the sponsor of the concert is insisting on irrational changes in the program.[4]

## The Manager as Resource Allocator

The third decisional role of the manager does not deal with change per se—whether voluntary or involuntary. Rather, it deals with how the resources of the organization are allocated. First there is the question of who in the organization will get what and who will do what. If you think about it for a moment, this is really the question of organizational design discussed in Section I: Who will perform the different tasks and who will coordinate them? In his role as *resource allocator,* therefore, the manager takes charge of the design of his organization's structure.

A second aspect of the resource allocator role relates to our discussion of Section II. A manager is the one who allocates the financial resources of the firm, namely, its money. He does this to some extent in the context of establishing budgets for different parts of the organization.

A third aspect of the resource allocator role involves the scheduling of the manager's own time. With his formal authority

[4] L. R. Sayles, *Managerial Behavior: Administration in Complex Organizations* (New York: McGraw Hill, 1964), p. 162.

and nerve-center information, a manager is an important individual in his organization. But his time is limited. He cannot give everyone all the time they request and believe they need. Therefore, time becomes one of the organization's most valuable (and scarcest) resources, and how he allocates his time—that is, how he schedules his day—becomes a key factor in determining how effective a manager will be and in turn how effective his organization will be in doing its work.

A fourth aspect of the resource allocator role is the authorizing of the decisions of others in the organization. Earlier we noted that managers supervise some improvement projects and delegate others. But as formal authority, the manager is ultimately responsible for every action taken in his organization. Thus to maintain some control over the action of his employees (and perhaps to ensure that this action is in line with his intended strategy), the manager may authorize certain of the more important decisions (that is, approve them before they are implemented). In other words, the manager does not concern himself with most parts of these decision processes (diagnosis of the issue, selection of design alternatives, and so on); he enters the process only near its end. The manager is presented with an alternative and is asked either to approve it or reject it:

**"Jack, how does this strike you? If you have no contrary thoughts, I'd like to see a thing like this go through."**

What are the factors that enter into the manager's choice-making behavior in allocating resources? Because requests for authorization are usually presented individually, they involve particularly difficult choices. The manager must feel sure in his own mind that the organization's resources will not be over-extended; he must consider whether the decision is consistent with other decisions; he must somehow test the feasibility of the proposals. Furthermore, the manager must consider factors of timing when deciding on requests for authorization. By authorizing too quickly, he may be denying himself important information—on events that will take place, on consequences of the decision that he did not at first consider, on other possible uses, yet to be suggested, for the same resources. By delaying authorization, the manager may be losing an opportunity, or he may be confusing subordinates who do not know whether to begin taking action or to forget about the request and start something else.

Despite the complexity of the choices that he must make, the very fact that the manager is approving rather than supervising these decisions suggests that he is not prepared to spend much time on them. Yet to make a choice quickly ("with the stroke of the pen," as one employee expressed it) is to risk discouraging an employee who may see a pet project, which has taken months to develop, destroyed in minutes. Clearly, the manager's success in his leader role depends in large part on the extent to which he does not inhibit innovative ideas that come to his in the form of requests for authorization.

Faced with these difficulties, the manager can beg the complexity by choosing the individual rather than the proposal. That is, the manager may approve proposals presented by employees who are perceived as capable and reject those presented by employees who are perceived as incapable. One manager commented, "I don't decide on the issues; I have people do that. All I do is ensure that I have good people. If they don't lead me well, I change them."

But most choices must be faced directly. Here the manager calls on his considerable store of nerve-center information. He must first make sure that a proposal complies with the values of the organizations's influencers—that it does not inappropriately violate the wishes of any power group and that it will carry the organization in the direction in which the influencers would like to see it move. Then the manager can draw on his extensive factual knowledge of the organization and its environment. Some of this is represented in terms of *models* and *plans* which the manager appears to develop in his mind to aid him in making choices.

A *model* is an abstraction of reality, a set of causal relationships by which the effects of given conditions can be predicted. One gets the impression, in listening to managers as they make decisions, that they carry an array of such models in their heads. One manager, for example, reacted to a question about product distribution by giving a detailed description—a model—of the distributor network. In effect, the manager absorbs the information that continually bombards him and forges it into a series of mental models—of the internal workings of his organization, the behavior of subordinates, the trends in the organization's environment, the habits of associates, and so on. When choices must be made, these models can be used to test alternatives. The manager can say to himself: Does this proposal make sense in terms of my understanding of the distribution network? Will the finance people be able to get along with marketing on this? What will happen to production if we introduce this one-week delay in shipping? The effectiveness of the manager's decisions is largely dependent on the quality of his models.

In many cases, the manager's *plans* are not explicit, documented in detail in the organization's files for all to see. Rather, crude plans seem to exist in the manager's mind in the form of a set of improvement projects that he would one day like to initiate. When asked about the future of his organization, one chief executive replied, "Well, once I get these foreign operations fully developed, I would like to begin to look into a reorganization." Such plans serve as a manager's vision of direction, as we saw specifically in the case of the entrepreneurial mode. By making choices with regard to them, the manager is able to interrelate various decisions and to ensure that they will all lead the organization in one general direction.

It should be stressed that the plans developed by the manager tend to be flexible, unlike those suggested in the planning mode. Because of unanticipated disturbances, unpredictable timing factors, possible new information, and alternatives, the manager often cannot afford the luxury of rigid plans. He must allow himself the flexibility to react to the environment. Thus his plans are made to be modified. And because they might readily be modified, the manager's plans often remain in his mind, never to be recorded on paper.

## The Manager as Negotiator

Our final role, the fourth of the decisional roles, describes the manager as the chief *negotiator* of his organization. Here again, we can see a direct tie-in to the other roles. Negotiation involves the organization with other organizations in the direct and real-time (that is, immediate) trading of resources. Organizations negotiate with suppliers, customers, unions, and governments.

When these negotiations are important ones for the organization, the manager must lead his organization's delegation, for a number of reasons:

1. As resource allocator, only he has the authority to commit the necessary resources.
2. As nerve center, only he has the information necessary for real-time negotiation.
3. As spokesman, only he can speak effectively on behalf of his organization and accurately reflect its goal system to outsiders.
4. As figurehead, his presence adds credibility to the proceedings.

Hence we hear examples of labor representatives stopping negotiations with companies to demand the presence of senior management, who they well know must ratify the final contract anyway. And we read of the president of the hockey team called in at the last minute to work out a contract with the hold-out superstar, or the head of a large corporation leading his group in negotiations for the acquisition of another firm.

Leonard Sayles, in his study of lower and middle managers in American industry, has noted that negotiations are a significant part of their job, intricately related to their liaison contacts:

> Sophisticated managers place great stress on negotiations as a way of life. They negotiate with groups who are setting standards for their work, who are performing support activity for them, and to whom they wish to "sell" their services. However, negotiations primarily concern costs, specifications, and time.[5]

This completes the discussion of the decisional roles. In closing, it is important to stress again the power that the manager of an organization has over the making of its strategy, power expressed by his ability to initiate and supervise improvement projects, by his handling of significant organizational disturbances, by his control over the allocation of organizational resources, and by his supervision of all major negotiations.

[5] Ibid., p. 131.

# Variations in Managerial Work

# 11

Do all managers play all the ten roles? We think we have shown that they do, that these ten roles describe the work of managers from foremen to presidents, from managers in corporations to those in school systems and governments (and, in some cases, even to those in street gangs). But saying that all managers play all ten roles is not to say that every manager gives equal attention to each role. In fact, we have evidence that different conditions give rise to different emphases among the roles. The factors that affect the attention that managers give to the different roles have been found to include the particular industry of the organization, the size of the organization, the function that a manager super-vise, the level of the manager's job in the hierarchy of the larger organization, the personality and style characteristics of the in-dividual manager in the job, and various factors related to time (such as the length of time a manager has been in the job).

Perhaps the most important factor is the function that the manager supervises. It has been found that sales managers, production managers, and staff managers seem to emphasize different groups of roles. Sales managers seem to place greatest emphasis on the interpersonal roles. For one thing, their units are more concerned with people, with the interpersonal aspects of convincing someone to buy something. Therefore, it is reason-able to expect that these managers should emphasize the inter-personal roles. Specifically, sales managers seem to spend more time than most other managers (1) dealing with important customers, largely in their figurehead role; (2) training their salesmen, in their role as leader; and (3) developing and main-taining contacts with people outside their units, in their liaison role.

In sharp contrast to the extrovert nature of sales managers, manufacturing managers tend to be much less concerned with people and much more concerned with production—with getting the products out. As a result, their focus tends to be on the decisional roles. They place particular emphasis on the (1) dis-turbance handler role because, as noted earlier, their prime concern is to keep the production system running and, to deal quickly with disturbances so that they will not impede production; and (2) the negotiator role, since they are constantly negotiating with people at the two ends of their production units, those who supply it with raw inputs and those who take the finished (or semifinished) outputs.

Managers of staff groups are different again. They tend to emphasize the informational roles, again for some very obvious reasons. Staff people are specialists, experts in giving some advice to other members of the organization. Thus the managers of these specialist groups must (1) devote considerable attention to the monitor role to build up their own expertise; and (2) spend considerable time in the spokesman role in giving advice on behalf of their units to other members of the organization.

Of course, managers' jobs vary not only by function but also by level in the organization, size of the organization, and so on. In general, both managers in small organizations and managers at lower levels of larger organizations tend to be closer to the operations of their organizations, and thus their jobs typically involve a greater handling of disturbances (since the key to efficient operations is to maintain routine) and fewer figurehead duties. Being close to the specific operations and not up on some removed, abstract level, they also tend to stress current and tangible information even more than other managers.

One study of the presidents of small companies found that they tend to perform two roles not common for managers of larger firms—those of *specialist* and *substitute operator*. The manager engages in the former role when he "deems that any one function is vital to the organization's well-being. . . ."

> [The president of a cosmetics company] implemented an inventory control system for his organization. He operated the system and felt that he was the most capable person in the organization to handle the position. As Mr. [Cosmetics] saw it, a well-run inventory control system was the heart of any business.
>
> [The president of a restaurant] acted as the purchasing agent for his firm. Here again the manager felt he was the most capable person to handle the assignment.[1]

The role of substitute operator reflects the derth of slack in small firms. As a generalist, the manager must be prepared to step into a job when any one of a number of needs arises—an employee is absent, the plant is operating at full capacity and an extra hand is needed, and so on. (The work of substitute operator can also be considered a part of the disturbance handler role. There may be merit, however, in clearly distinguishing this work when it assumes the special importance that it does for the head of small organizations.)

Personality is another factor in determining how managers attend to the different roles. Some managers simply prefer to

[1] Choran, cited in H. Mintzberg, *The Nature of Managerial Work* (New York: Harper & Row, 1973), p. 107.

focus on some roles and give less attention to others. In one study of a psychiatric hospital, there was one designated chief executive, but in fact he shared his job with two of his employees. This job sharing was found to be related to task as well as emotional issues. The superintendent tied his organization to its environment (liaison, figurehead, spokesman, and negotiator roles) and was both assertive and controlling. The clinical director operated internal clinical services (disseminator, disturbance-handler, and resource-allocator roles) and was the supportive one (leader role). The assistant superintendent dealt with nonroutine innovation (entrepreneur role) and expressed friendship and equalitarian norms (another approach to the leader role).[2]

Another common way to share a managerial job is by designating those roles clearly related to the outside (liaison, spokesman, and negotiator) to the more outgoing manager, whereas the inside roles (leader, disseminator, and resource allocator) can go to the more production-oriented personality. Of course, some roles, such as those of monitor and disturbance handler, relate to both inside and outside. Thus the two managers must be able to get along easily in performing these roles and, in particular, to share the privileged information. Information related to both the inside and the outside must be brought to bear on the same decisions.

Various time factors also affect what managers do. Many other jobs are far more influenced by time than that of the manager, one case being farmers, who sow in the spring and reap in the fall (and repair barns in the winter). But some time factors have been found to influence managers' jobs as well. For example, managers of accounting departments are influenced by the reporting cycle: They are busier when the reports are due at the month's end and freer at the beginning of the month.

Since change does not seem to happen steadily in organizations, but rather appears in cycles or waves, we would expect managers' work to react accordingly—emphasis would be placed on the entrepreneur and the negotiator roles during periods of change, and on the leader and the disturbance handler roles during periods of the consolidation of change.

[2] R. C. Hodgson, D. J. Levinson, and A. Zaleznik, *The Executive Role Constellation* (Boston: Harvard Business School, Division of Research, 1965).

Another time-related factor of interest is the manager's experience, his time in the job. There is evidence that managers in new jobs adopt behavior patterns that change as they gain experience. For one thing, the new incumbent lacks the contacts and the information that will enable him to play the spokesman and the disseminator roles effectively. Therefore, one would expect him to spend much of his time developing these contacts and collecting information (in the liaison and monitor roles). As information and contacts develop, but while the manager is still quite new in his job, attention probably shifts to the entrepreneur role; as a newcomer, the manager is sensitive to what should be improved and desirous of putting his personal stamp on his organization. Once this is done, he may settle down to the more balanced work of carrying out the ten roles. We may then consider him experienced in the job.

Perhaps the best way to summarize what we know about variations in managers' work is to classify different managerial jobs. Following are eight common types:

*The Contact Man.* Some managers spend much time outside their organizations, dealing with people who can help them by doing them favors, giving them sales orders, providing privileged information, and so on. In addition, this type of manager expends much effort developing his reputation, and that of his organization by giving speeches or doing favors. We may call him the "contact man." His two primary roles are *liaison* and *figurehead.* Many sales managers fit this description, as do many ex-military chiefs who hold executive positions in defense-contracting firms. Some chief executives as well, particularly in service industries, tend to fit this description.

*The Political Manager.* This is another type of manager who also spends much of his time with outsiders, but for different purposes. He is caught in a complex managerial position where he is required to reconcile a great many diverse political forces acting on his organization. This manager must spend a great part of his time in formal activities, meeting regularly with directors or the boss, receiving and negotiating with pressure groups, and explaining the actions of his organization to special-interest parties. His key roles are those of *spokesman* and *negotiator.*

This description is probably typical of managers at the top of most governments and institutions, including hospitals and universities, where the political pressures from below are as great as those from outside. The widening number of influencers of all organizations suggests that there will be more of the political manager in all chief executives of the future, whether they work in the private or the public sector. In addition, we may find something akin to the political manager in the middle levels of some large organizations. Such managers may be required to spend considerable time on organizational politics when the duties of their units are vague (so that no one can be sure how effectively they are performing), when there is enough slack in the system to allow for such political activity, and when the organizational climate promotes it.

*The Entrepreneur.* A third type of manager spends much of his time seeking opportunities and implementing changes in his organization. His key role is that of *entrepreneur*, but he must also spend considerable time in the *negotiator* role to implement his proposed changes. The entrepreneur is commonly found at the helm of a small young business organization, where innovation is the key to survival. He may also be found at the head of, or within, a large organization that is changing rapidly. But his tenure here is probably short lived. A large organization can tolerate extensive change only for a short time before a period of consolidation must set in. When it does, the entrepreneur is likely to become an insider, as described next.

*The Insider.* Many managers are concerned chiefly with the maintenance of smooth-running internal operations. They spend their time building up structure, developing and training their subordinates, and overseeing the operations they develop. They work primarily through the *resource allocator* role and, to a lesser extent, the *leader* role. The typical middle- and senior-level production or operations managers are probably insiders in that they work to build up and maintain a stable production system. We can also include here those managers who are attempting to rebuild their organizations after a major crisis or to settle them after a period of disruptive change.

*The Real-Time Manager.*   Akin to the insider is another type whose primary concern is also with the maintenance of internal operations, but whose time scale and problems are different. We can use the term *real-time manager* to describe that person who operates primarily in the present, devoting his efforts to ensuring that the day-to-day work of his organization continues without interruption. Hence primacy is given to the *disturbance handler* role. The work of the real-time manager exhibits all the regular characteristics in the extreme—contacts are very many and very brief, there is little time given to mail or reports, and so on. This manager always appears to be exceedingly busy; he has his "finger in every pie"; he is prepared to substitute for any employee, and do any necessary job himself. The real-time manager is usually found in the basic line-production job (foreman), as the head of a small, one-manager business, at the helm of an organization (or organizational unit) in a dynamic, competitive, and high-pressure environment.

*The Team Manager.*   There is another type of manager who is oriented to the inside, but he has a special concern. He is preoccupied with the creation of a team that will operate as a cohesive whole and will function effectively. The team manager is found where the organizational tasks require difficult coordination among highly skilled experts. Obvious examples of team managers are hockey coaches and heads of research-and-development groups charged with complex projects. The team manager is primarily concerned with the *leader* role.

*The Expert Manager.*   In some situations a manager must perform an expert role in addition to his regular managerial roles. As head of a specialist staff group this manager must serve as a center of specialized information in the larger organization. He advises other managers and is consulted on specialized problems. His key roles are *monitor* and *spokesman;* his related duties, the collection and dissemination outward of specialized information. Because much of his work is associated with his specialty function, the usual managerial work characteristics appear less pronounced for him (although they are present, nevertheless). He does more desk work, is alone more of the time, does more reading and writing, and encounters less pressure. He spends more time in nonline relationships—in advising others, for example.

*The New Manager.* Our last type of manager is the one in a new job. Lacking contacts and information at the beginning, the new manager concentrates on the *liaison* and *monitor* roles in an attempt to build up a web of contacts and a data base. The decisional roles cannot become fully operative until he has more information. When he does, he is likely to stress the *entrepreneur* role for a time, as he attempts to put his distinct stamp on his organization. Then he may settle down to being one of the other managerial types—contact man, insider, or some other type.

> EXERCISE: What roles do you think the following managers tend to emphasize: the president of a small dress manufacturing firm, a fire chief, an Indian chief (today, in 1850, and in 1491), an army general (in peacetime and wartime), an army sergeant (in peacetime and wartime), a leader of a pacification movement (in peacetime and wartime, comparing particularly his job with that of the sergeant), the Pope, a coach of a hockey team (before the big game and during it), queen bee (As a manager, does she play any of the roles?)? Can any of these managers (aside from queen bee) totally ignore any of the roles? What would happen if any one did?

To conclude, we must reiterate an earlier point, which is well illustrated by the description of the new-manager type. The ten roles of the manager form a gestalt, an integrated whole. They cannot be divided. All ten roles are important in all managers' jobs, no matter which ones particular managers emphasize. The manager's job is like a chain, with authority giving rise to interpersonal contacts that provide information, and these in turn enable the manager to make decisions. No link, no role, can be pulled out and leave the chain intact.

# 12

# Some Conclusions About Managerial Work

Managing an organization can certainly be interesting work, but it is no bed of roses (unless one counts the thorns). A number of difficulties present themselves in almost every manager's job. Let us look at some of these and consider how managerial work might change in the future to deal with them.

1. *A manager's job is inherently a heavy and high-pressured one, with little time to relax.* Studies have shown that the pace of managerial work is a hectic one and that the amount of work managers feel compelled to do during the working hours is great. In one study of foremen, it was found that they engaged in be-

tween 237 and 1073 distinct incidents per day (an average of 583) without a break in the pace:

> Obviously, these foremen had little idle time. They had to handle many pressing problems in rapid-fire order. They had to "take" constant interruption, to retain many problems in their minds simultaneously, and to juggle priorities for action.[1]

The studies of the five chief executives similarly showed no break in the pace of activity during office hours. Their mail (on the average, 36 pieces per day), telephone calls (about 5 per day), and meetings (about 8 per day) accounted for almost every minute from the moment these men entered their offices in the morning until they departed in the evening. A true break seldom occurred. Coffee was taken during meetings, and lunchtime was almost always devoted to formal or informal meetings. When free time appeared, ever-present employees quickly usurped it. If these managers wished to have a change of pace, they had two means at their disposal—the observational tour and the light discussions that generally preceded scheduled meetings. But these were not regularly scheduled breaks, and they were seldom totally unrelated to the issue at hand—managing the organization.

Thus the work of managing an organization may be described as taxing. The quantity of work to be done, or that which the manager chooses to do, during the day is substantial, and the pace is unrelenting. After hours, many managers are simply unable to escape either from an environment that recognizes the power and status of their positions or from their own minds, which have been well trained to search continually for new information.

Why do managers adopt this pace and work load? One reason of course is in the roles themselves. It simply takes considerable time to maintain a large network of interpersonal contacts, to process the large quantity of incoming information, and to take prime responsibility for the organization's strategy formulation system, carrying out the heavy burdens of the roles of disturbance handler, negotiator, resource allocator, and entrepreneur. But there are two other more specific and important

[1] R. H. Guest, "Of Time and the Foreman," *Personnel* (1955–56: 480).

reasons that explain the manager's work load. These are discussed in our next two points.

2. *The manager can never relax in the knowledge that all is
well, or even that a job has come to an end.* The job of managing
an organization is inherently an open-ended one. The manager is
responsible for the success of his organization, and there are
really no tangible mileposts where he can stop to say, "Now my
job is finished." The engineer finishes the design of a casting on
a certain day, the lawyer wins or loses a case at some moment.
But the manager must always keep going, never sure when he
has succeeded, never sure that his whole organization will not
come down around him because of some miscalculation. As a
result, the manager is a person with a perpetual preoccupation.
He can never be free to forget his job, and he never has the
pleasure of knowing, even temporarily, that there is nothing
else he can do. No matter what kind of managerial job he has,
he always has the nagging suspicion that he might be able to
contribute just a little bit more. Hence he assumes an unrelenting
pace in his work.

3. *The manager is damned by his own information system
to a life of overwork or one of frustration.* These are strong words,
but they point to a prime dilemma of managerial work, which
we shall call the "dilemma of delegation." Managers have often
been found to be reluctant to delegate their work. Traditionally,
this was explained in terms of power: managers hold on to their
tasks in order to hold on to their power; delegating too much to
employees could create power centers that could one day threaten
the managers. There may be some truth to this in some cases, but
it certainly does not explain why managers with self-confidence
are also sometimes reluctant to delegate tasks.

The main reason seems to relate to the nature of the manager's information. Consider the following incident:

> An employee calls to ask the chief executive if a certain ap-
> pointment should be cleared through a particular committee.
> The executive replies that it should not. To a second question on
> another appointment, he gives an affirmative reply. Finally, the
> employee asks about a third man, and receives another nega-
> tive reply. Asked why he did not give consistent decisions, the
> chief executive replies that his knowledge of the personalities

**of the three men and of the committee members necessitated that he make individual decisions.**

But what is the result of this action? The next time such a situation arises the chief executive will have to be consulted again. Not only did he give the employee no basis on which to make a future decision, but he actually discouraged him from doing so by providing no rationale for his own decisions. Quite clearly (although perhaps not consciously), he chose not to delegate responsibility for this kind of decision but to retain it for himself. The obvious reason is that he considered himself better informed.

Earlier we noted that the manager is the nerve center of his organization, its best-informed member. But we also noted that a great deal of this information arrives through the verbal media and can therefore be stored only in the manager's mind (as opposed to on paper or in a computer memory bank, etc.). Now what happens when a task must be delegated? If it is related only to the work of one employee, then that person probably has the necessary information to deal with it (for example, the president can delegate manufacturing problems to the manufacturing vice president). But what of problems that cut across specialties, or that involve the manager's special privileged information? To delegate these, he must disseminate the information that goes with them. But because the information is verbal, it takes time to disseminate it. It is not as if the manager can hand over a dossier or report and say, "Here's what you need to do the task." No, he must take the time to "dump memory," to tell all he knows about the issue. But that may take so long that the manager may be better off doing the task himself.

Hence we have the dilemma of delegation. By the very nature of his information system, the manager is required to do too many tasks, to spend too much of his time disseminating information along with the tasks he wishes to delegate, or to delegate without dissemination, in which case the manager must watch in frustration as the task is done without the information that it requires. Thus the manager's information system damns him to a life of overwork or to one of frustration.

4. *The manager's activities are characterized by brevity, variety, and fragmentation; as a result, managers have difficulty giving complex issues the concentrated attention they require.*

These findings relate back to our first three points. The pace and work load, the open-ended nature of the job, and the dilemma of delegation—all put the manager under pressure. This is not a job of concentration or repetition, like that of the watchmaker, who works uninterrupted from 8 A.M. to 5 P.M., the researcher in the lab, who probes deeply into his work, sometimes uninterrupted into the early hours of the morning, the salesman who spends his working life selling one product, or the assembly-line worker who bolts the same fender onto car after car, hundreds of times every day, year after year. Rather, studies of managers' work show that their activities are characterized by brevity, variety, and fragmentation—in other words, that these activities tend to be short, to range widely across issues in the course of a day, with no apparent pattern, and to be frequently interrupted or cut short.

Earlier, we saw in the ten roles the variety of tasks that all managers must perform. A typical morning for the chief executive of a large organization might proceed as follows:

> An employee calls to report a fire in one of the facilities; then the mail, much of it insignificant, is processed; an employee interrupts to tell of an impending crisis with a public group; then a retired employee is ushered in to receive a plaque; later there is a discussion on bidding on a multi-million dollar contract; after that, the manager complains to another employee that office space in one department is being wasted; and so on.

Throughout each working day, the manager encounters this great variety of activity. Most surprising, the significant activity is interspersed with the trivial in no particular pattern. Hence the manager must be prepared to shift moods quickly and frequently.

Consider the specific evidence on brevity and fragmentation in studies of managers' work:

> The foremen cited earlier averaged only 48 seconds on each activity they carried out. Guest, one of the researchers in this study, noted: "Interestingly enough, the characteristics of a foremen's job—interruption, variety, discontinuity—are diametrically opposed to those of most hourly operator jobs, which are highly rationalized, repetitive, uninterrupted, and subject to the steady unvarying rhythm of the moving conveyor."[2]

[2] Ibid., p. 481.

**The five chief executives studied averaged 36 written and 16 verbal contacts each day, almost every one dealing with a distinct issue. Half of these activities were completed in less than nine minutes and only one in ten took more than one hour. Telephone calls averaged 6 minutes, unscheduled meetings 12 minutes, and sessions of working alone at their own desks, only 15 minutes. And these were the heads of large, important organizations!**

**In the study of 160 senior and middle managers in British industry it was found that on average less than once every two days did they work for one-half hour or more without interruption.**

Some researchers who have studied managerial work have pointed out a number of ways in which managers can cut down the interruptions, for example, by making better use of their secretaries to block phone calls and unexpected guests. But these researchers beg one important question. Are brevity, variety, and fragmentation forced on managers or do they in fact choose to work in this way?

Indeed, managers seem to *choose* these ways of working. It is they who determine in large part the duration of their activities. For example, in the study of the five chief executives, the tours that they chose to take could not be interrupted by the telephone, yet they lasted, on an average, only 11 minutes. Furthermore, these chief executives, not the other parties, terminated many of the meetings and telephone calls, and they frequently left meetings before they ended. They frequently interrupted their desk work to place telephone calls or to request that employees come by. One chief executive located his desk so that he could look down a long hallway. The door was usually open, and his employees were continually coming into his office. He fully realized that by moving his desk, closing his door, or changing the rules his secretary used to screen callers, he could easily have eliminated many of these interruptions.

Why, then, is there an indication that managers prefer brevity, variety, and interruption in their work? To some extent, certainly, managers tolerate interruption because they do not wish to discourage the flow of current information. Furthermore, managers may become accustomed to variety in their work, and they may find that boredom develops easily. But it would appear that these factors can only partly explain managers' behavior.

A more significant explanation might be that managers become conditioned by their work loads. They develop a sensitive appreciation for the *opportunity cost* of their own time—the benefits forgone by doing one thing instead of another. Thus they take on much work because they realize their own worth to the organization. In addition, they are aware of the ever-present assortment of obligations associated with the job—the mail that cannot be delayed, the callers who must be attended to, the meetings that require their participation. In other words, no matter what they *are* doing, managers are plagued by what they *might* do and what they *must* do.

In effect, managers are encouraged by the realities of their work to develop a particular personality—to overload themselves with work, to do things abruptly, to avoid wasting time, to participate only when the value of participation is tangible, and to avoid too great an involvement with any one issue.

All of this suggests that the pressures of their jobs drive managers to be superficial in what they do, not to give concentrated attention to issues but to get them done. Every job has its "occupational hazards"—lung disease in coal mining, a callousness to human suffering in law, a propensity to talk too much in teaching. In managerial work the prime occupational hazard is superficiality. In order to succeed, then, managers must presumably become proficient at their superficiality.

5. *Managerial work is that of action, not reflection, leading to a planning dilemma.* We have already seen repeatedly that this is a job of live action, not one of calm reflection. We have noted this, for example, in discussing the treatment of the mail. The manager's is a talking job, not a reading one. We have seen the action orientation again in the manager's thirst for current, tangible information. There is other evidence too. For example, in the study of the five chief executives, of 368 verbal contacts, only 1 dealt with an issue that could be called general planning. All of the rest focused on tangible activities with clearly defined purposes (such as to pass on specific information, to make specific decisions, etc.). And only 7 percent of these verbal contacts were regularly scheduled (such as a weekly meeting); all the rest were scheduled on ad hoc bases for one or more specific

purposes. Neustadt, in his study of U.S. presidents, has concluded that even in the case of the head of state, "Deadlines rule his personal agenda,"[3] and Sune Carlson, who studied the nine Swedish managing directors, has concluded:

> There is a tendency for business executives to become slaves to their appointment diaries—they get a kind of "diary complex." One can seldom see two business executives talking together without their diaries in their hands, and they feel rather lost unless they know that they have these diaries within easy reach. When they start their working day they will look up what they have to do, and whatever is in the diary they will fulfil punctually and efficiently. If one wants to be sure of getting something done by this group of people, one has to see that it gets into their diaries. One should never ask a busy executive to promise to do something e.g. "next week" or even "next Friday." Such vague requests do not get entered into his appointment diary. No, one has to state a specific time, say, Friday 4:15 p.m., then it will be put down and in due course done. The more exactly the time is specified, the more certain it will be that the task will be attended to.[4]

Clearly, the manager is not a relaxed, reflective planner, as a great many people believe. Rather, the job breeds adaptive information manipulators who prefer the live, concrete situation. If the manager plans at all, it is not by locking his door, puffing on a pipe, and thinking great thoughts. Rather, the manager's planning is informal and in large part in his own head, bound up with his daily actions. Action and planning cannot easily be separated in this job.

But what of the issues that need reflection, concentration, and perhaps even formal planning? Is the manager the one to handle them? Here we find a second major dilemma of managerial work, which we shall call the "planning dilemma." The manager has both the authority to make the plans and the nerve-center information they require, but he lacks the time to focus intensively on complex issues. In turn, the planner, who has the time and skill to do systematic analysis, lacks the authority and

[3] R. E. Neustadt, *Presidential Power: The Politics of Leadership* (New York: Wiley, 1960), p. 155.
[4] S. Carlson, *Executive Behavior* (Stockholm: Strombergs, 1951), p. 71.

information that planning needs. In effect, the planning mode often loses out because it is unnatural in managerial work. Thus organizations must often rely on the adaptive or entrepreneurial modes. But these approaches, with the manager chasing opportunities when he is not being chased by disturbances, with improvement projects being considered independently and intermittently, with plans existing only in the manager's head, are inadequate in many situations. Clearly, then, there is the need to couple the skills of the manager with those of the staff specialist.

## Management as a Science

Where will managerial work go from here? What form will it take in the future? First, we might ask whether the practice of management is a science today. From all that we have said in this section, the answer is a resounding no. That is to say, managers do not work according to procedures that have been prescribed by scientific analysis. Indeed, except for his use of the telephone, the airplane, and the dictating machine, it would appear that the manager of today is indistinguishable from his historical counterparts. He may seek different information, but he gets much of it in the same way—by word of mouth. He may make decisions dealing with modern technology, but he uses the same intuitive (that is, nonexplicit) procedures in making them. Even the computer, which has had a great impact on other kinds of organizatioal work, has apparently done little to alter the working methods of the general manager.

The fact of the matter is that we really know very little about the essence of managerial work, namely, the procedures (or *programs*) that managers use. How do they really collect information; how do they negotiate; how do they handle disturbances? It is clear that we shall not develop a science of managing until we can get inside these programs and describe their contents precisely. Only then shall we be able to develop a true science of managing. (In effect, this means that the black box we opened in this Section III has simply led us to describe a series of smaller black boxes inside. Every time we open a black box, we learn something important, but we also find out other things that we must learn next.)

To develop a science of managing, then, we shall have to know more about leadership, information processing, decision-making, and so on. But what are we to do in the meantime to improve the practice of management?

First we can develop ways by which the staff specialist—whether he be a planner, an information systems designer, an operations researcher, or whoever—can work more closely with the manager. The manager can benefit from the specialist's techniques and especially from his available time (an organization normally has only one manager as its head, but it can have any number of staff specialists aiding that manager). As has been evident in our discussion, this manager-specialist relationship hinges on one key issue—whether or not the manager can share his privileged information with the specialist. If he cannot, the specialist will remain forever detached from the key issues confronting the manager and therefore will be of little help to him. But if information can be shared, the specialist can play a key role in aiding the busy manager. By himself, the manager can do little to alleviate his work load; working with well-informed staff specialists, however, he may be able to accomplish much.

The staff specialist must study and understand the work of the person for whom he designs systems and solves problems. He must gain access to the manager's hitherto undocumented information before he can be able to design useful systems for him. In this way, he will find that the manager generally has great need, not for the quantitative, routine, internal information that the information system has always provided, but for uncertain, ad hoc, external information. He will find, for instance, that the manager can use, not static long-range plans, but flexible plans that can be modified en route. He will also learn that "quick-and-dirty" analysis, providing results in real time, can be more useful in the event of a crisis than statistically significant data.

Managers can of course do a number of things on their own to work more effectively. For example, one way the manager can alleviate the dilemma of delegation is to get into the habit of regularly sharing his privileged information with his employees. Then when a task must be delegated to one of them, the employee will already be well informed.

For the occupational hazard of superficiality, there are of course no simple answers. But the manager who is aware of this problem will be better able to deal with it. He can pass over the less important issues quickly, reserving his efforts for those that need more concentrated attention. He can know that he must work with information that is current and tangible, but at the same time he can recognize the need to put this information into a broad context, to see the "big picture" of his organization and not always be lost in a welter of details.

Above all, to perform effectively the manager can come to know his own job intimately, to recognize the roles he must play, the pressures of his job, the difficulties and dilemmas inherent in it, his own strengths and weaknesses vis-à-vis these pressures, the influence of what he does and how he works on his own organization. "Know thyself" (and thy job) is perhaps the most important message that comes out of all we have said about the work of the manager. And that of course is why this section has been included in this book and placed at the end of it, the last word before launching the training of managers-to-be.

# Index

78 79 80 9 8 7 6 5 4 3 2 1